ATTOO Lettering & Banners

Classic and Modern Script Designs

Britt Johansson

Schiffer Publishing Ltd®
4880 Lower Valley Road • Atglen, PA 19310

Library of Congress Control Number: 2016949809

Designed by Justin Watkinson
Type set in Minion Pro/BaseTwelveSerif

ISBN: 978-0-7643-5215-7
Printed in China

Published by Schiffer Publishing, Ltd.
4880 Lower Valley Road
Atglen, PA 19310
Phone: (610) 593-1777; Fax: (610) 593-2002
E-mail: Info@schifferbooks.com
Web: www.schifferbooks.com

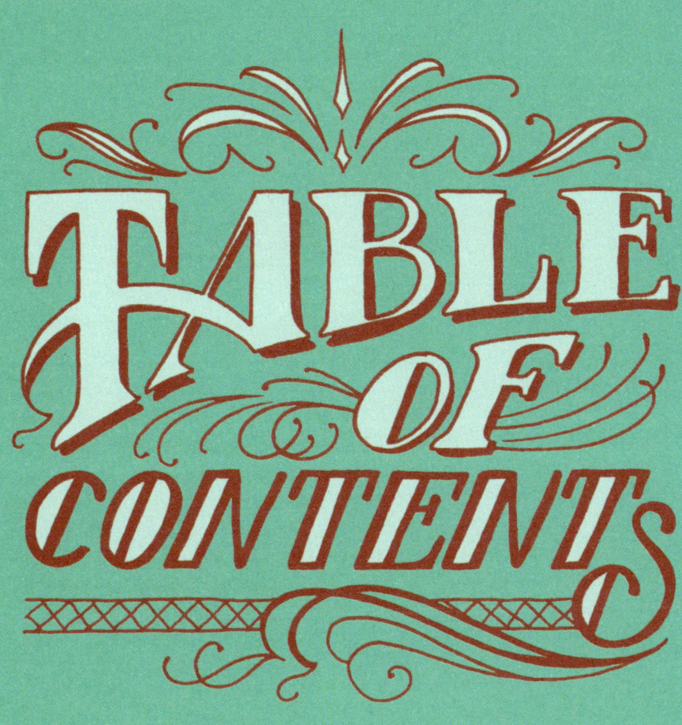
TABLE
OF
CONTENTS

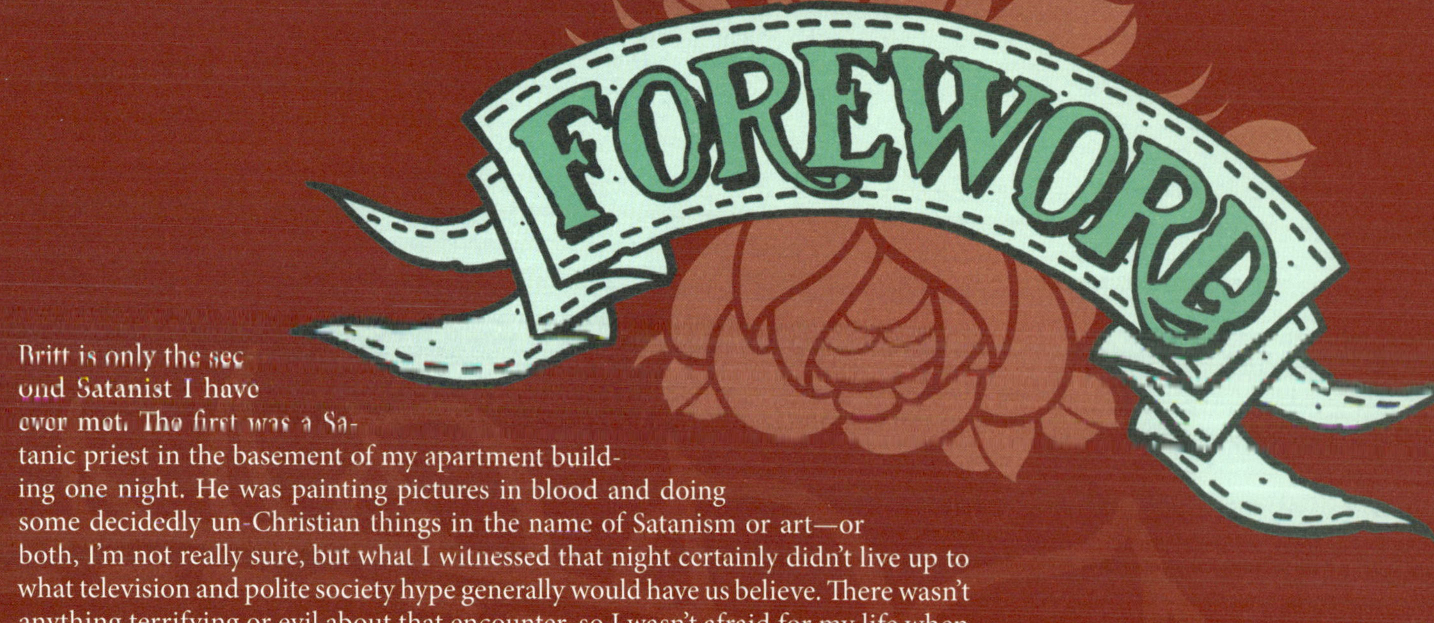

Britt is only the second Satanist I have ever met. The first was a Satanic priest in the basement of my apartment building one night. He was painting pictures in blood and doing some decidedly un-Christian things in the name of Satanism or art—or both, I'm not really sure, but what I witnessed that night certainly didn't live up to what television and polite society hype generally would have us believe. There wasn't anything terrifying or evil about that encounter, so I wasn't afraid for my life when I met Britt.

I know Britt from the relatively brief encounters we have had over the last couple of years, which have been as a tattooer and client. That is to say, Britt has been traveling to see me every few months to complete a tattoo on her arm, and each time we met, I have gotten to know a little more about her and her life, which by all accounts seems pretty ordinary to me. That is not to say she doesn't live an extraordinary life! From what I know about her, apart from worshipping fallen angels, she is an avid collector of *objets d'art* and rare medical conditions, of which she has both in abundance. She is by all accounts a fairly down-to-earth person. She is quiet, polite, quirky, and very friendly. Swedes tend to have a reputation as being socially reserved and private people, and Britt doesn't stray too far from that stereotype, but like so many of her countryfolk, she is charming and funny and very likeable. She is also very generous and giving. On our second meeting, she presented me with an original painting she had made for me, which has hung proudly in my studio ever since.

Britt asked me to write the foreword for this book, ostensibly to lend some kind of tattooing credentials to the project, which is both flattering and embarrassing at the same time. I don't feel qualified or fit to bear the lofty responsibility of such a task, and I have only seen snippets of what the final book may contain. My impression is of someone who is very passionate about her work, and who has spent countless hours in the pursuit of achieving her creative goals. Britt truly does believe in giving 110 percent of herself to this business, and it is abundantly evident in the prolificacy of her work.

Twenty years ago there were barely a handful of books on the subject of tattooing. These days bookshops have whole shelves related to tattooing. Some books have some value, others are merely riding the wave of current trends, so it is refreshing to know first hand the passion and dedication given to the one you are holding. Britt is driven, committed, and truly immersed in her work. Our conversations often turn to how she may be able to improve the overall quality of her work and service to her customers, the sentiment of a true professional interested in improving and honoring her craft.

It has been my pleasure to have her as a customer myself, and when our exchange is finished, it will be nice to know that somewhere, in a small village in the vast expanses of Sweden, another craftsperson is waking to a new day, filled with hope and commitment, to be the best she can be, and pay tribute to her trade. And maybe sacrifice a goat or two.

Judd Ripley

DENMARK 2015

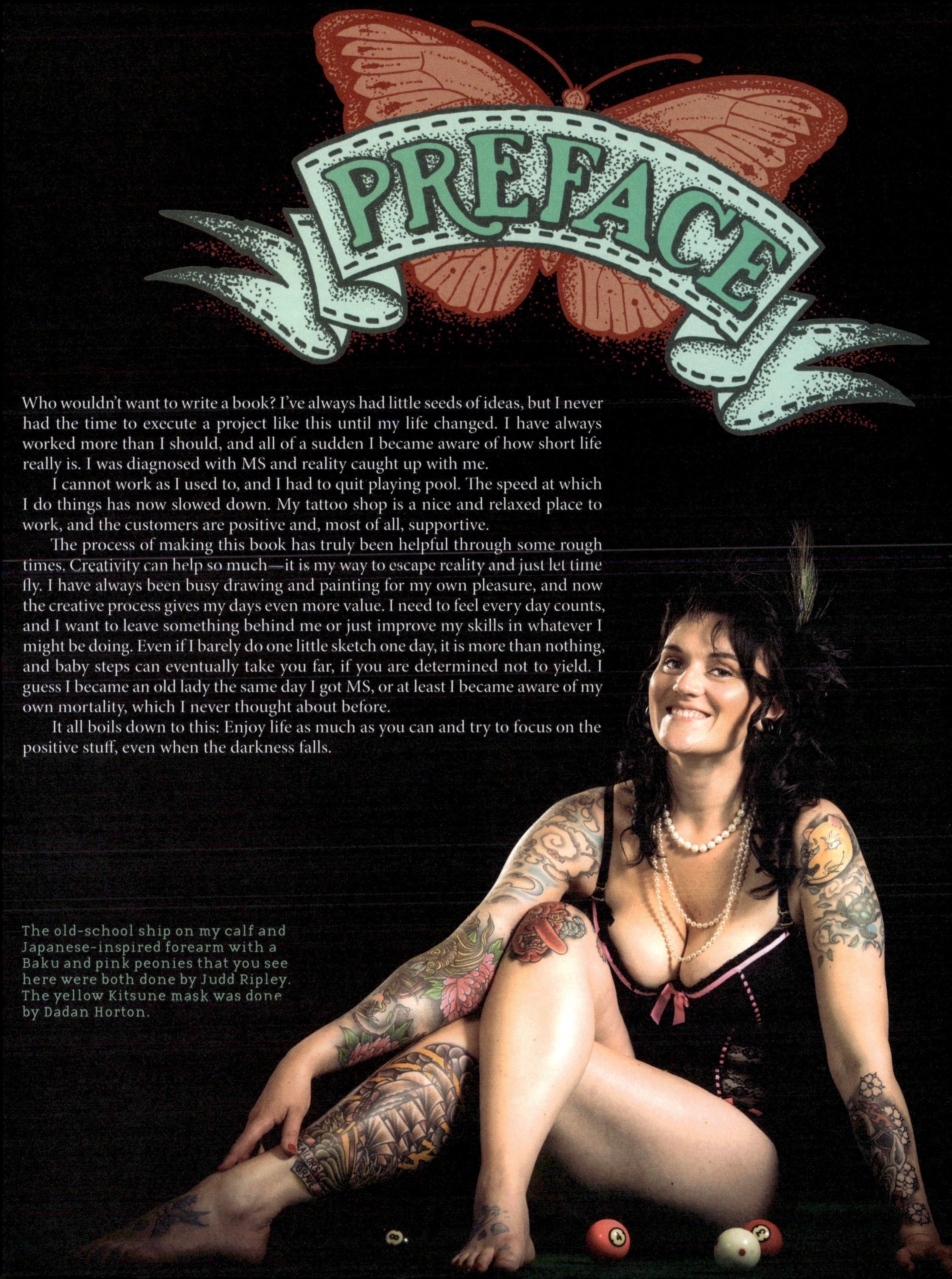

PREFACE

Who wouldn't want to write a book? I've always had little seeds of ideas, but I never had the time to execute a project like this until my life changed. I have always worked more than I should, and all of a sudden I became aware of how short life really is. I was diagnosed with MS and reality caught up with me.

I cannot work as I used to, and I had to quit playing pool. The speed at which I do things has now slowed down. My tattoo shop is a nice and relaxed place to work, and the customers are positive and, most of all, supportive.

The process of making this book has truly been helpful through some rough times. Creativity can help so much—it is my way to escape reality and just let time fly. I have always been busy drawing and painting for my own pleasure, and now the creative process gives my days even more value. I need to feel every day counts, and I want to leave something behind me or just improve my skills in whatever I might be doing. Even if I barely do one little sketch one day, it is more than nothing, and baby steps can eventually take you far, if you are determined not to yield. I guess I became an old lady the same day I got MS, or at least I became aware of my own mortality, which I never thought about before.

It all boils down to this: Enjoy life as much as you can and try to focus on the positive stuff, even when the darkness falls.

The old-school ship on my calf and Japanese-inspired forearm with a Baku and pink peonies that you see here were both done by Judd Ripley. The yellow Kitsune mask was done by Dadan Horton.

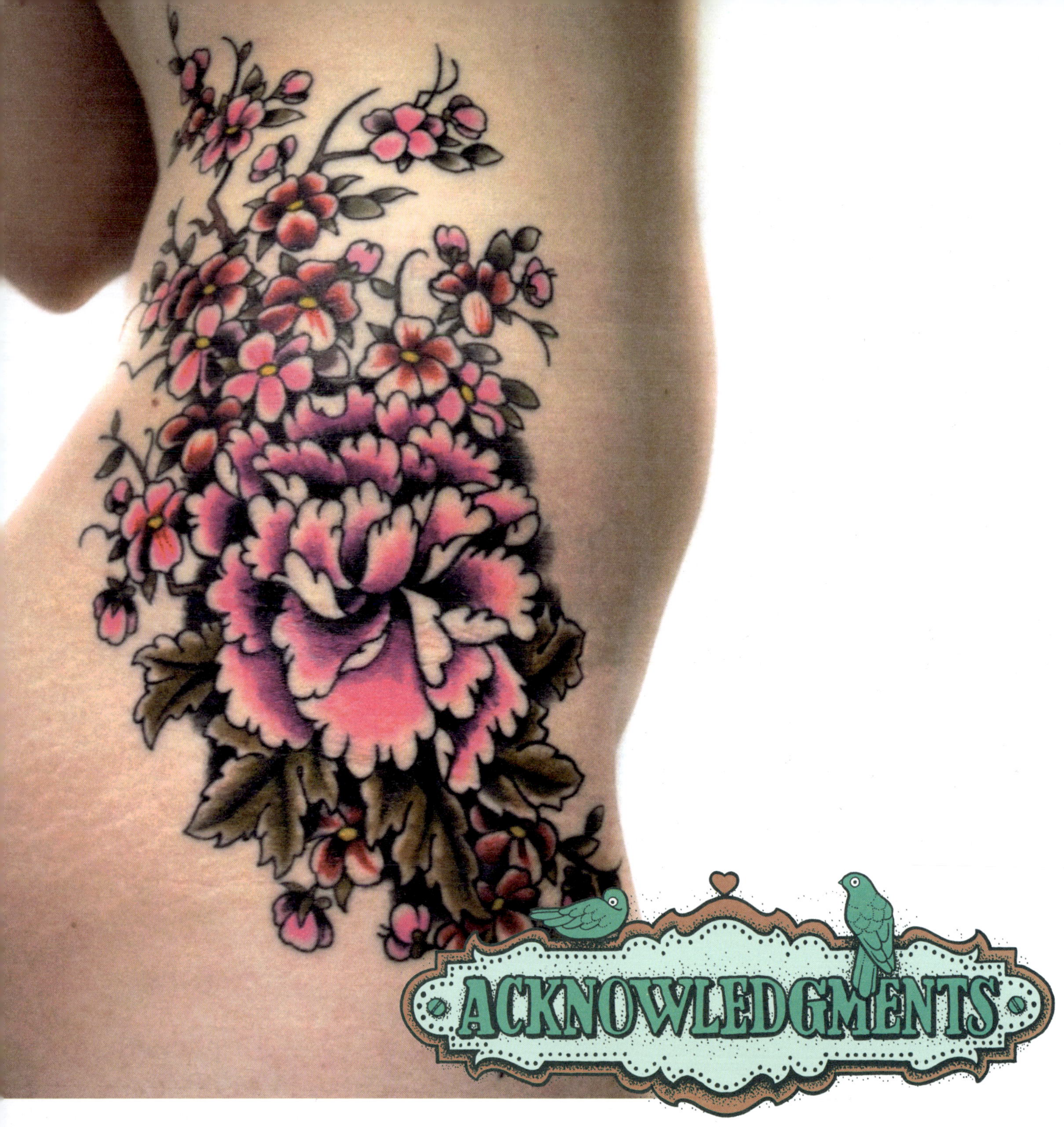

Peony and Sakura tattoo on Alexandra Björck, Ljungby.

I would like to thank my friends, my customers, and all the great people around me, not only for their support whenever I need it, but also for helping out in the creation of this book: Staffan, the underground artist, who taught me the basics of tattooing, Costan and family for friendship and teaching me about life and always giving great advice, my dentist Stefan Lodén for help and support, Lars and the MS team for keeping me up on my feet, Said for fitness and health, David at Ljungby Textiltryck & Brodyr, Rulles Foto and photographer Josefine, Peter Wallin for taking photos of me for this book, and the tattoo artist Judd Ripley and family and crew at the Sailors Grave in Copenhagen. Special thanks to the love of my life, Stefan, for his exquisite taste and impeccable points of view and for always being there to help out and make me a better person.

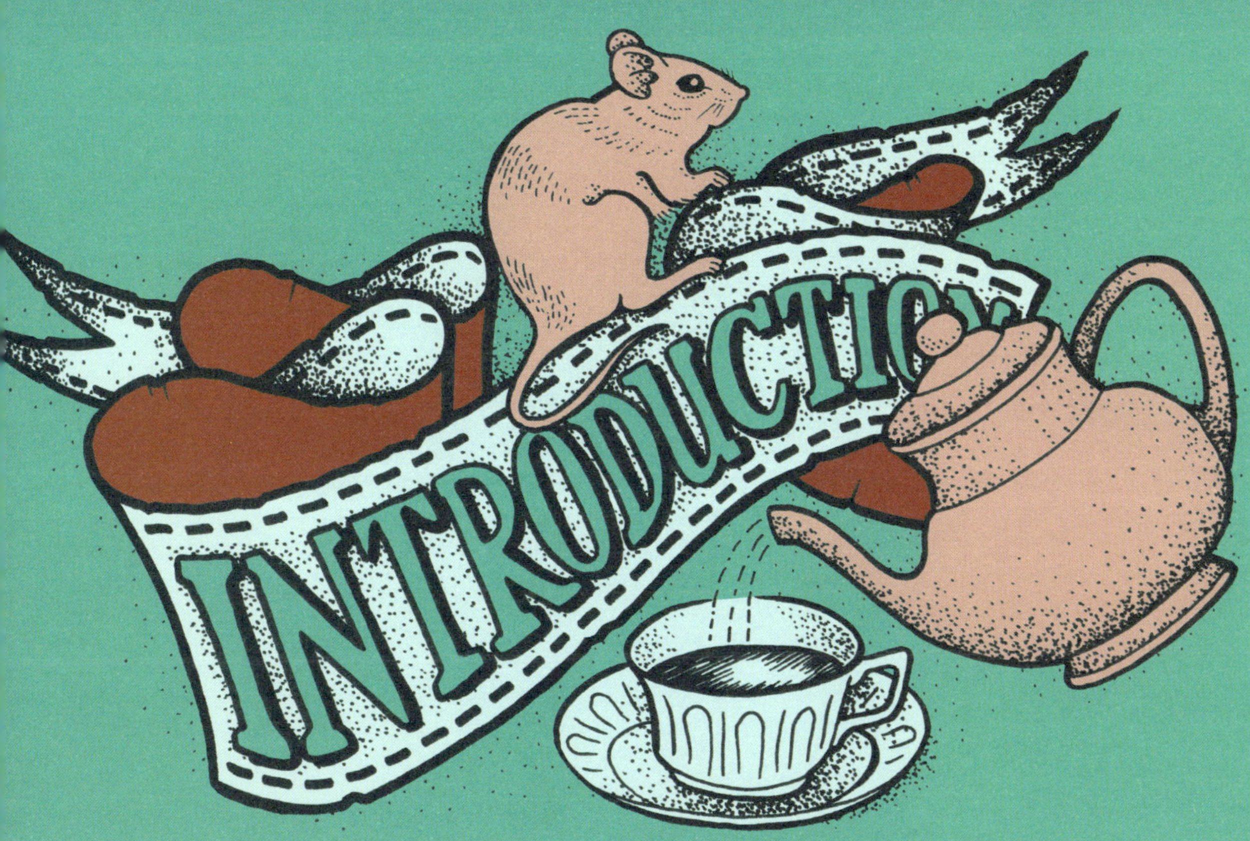

Nice lettering doesn't come easy. It takes a lot of practice, even if you're talented. This book will hopefully help set you in the right direction.

Improved writing and calligraphic skills come in handy, both in everyday life and in arts and crafts. When making script designs, you add your own personality to the words. It doesn't have to be excessive!

These pages will give you new ideas on how to match your own lettering to your artwork and more. You'll find some new styles to work with, without losing yourself on the way or setting your hopes too high. Always try to do your own thing and never copy. That is the true way to self-fulfilment. Every artist is unique and different, and sometimes we just need encouragement from others to keep on going.

Seek your own path and don't worry if you're not doing your stuff like everybody else. It's ok to steal a little here and there—we all do, or at least we're all influenced and inspired by each other. Without the guidance and knowledge of others, none of us can go very far.

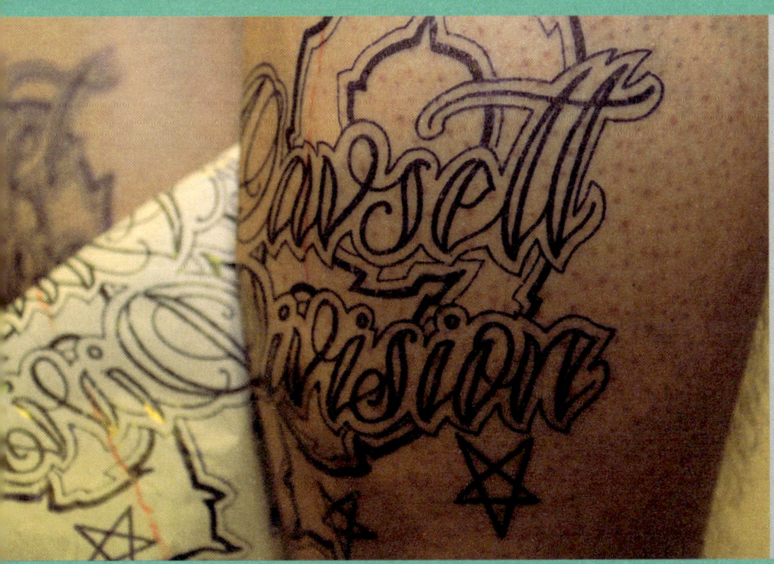

Putting on the stencils before the needle goes into the skin.

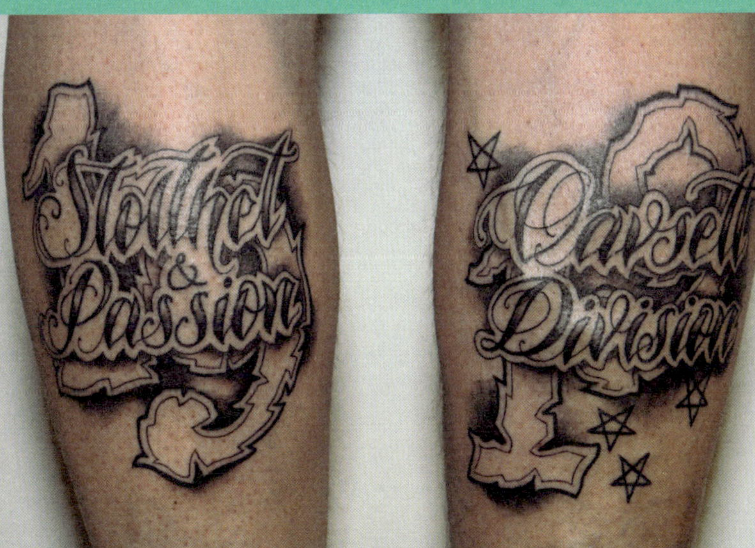

Finished tattoos on Nicklas Engström.

Chapter ONE

LETTERS AND NUMBERS

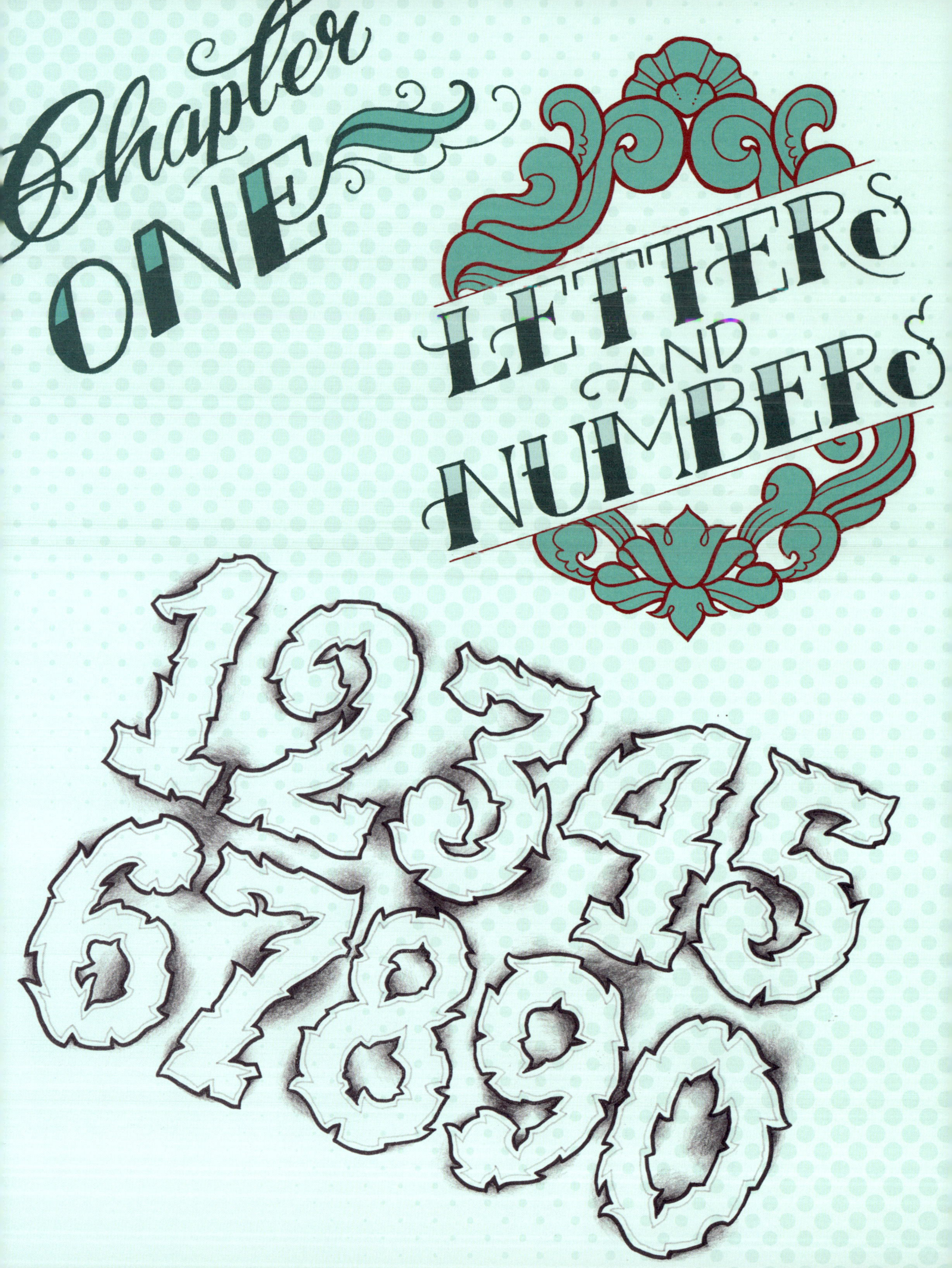

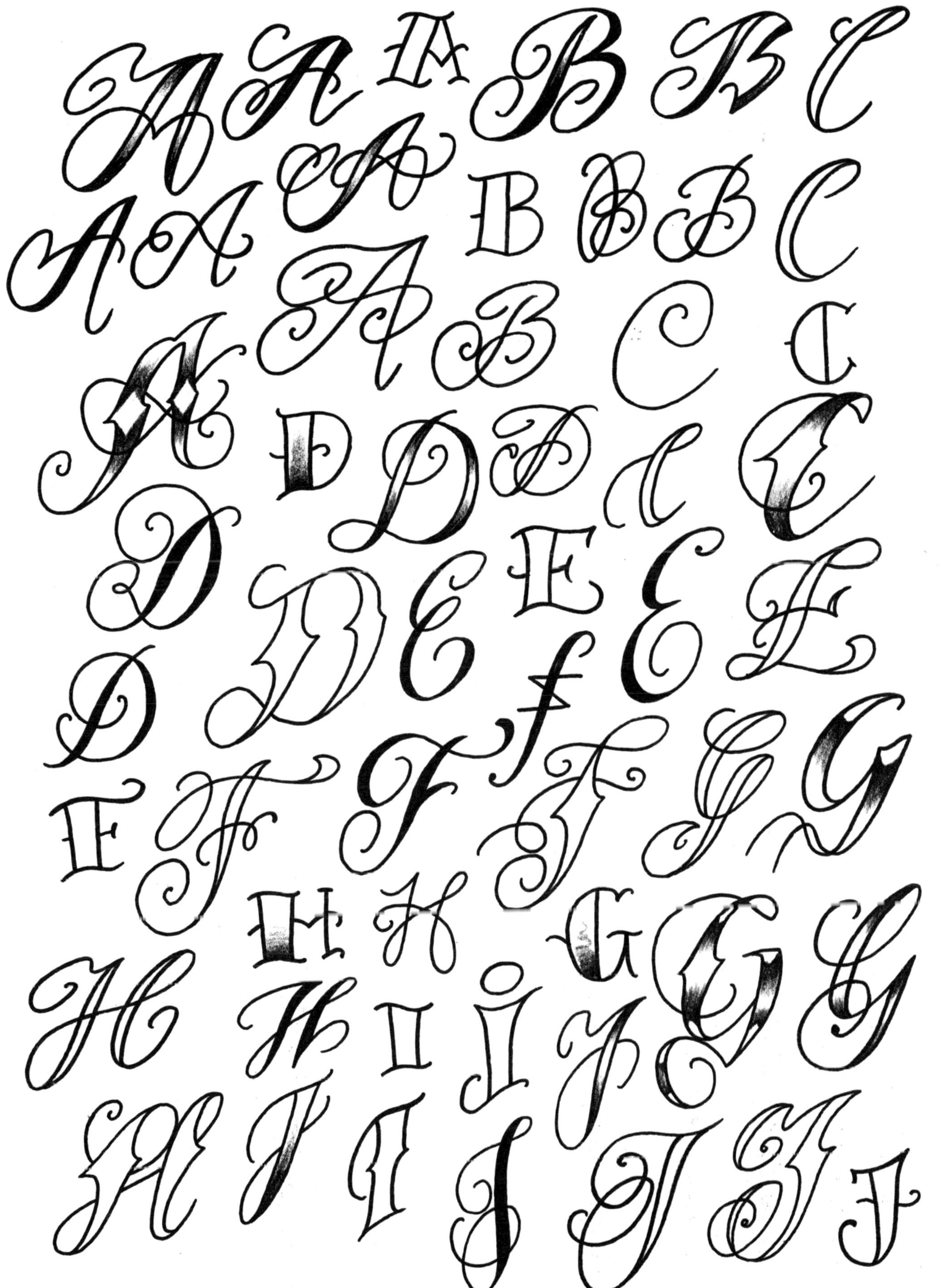

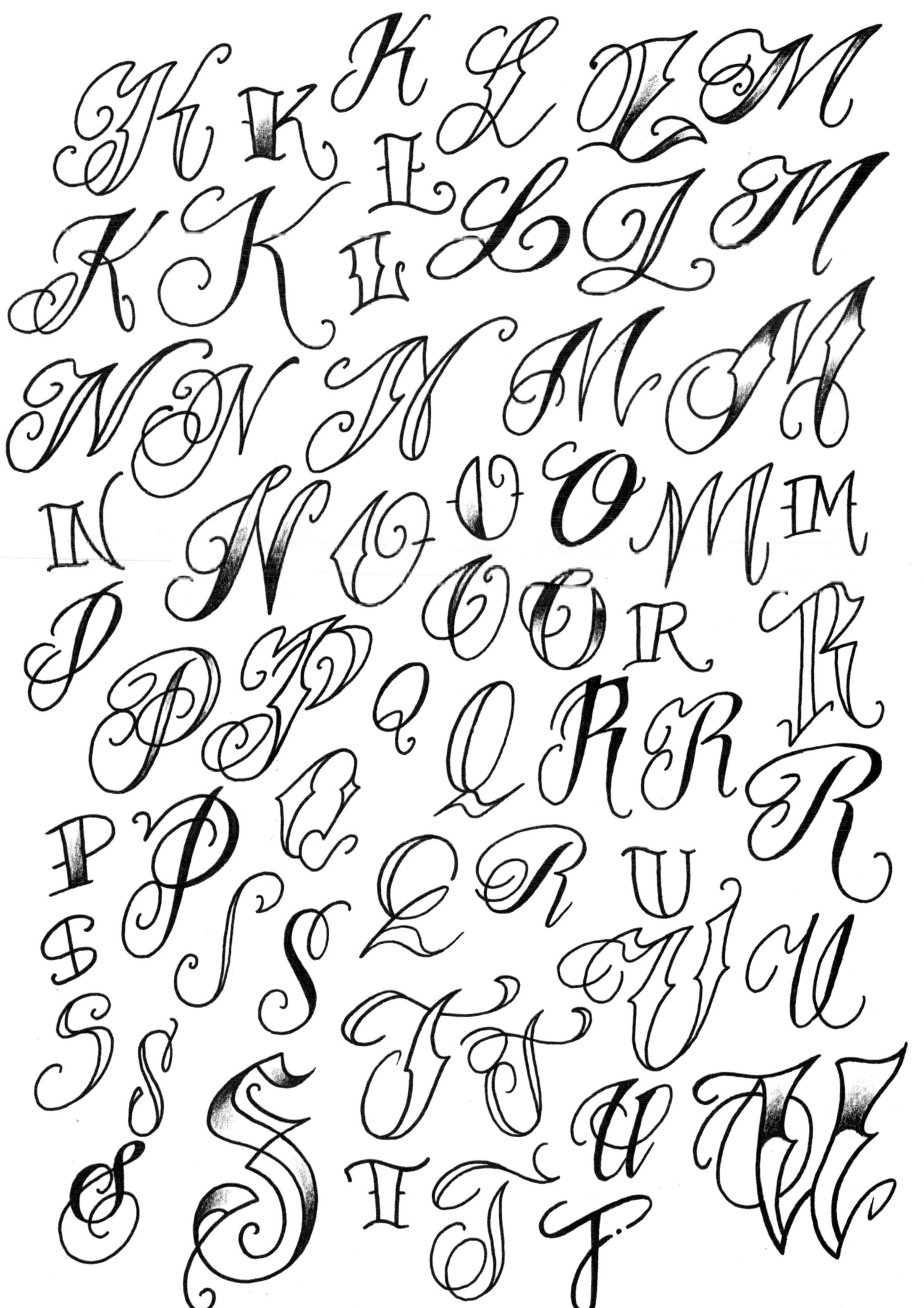

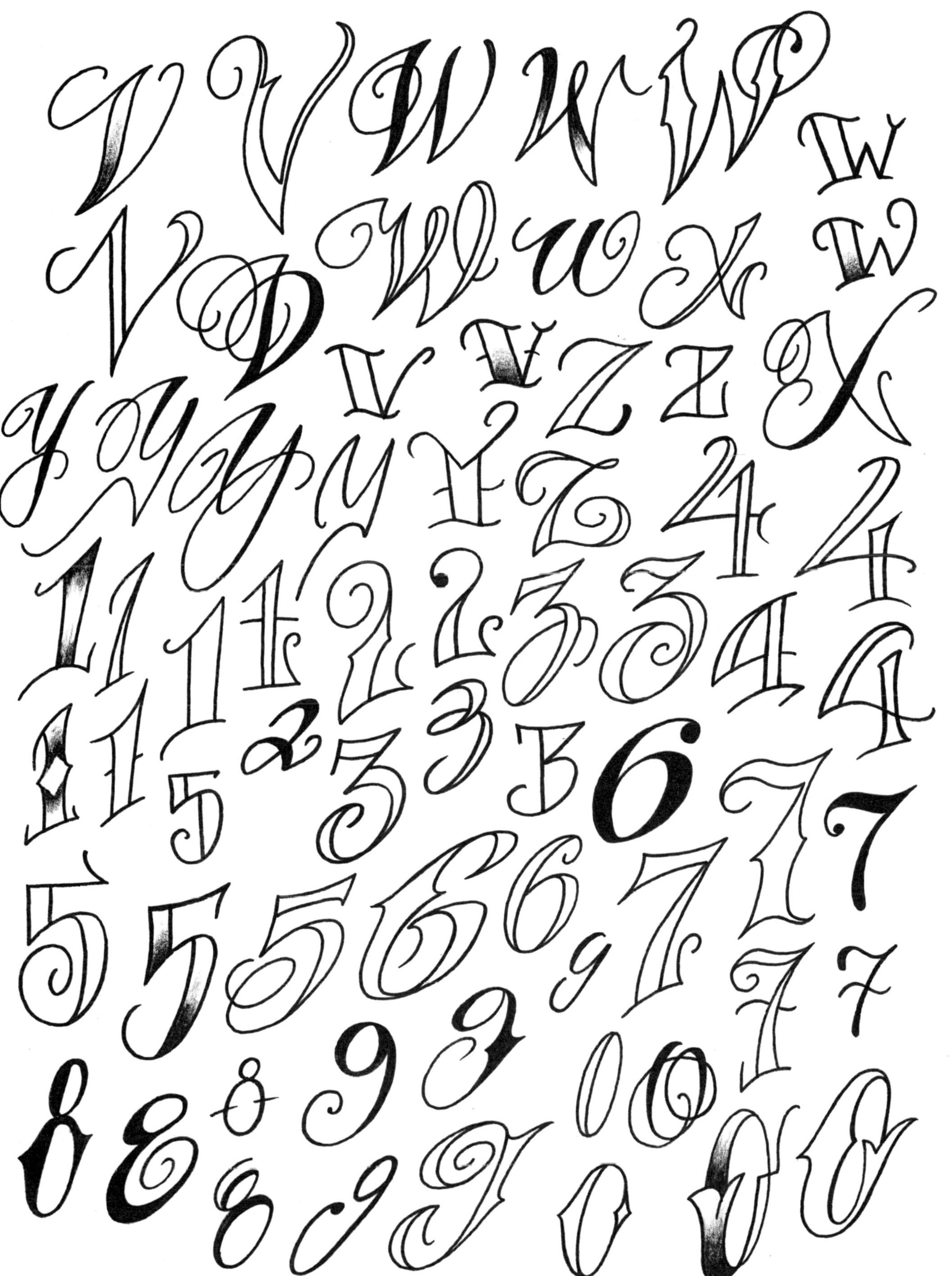

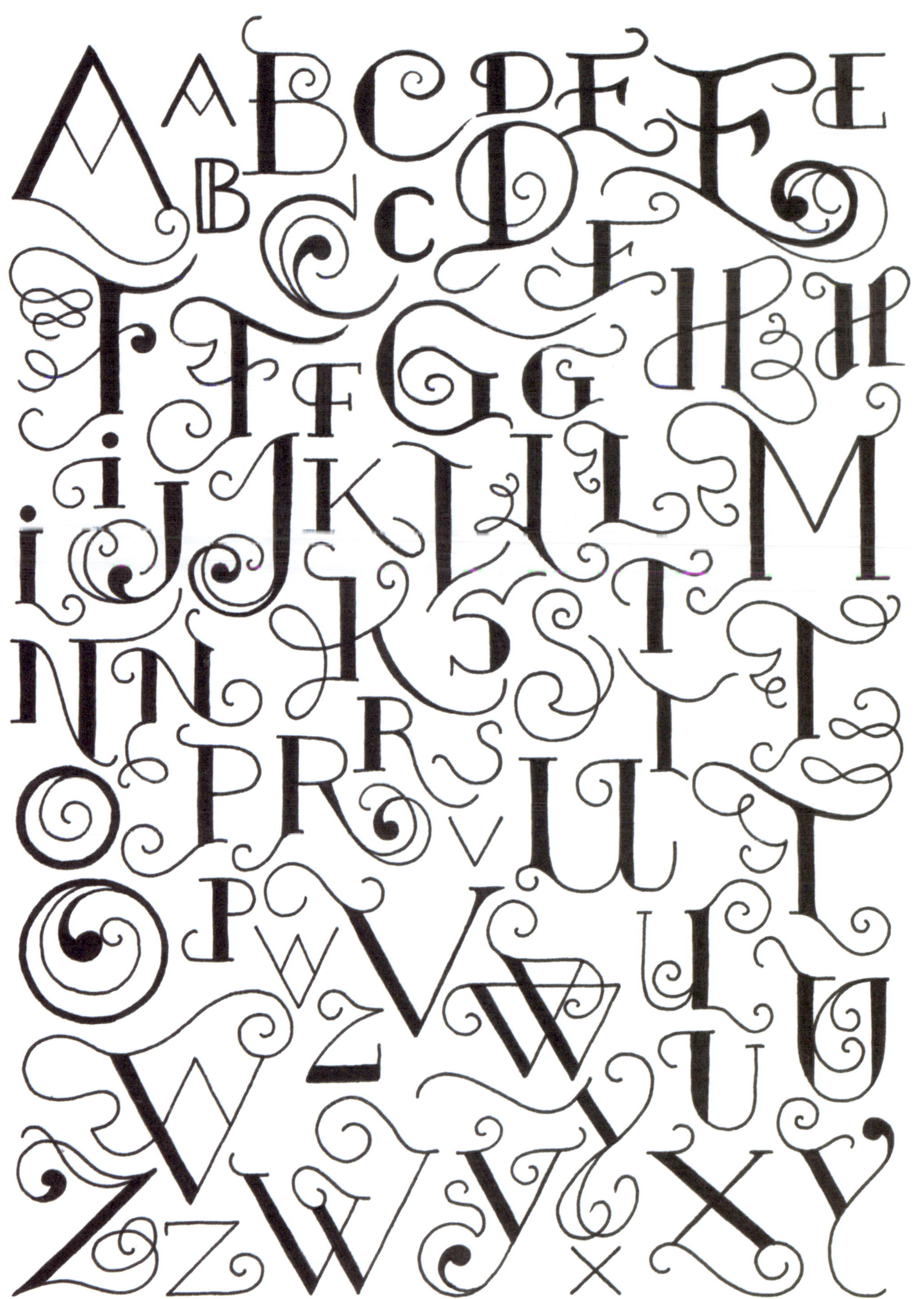

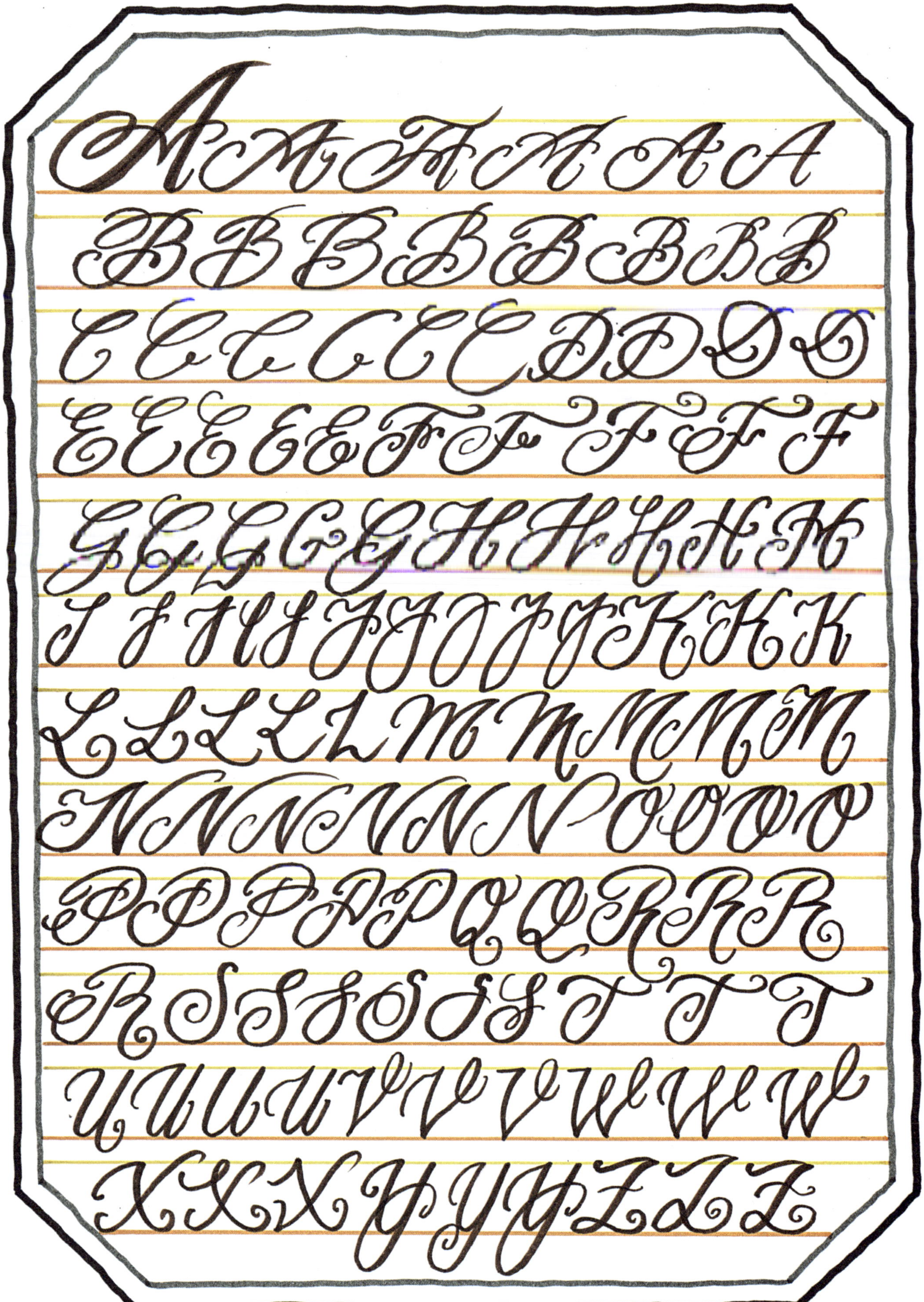

A A A A A A A A

B B B B B B B B B

C C C C C C D D D D

E E E E E F F F F F

G G G G H H H H H

I I I I J J J J K K K

L L L L L M M M M M M

N N N N N N N O O O O

P P P P P Q Q R R R

R S S S S S T T T T

U U U U V V V W W W W

X X X Y Y Y Z Z Z

Applepie Blowfish
Blueberry Blues Cup
Coffee & Cookies Candybar
Cherries Chocolatechip
Diamond Dresses Dove
Eggshell Earring Ebony
Easterbunny Eternity
Fashion Freedom
Garden Honeyrum
Ivory Juicy Jazz

Knife Loveletter

Lollipop Lace Monkey

Masquerade Nightingale

Nostalgia Opera Poolcue

Pineapple Pearlnecklace

Peony Roses Submarine

Stockings Spongecake

Tomatosalad Thick'n'Thin

Tattoo Together Umbrella

Ukelele Valentine Witch

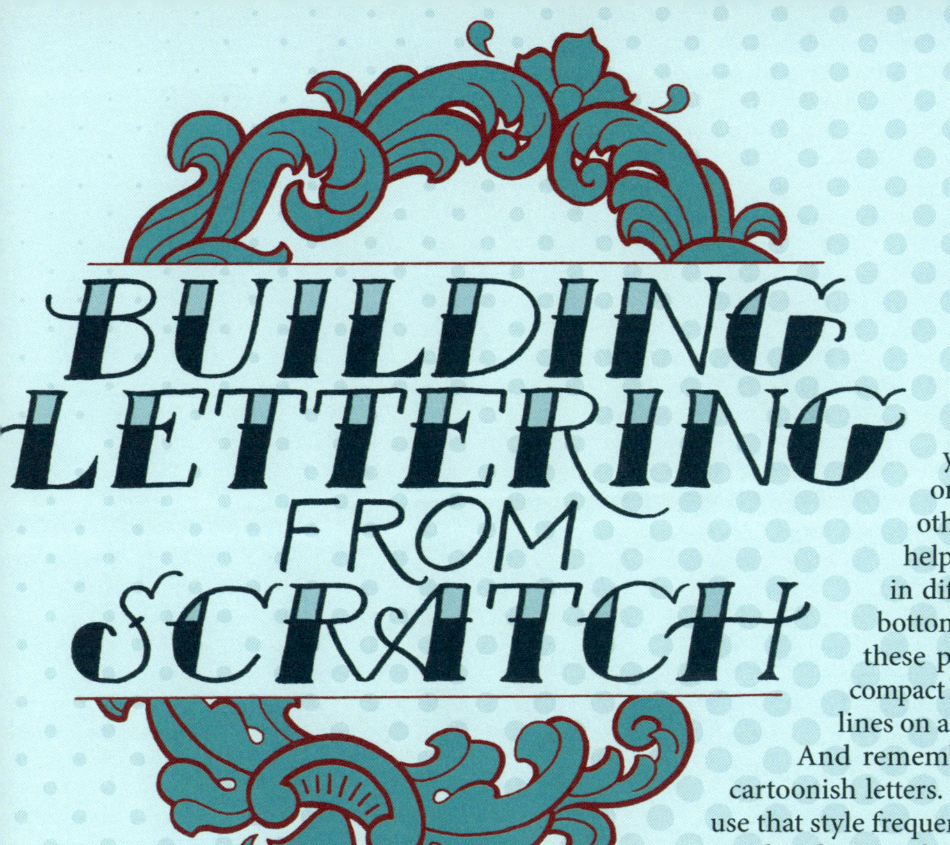

Building Lettering from Scratch

As you turn the pages, you'll find little step-by-step drawings here and there. For some of you, one quick look at an example of lettering or drawing might be enough to get inspired. For others, here are some ideas and tricks that might help. Transparent paper is just fantastic and comes in different weights. If you are starting from rock bottom, put a piece of transparent paper on top of these pages and start practicing your lettering. A compact light table is useful, too. Putting a few supportive lines on a piece of paper is a great way to start a design. And remember: There is nothing wrong with straight, cartoonish letters. They are basic in old school tattooing, and I use that style frequently.

For handwriting-based styles, here are more tips. To create letters that are fat, put some extra lines on the vertical parts of the letter, and build up on both sides to fatten the letter. Keep the letter thinner close to the bottom and top. In many styles, the horizontal lines should not be fat.

If you are insecure about how to angle letters vertically, keep the letters straight by using a squared paper underneath. If you want cursive text, change the supportive lines to create the perfect angle.

Wave-shaped lettering sometimes looks more vibrant. The S-shape is standard for beauty and curve. Imagine female legs and feet in high heels. Using the wave-shaped supportive line, your words come to life.

Always start at the bottom, working your way up, to create positive energy. You can keep the letters the same size or start big to go smaller. Again, there are no rules. These are just my own guidelines.

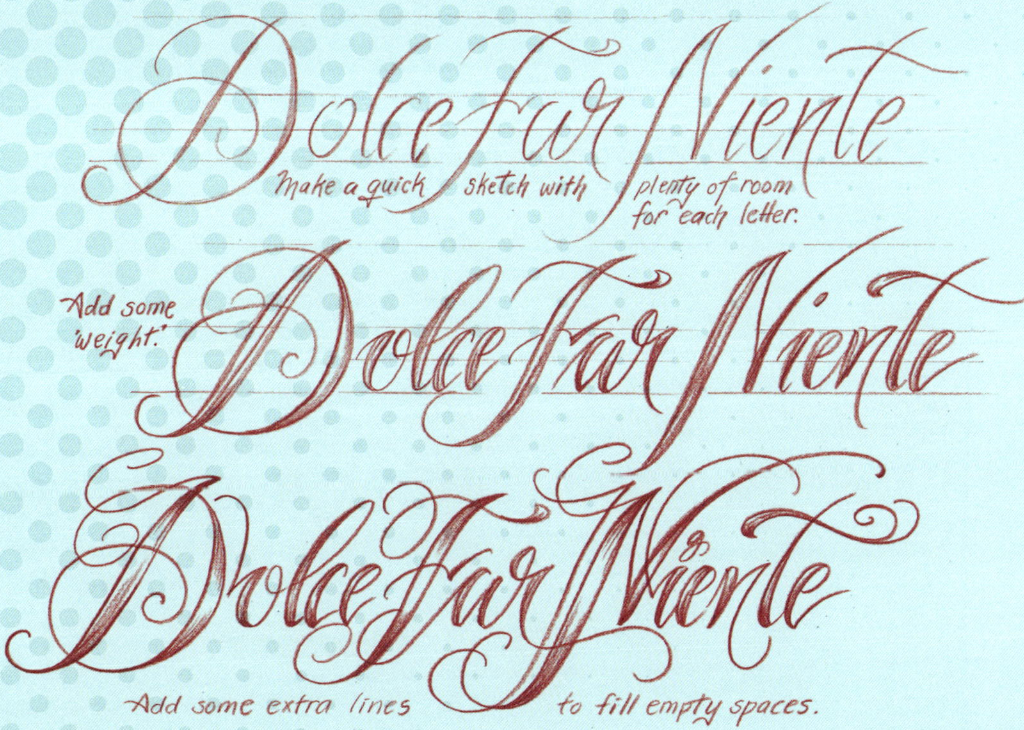

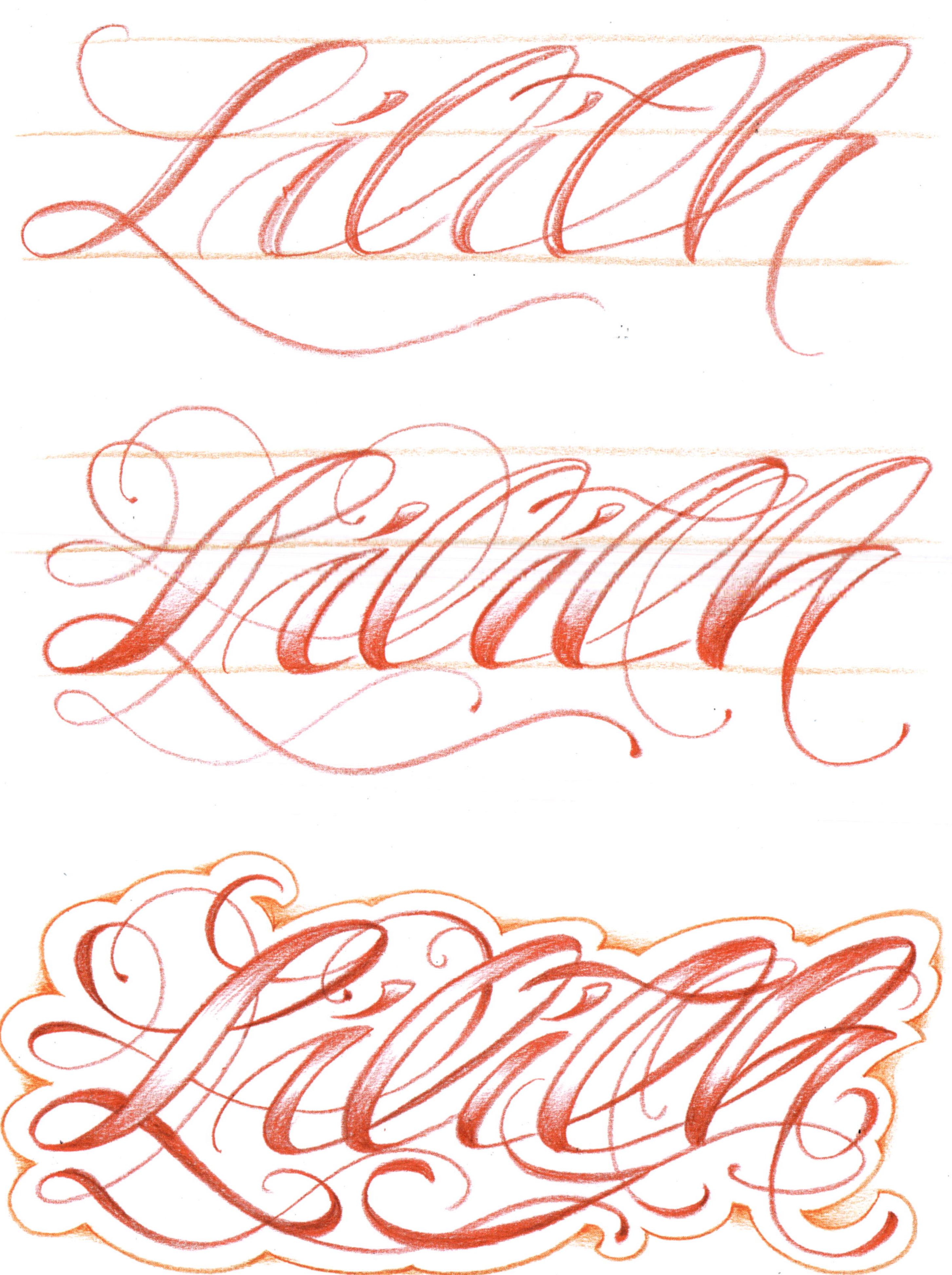
Lilith
Lilith
Lilith

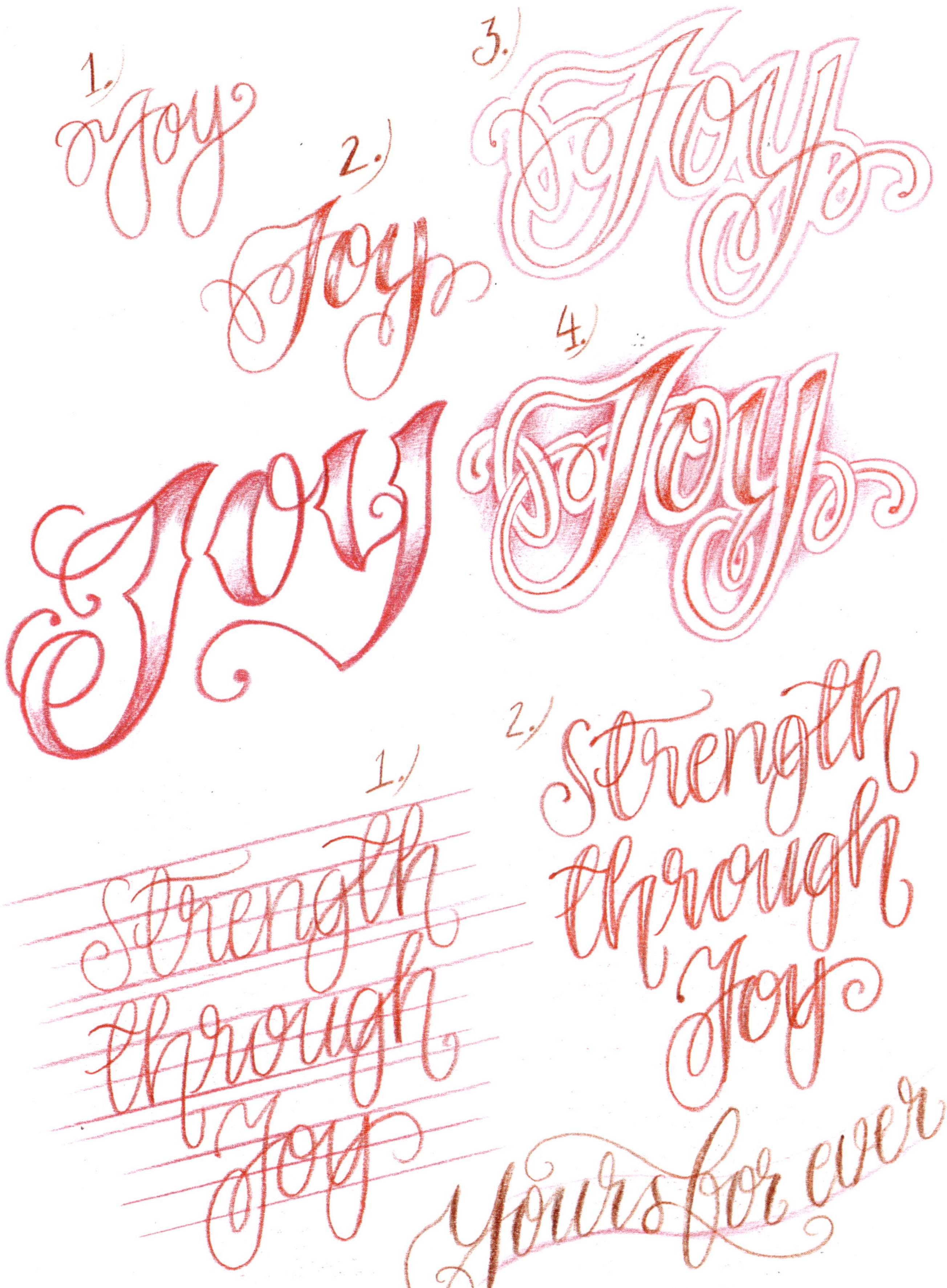

1. Joy

2. Joy

3. Joy

Joy

4. Joy

1. Strength through Joy

2. Strength through Joy

Yours for ever

Never Forgive

Never Forgive

Never Forgive

Never Forgive

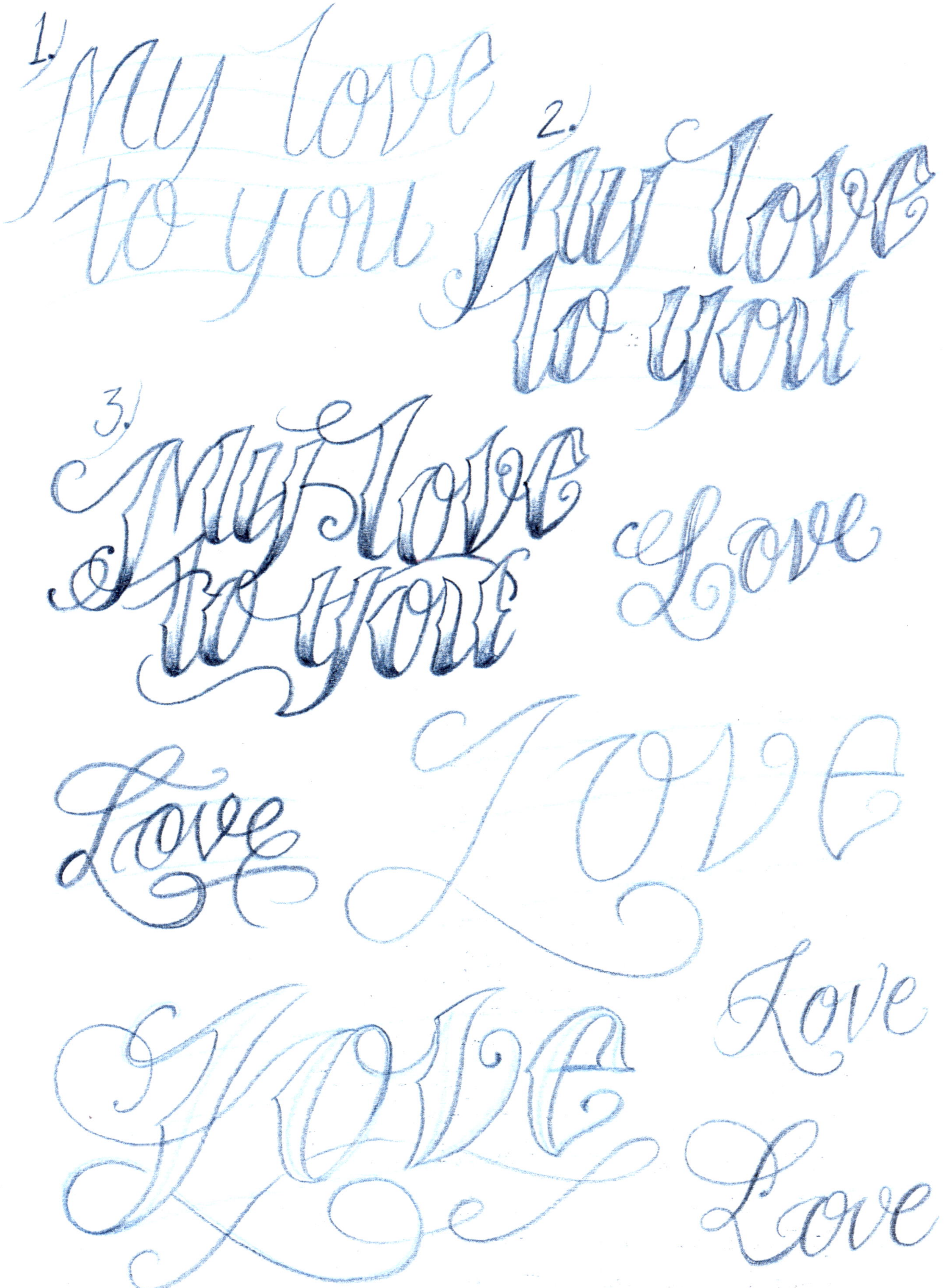

1.) My love to you

2.) My love to you

3.) My love to you

Love

Love

Love

Love

Love

Love

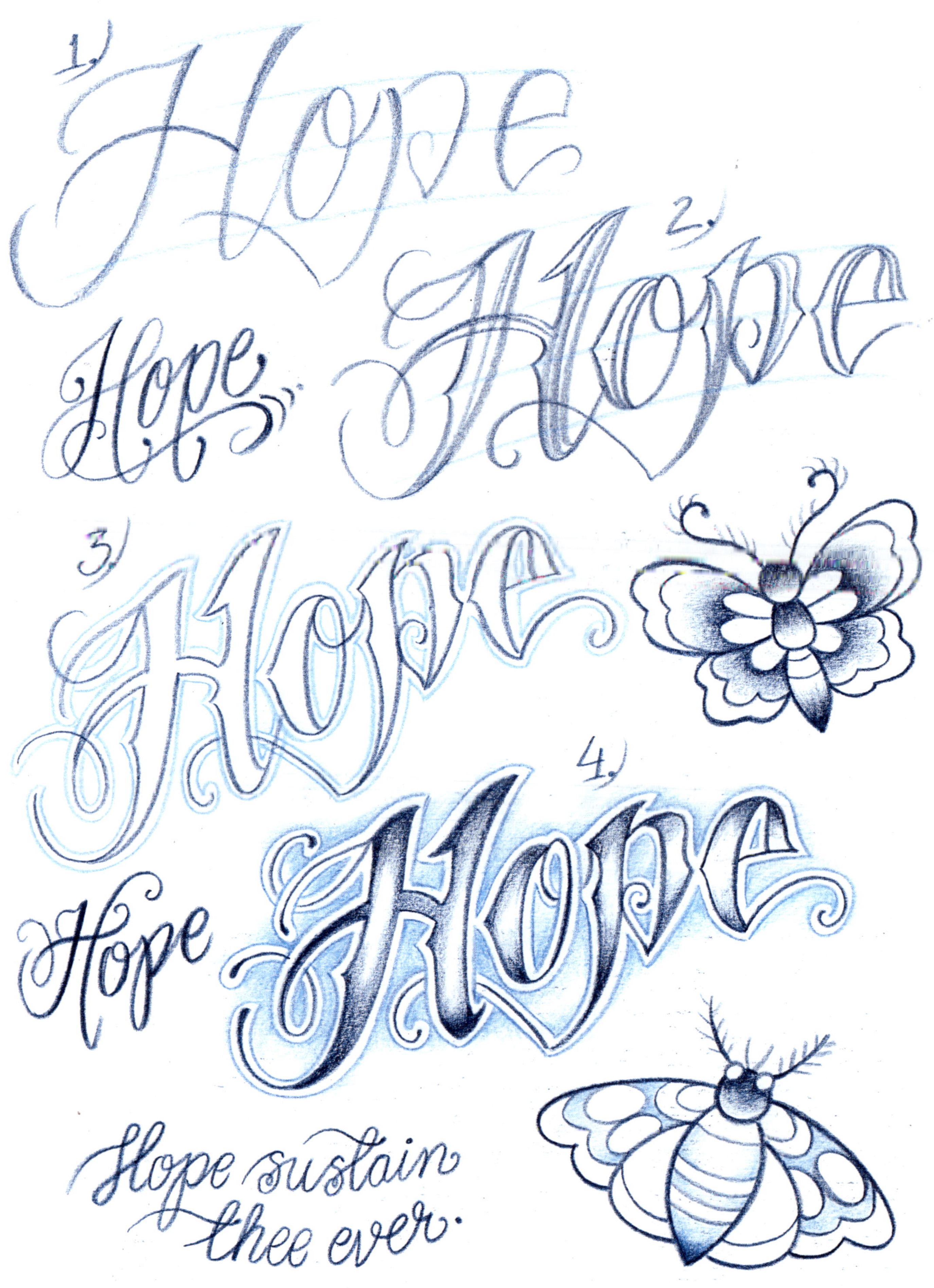
1.
Hope
2.
Hope
Hope
3.
Hope
4.
Hope
Hope
Hope sustain
thee ever.

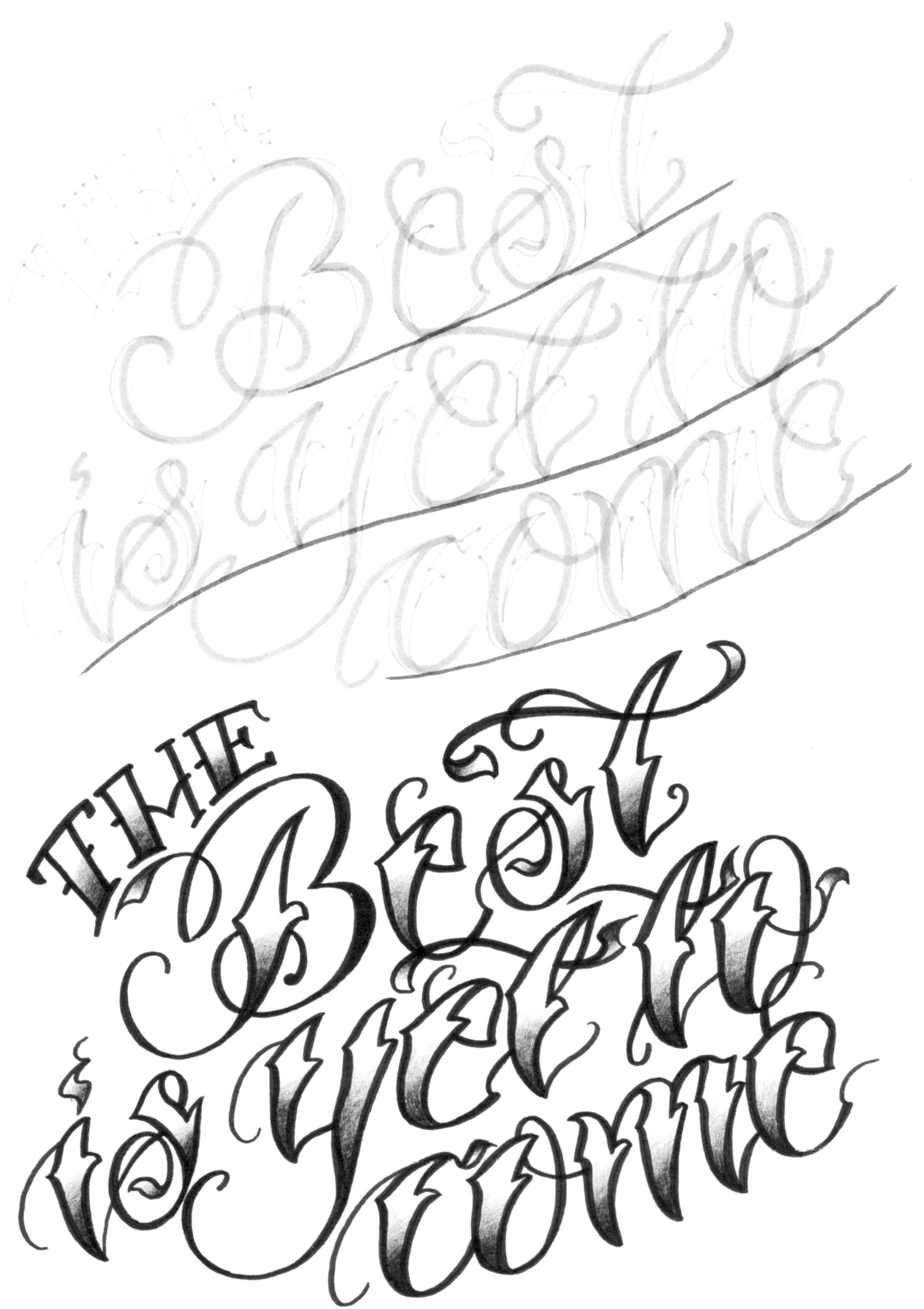
The Best is yet to come

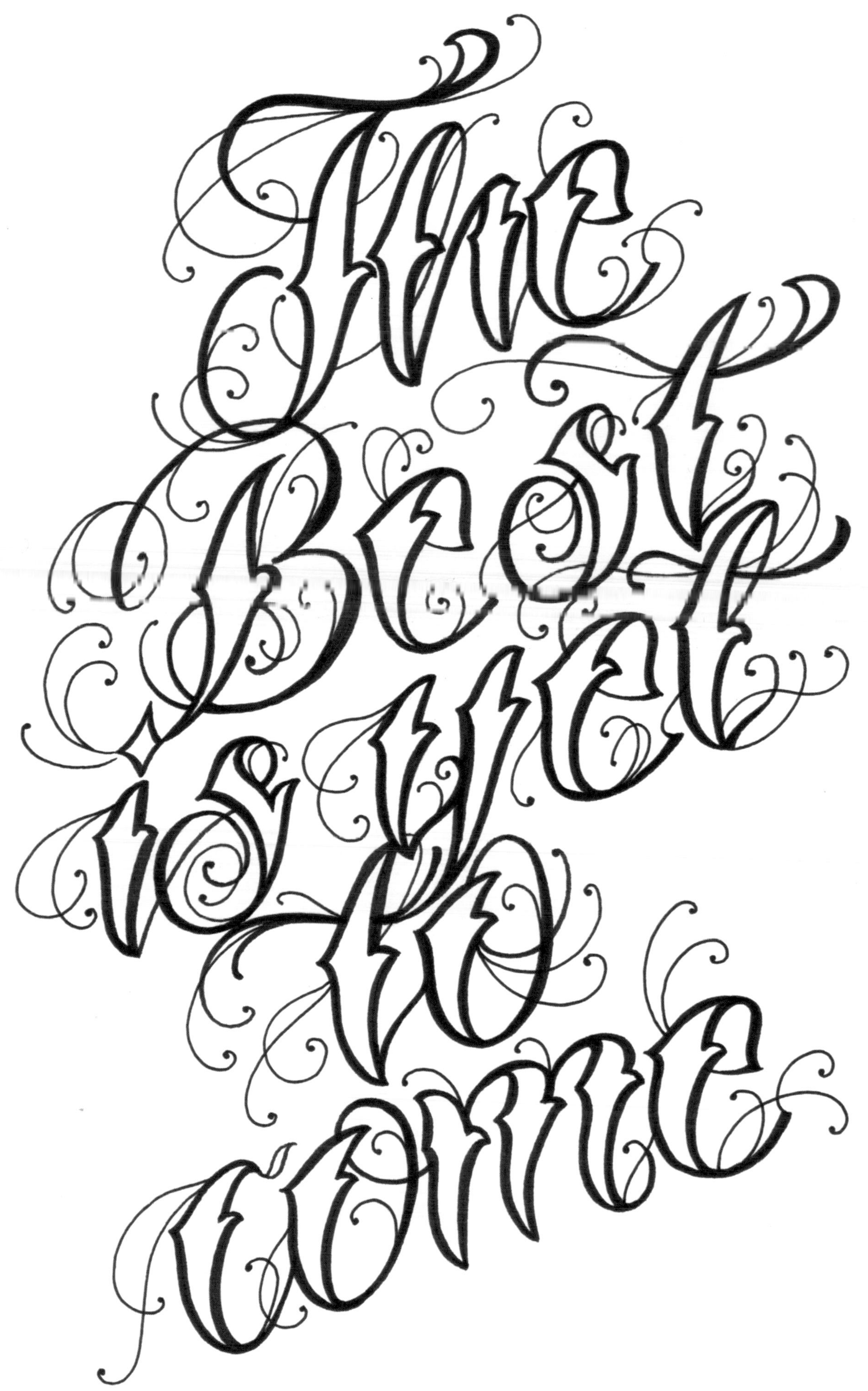
The Best is yet to come

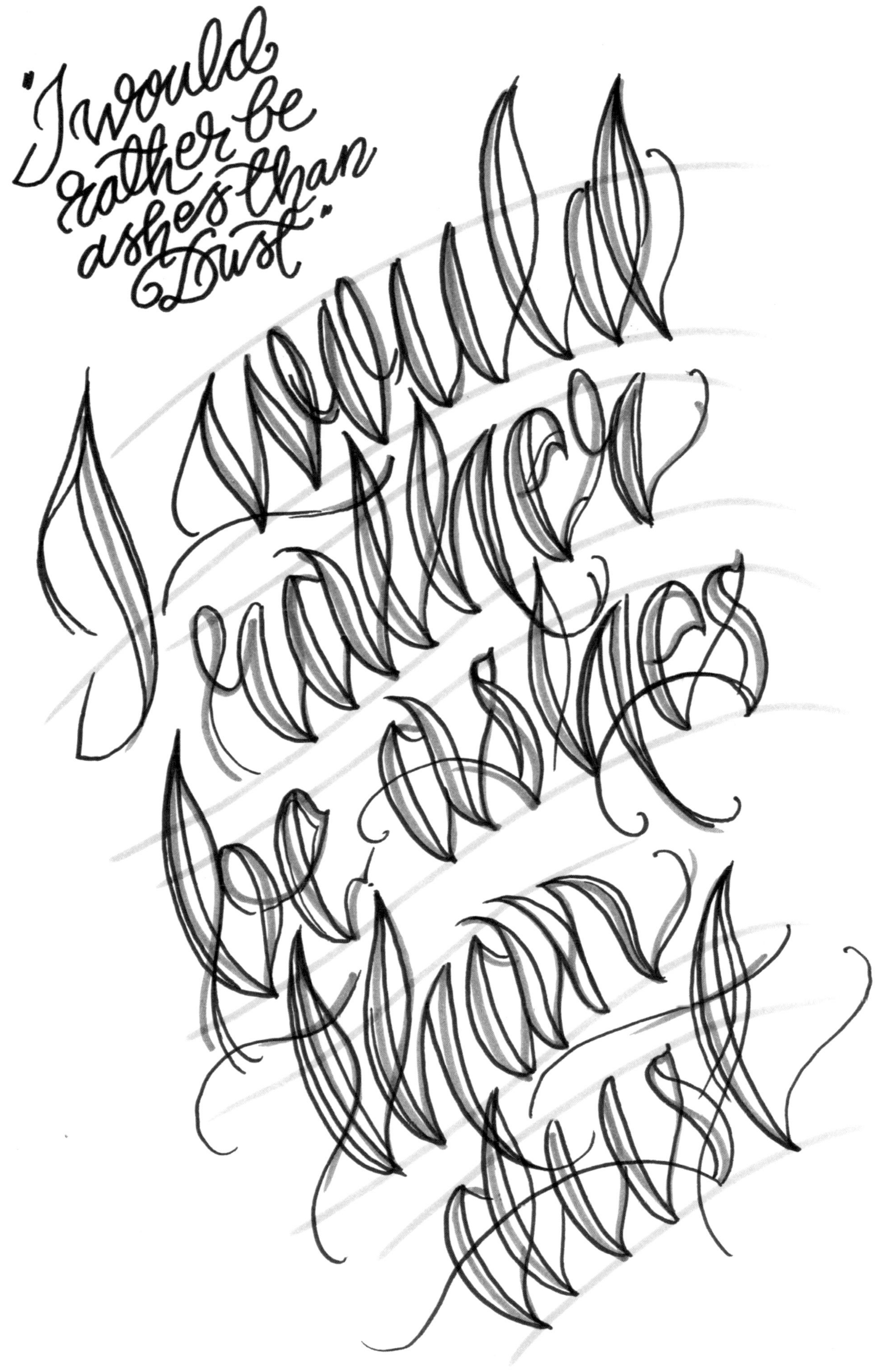
"I would rather be ashes than Dust."
I would rather be ashes than dust

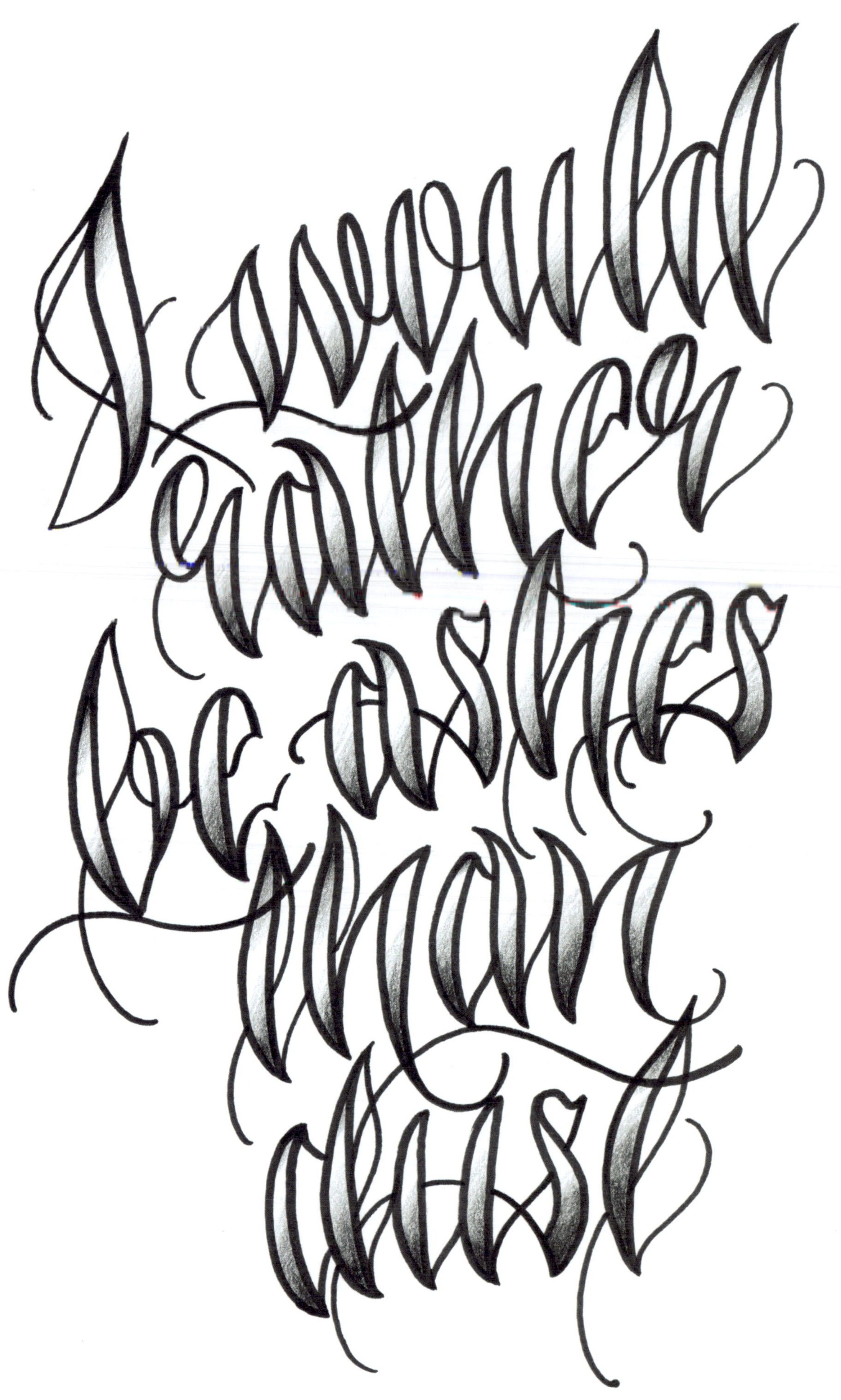
I would
rather
be ashes
than
dust

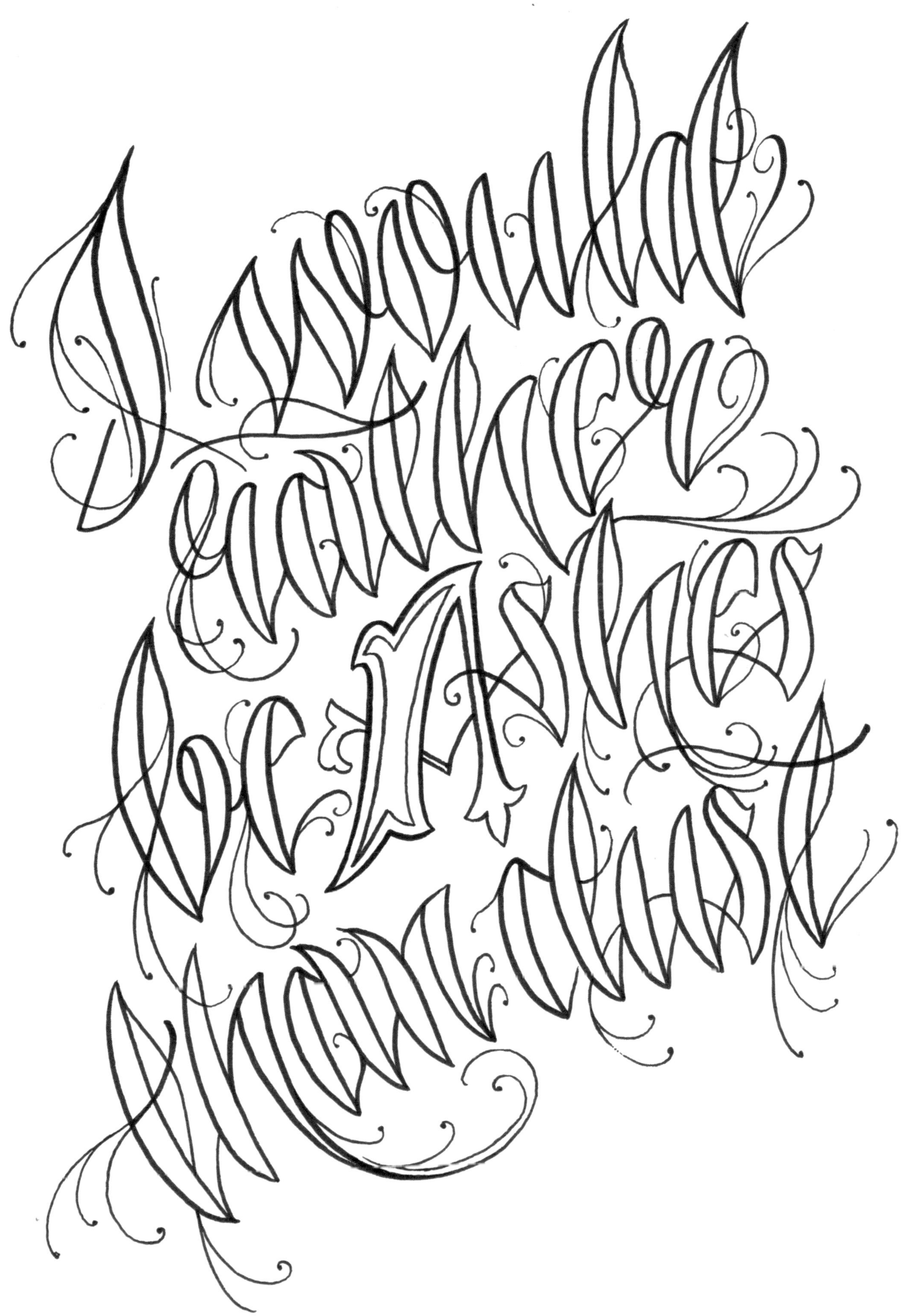
I would
rather
be Ashes
than dust

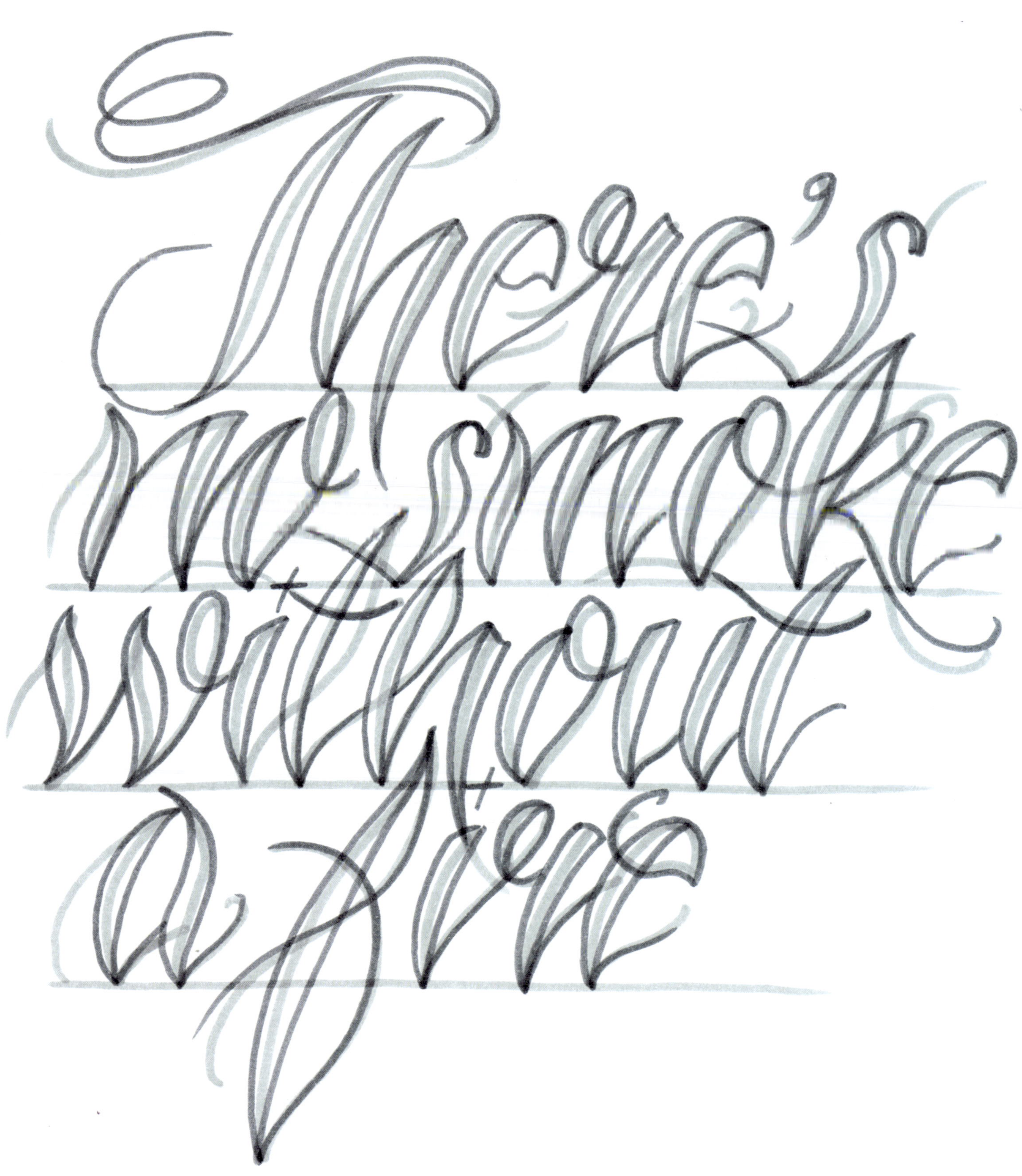
There's
no smoke
without
a fire

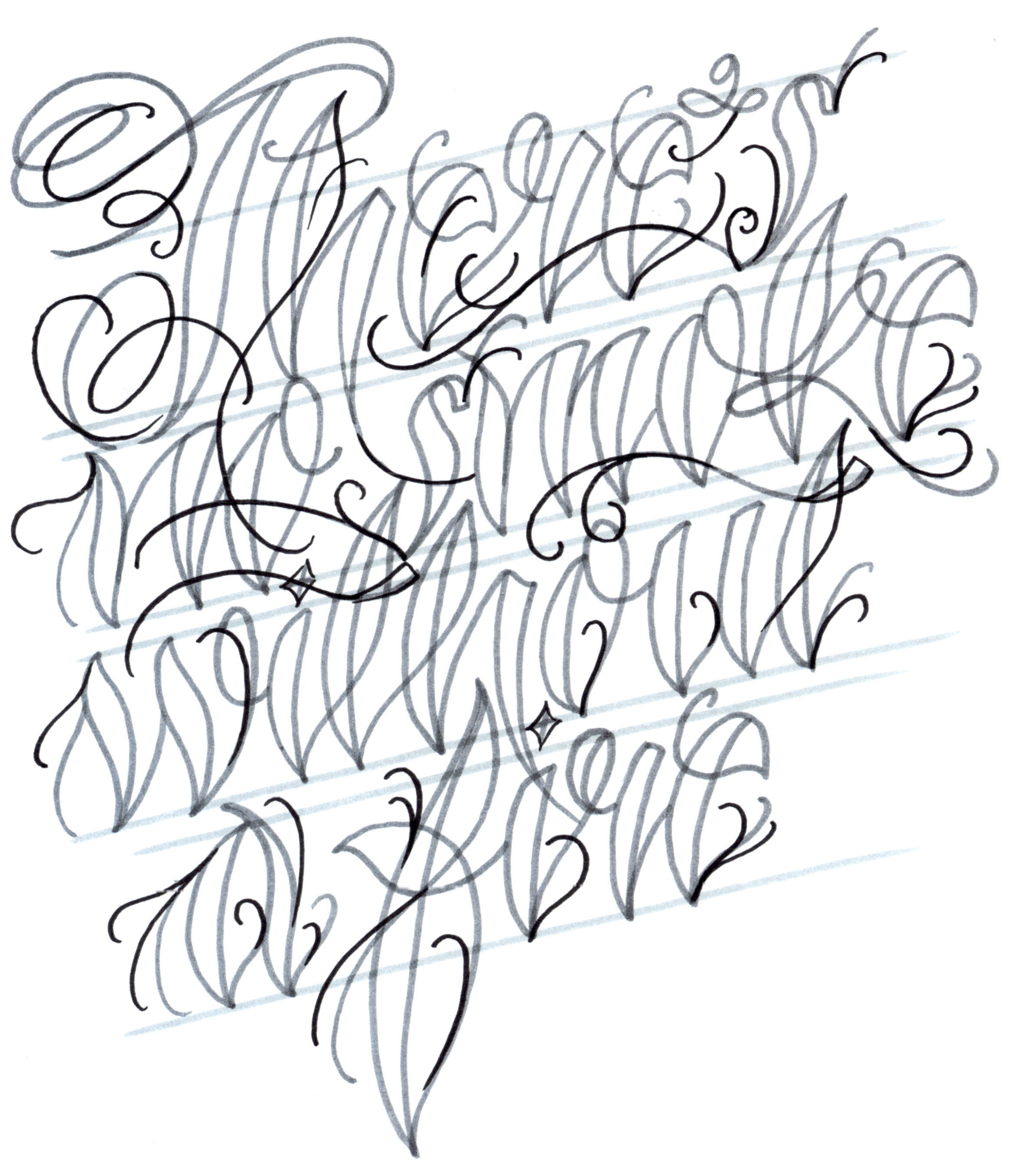

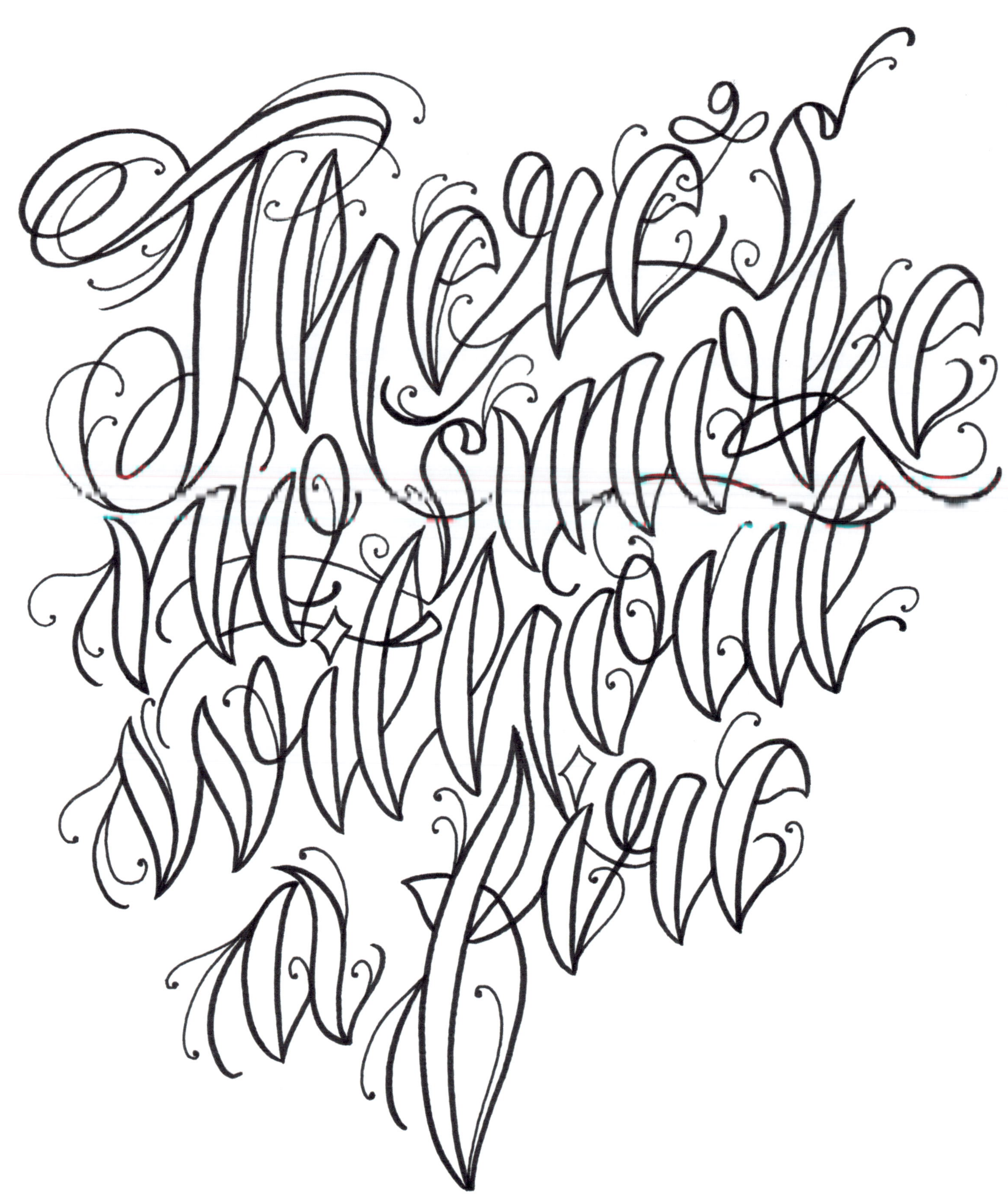

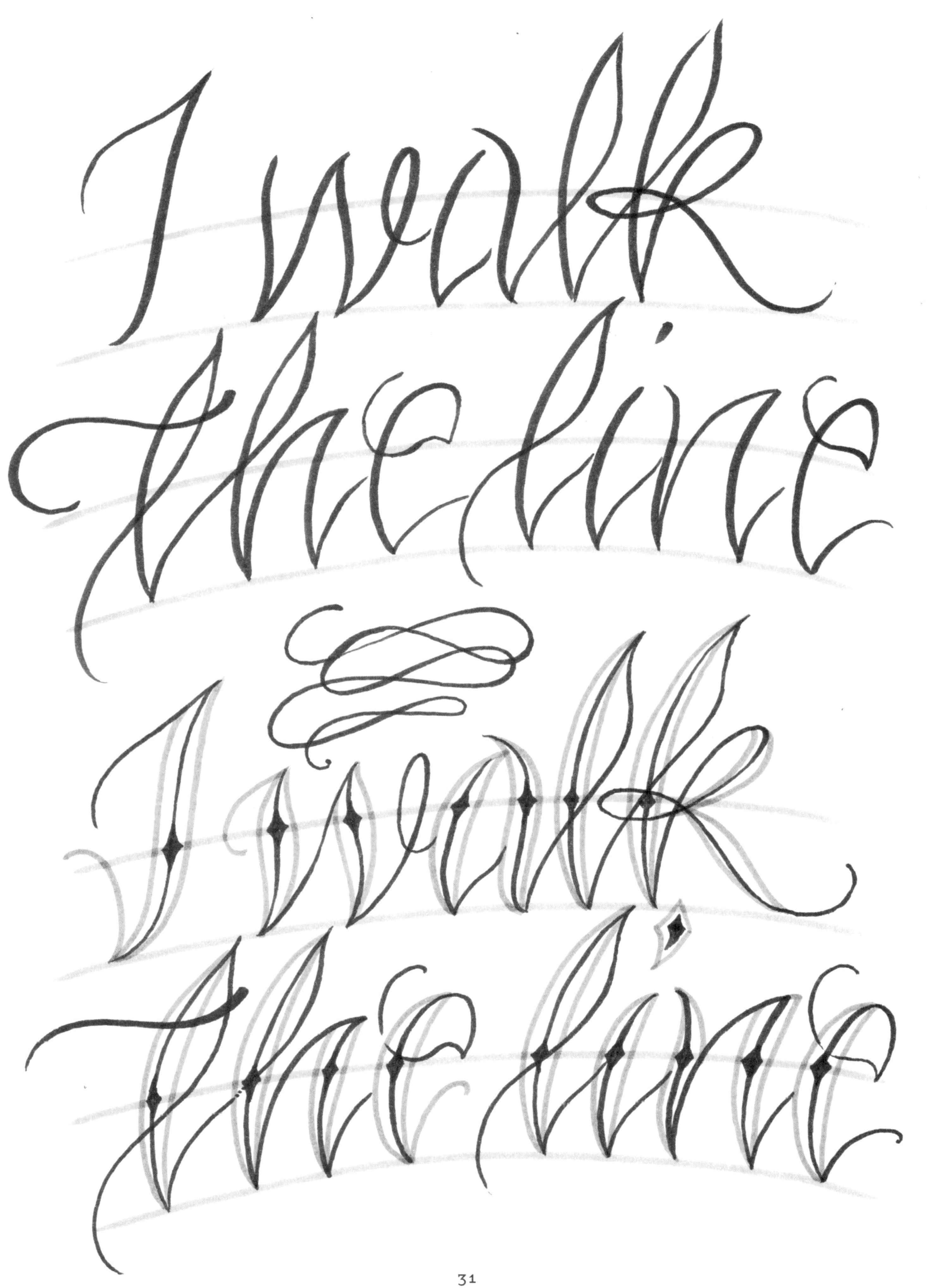
I walk
the line
I walk
the line

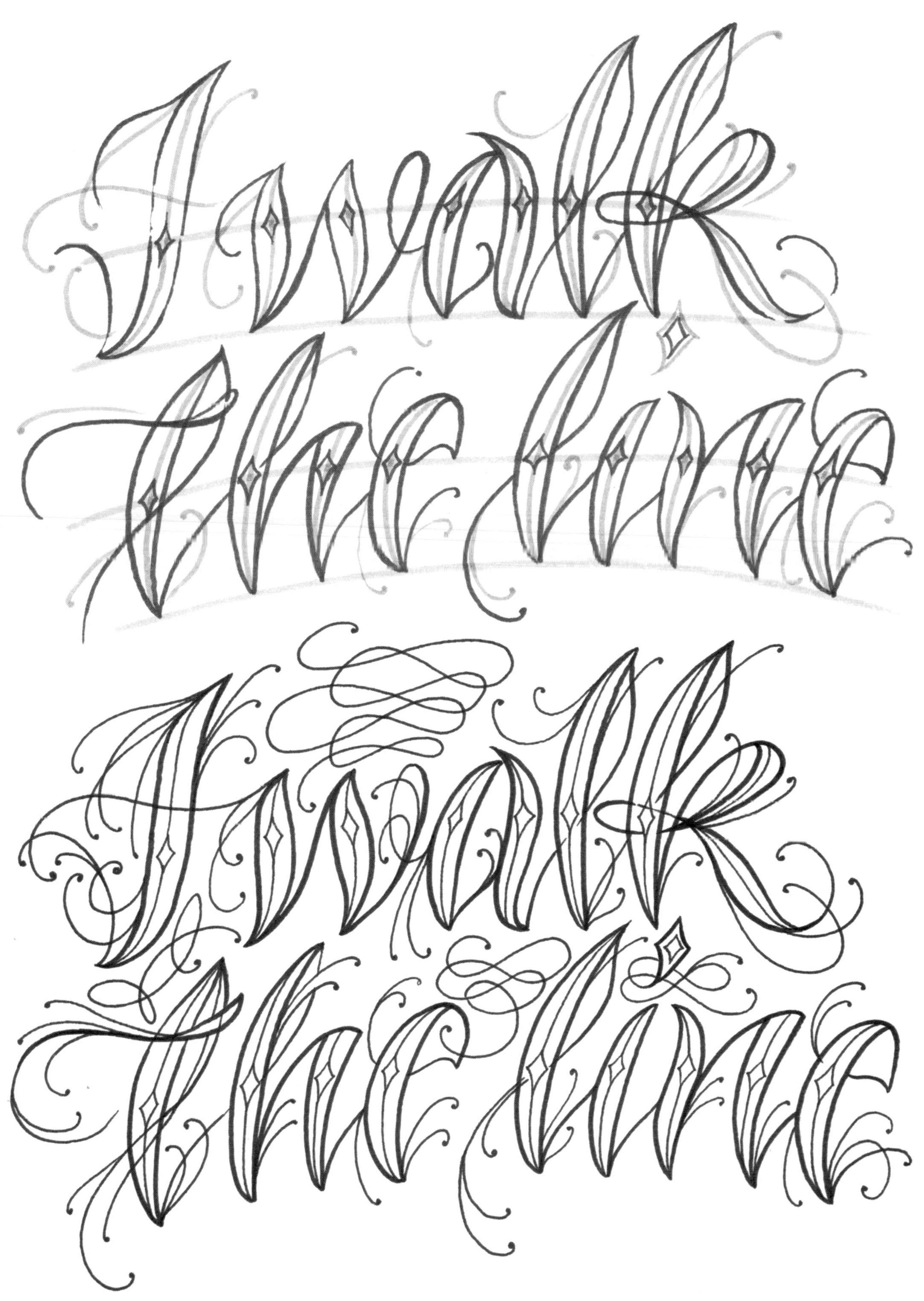
I walk
the line
I walk
the line

A friend to all is a friend to none

No worries

No worries

No worries

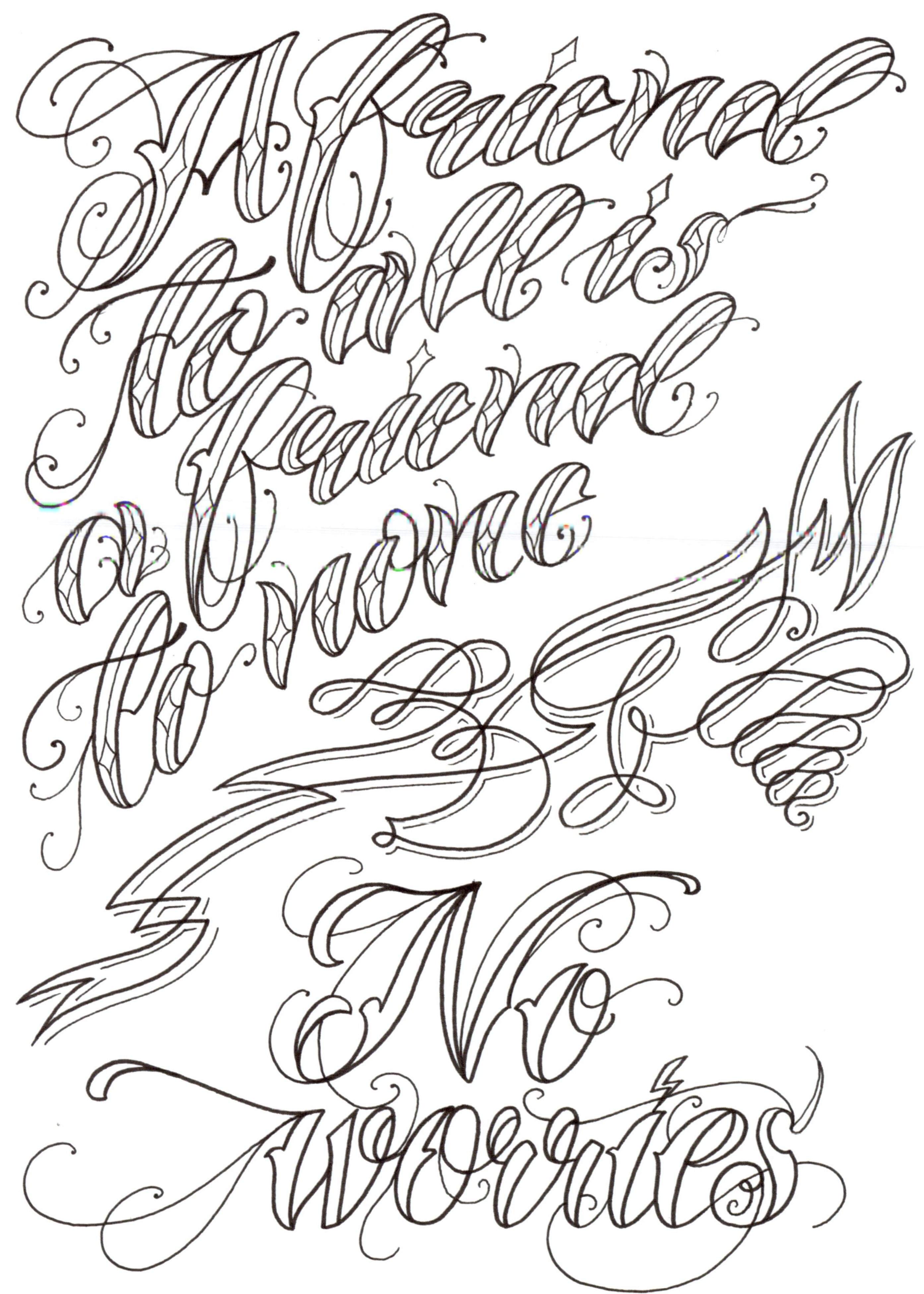
A Friend To All Is A Friend To None
No Favorites

Chapter TWO
LETTERING WITH CONTOURS

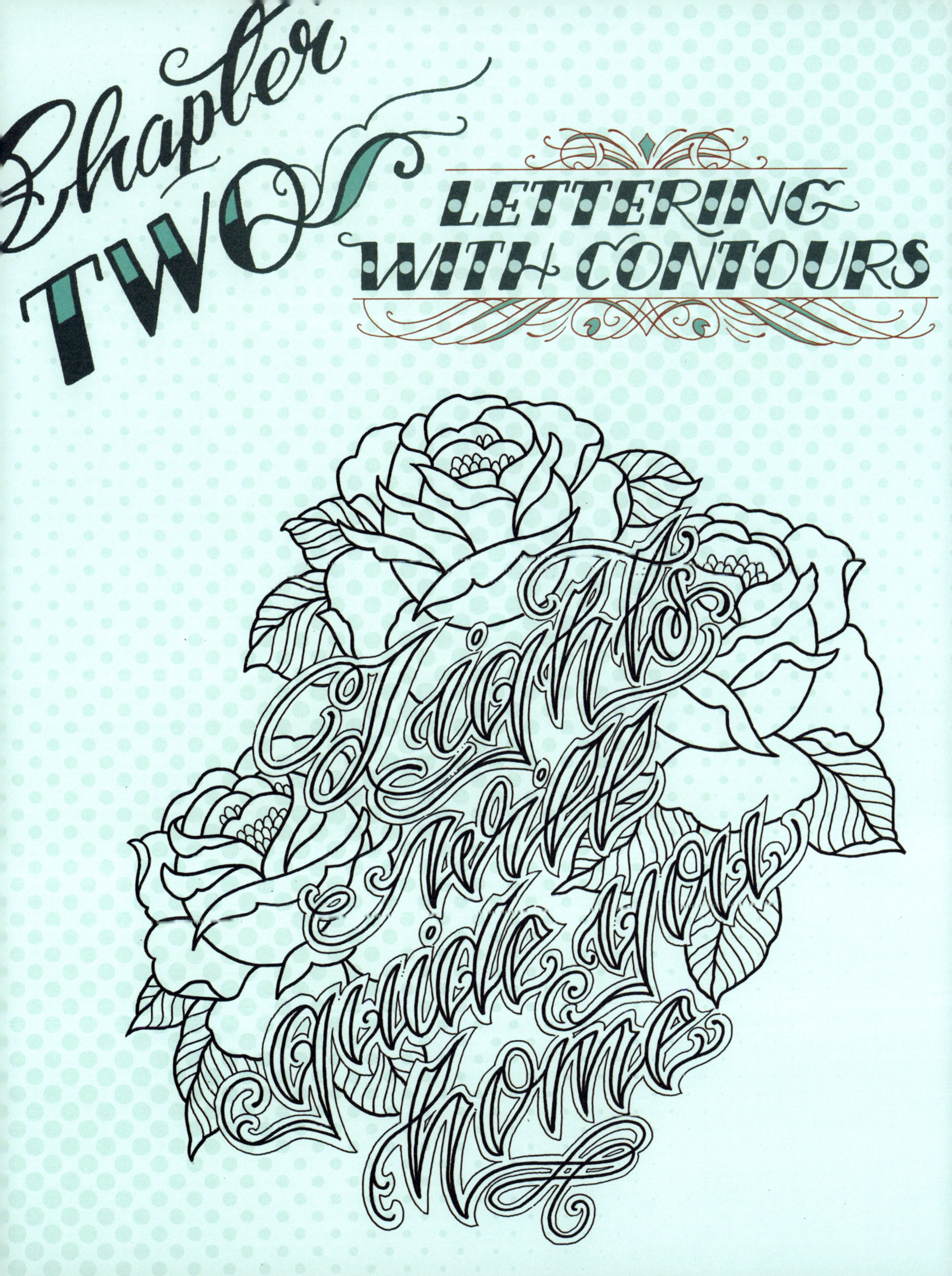

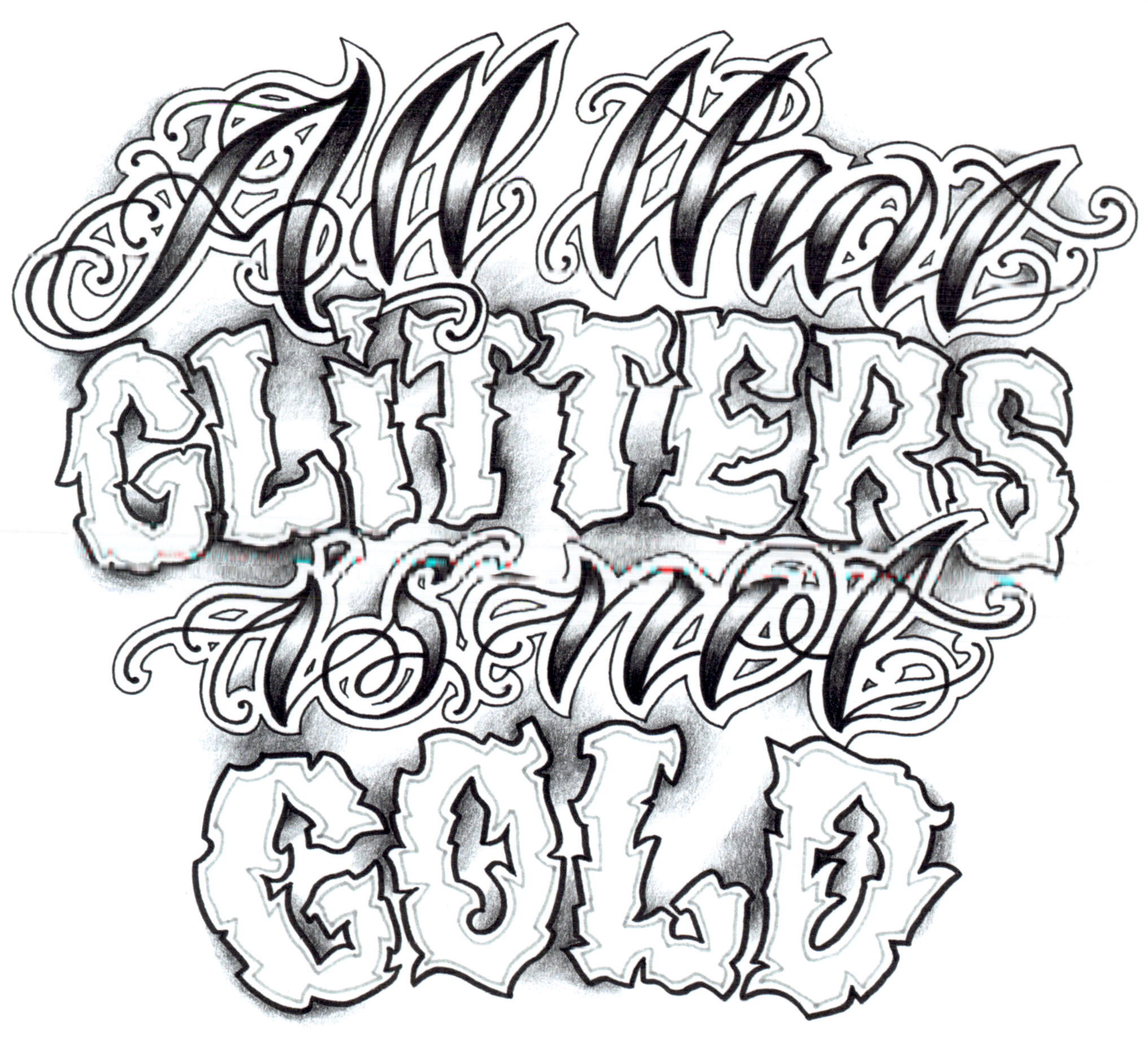

When mixing lettering and drawings, it is nice to keep them from blurring together. One easy way is to draw a line around the words, following the contours. If you don't go too close to the text, you'll create some space around it, which will visually make the text pop more. If you feel no urge to separate the text from what is around it, or simply want to achieve a complicated look, draw the line closer to the contours and fill all gaps inside the letters, too.

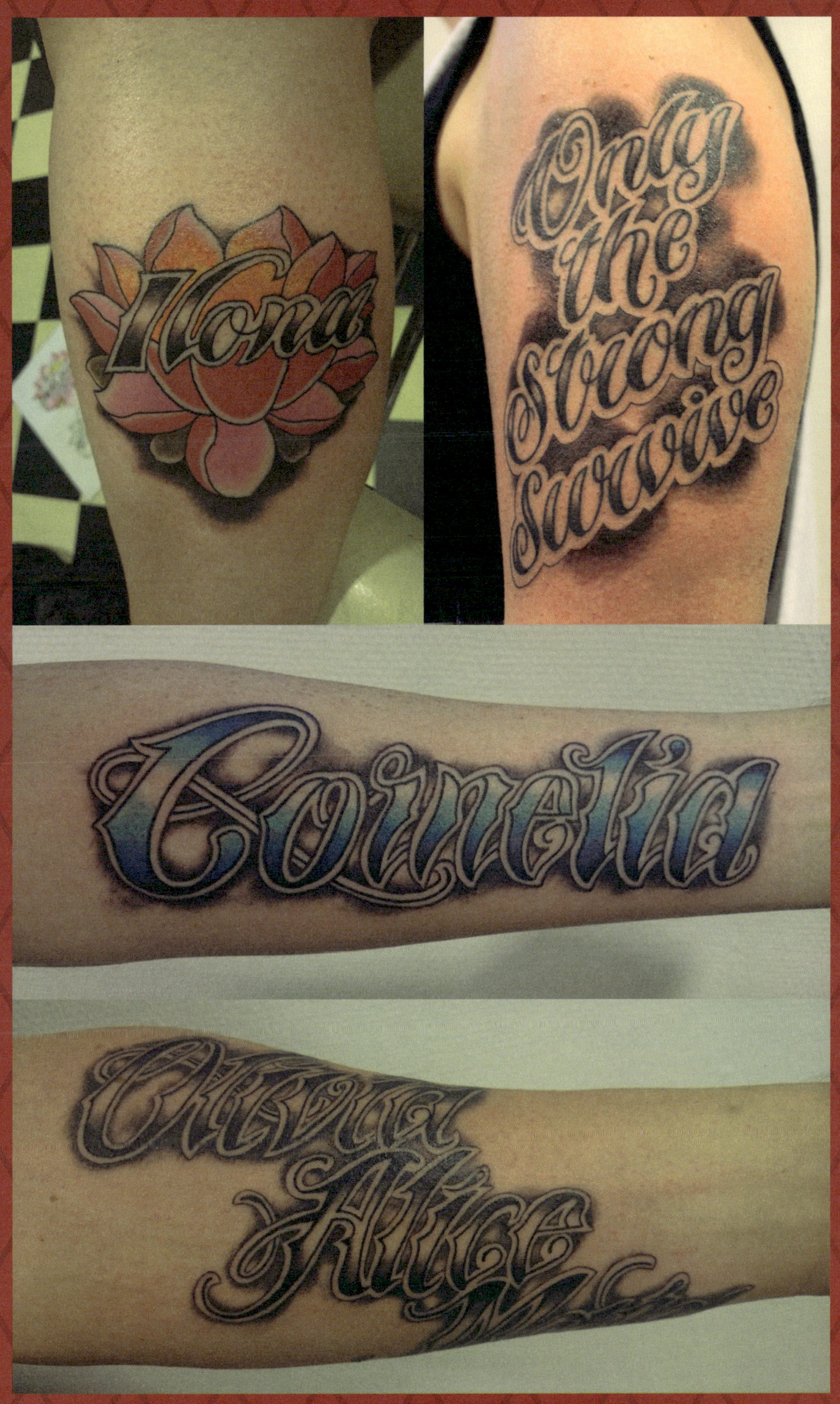
Ilona
Only the strong survive
Cornelia

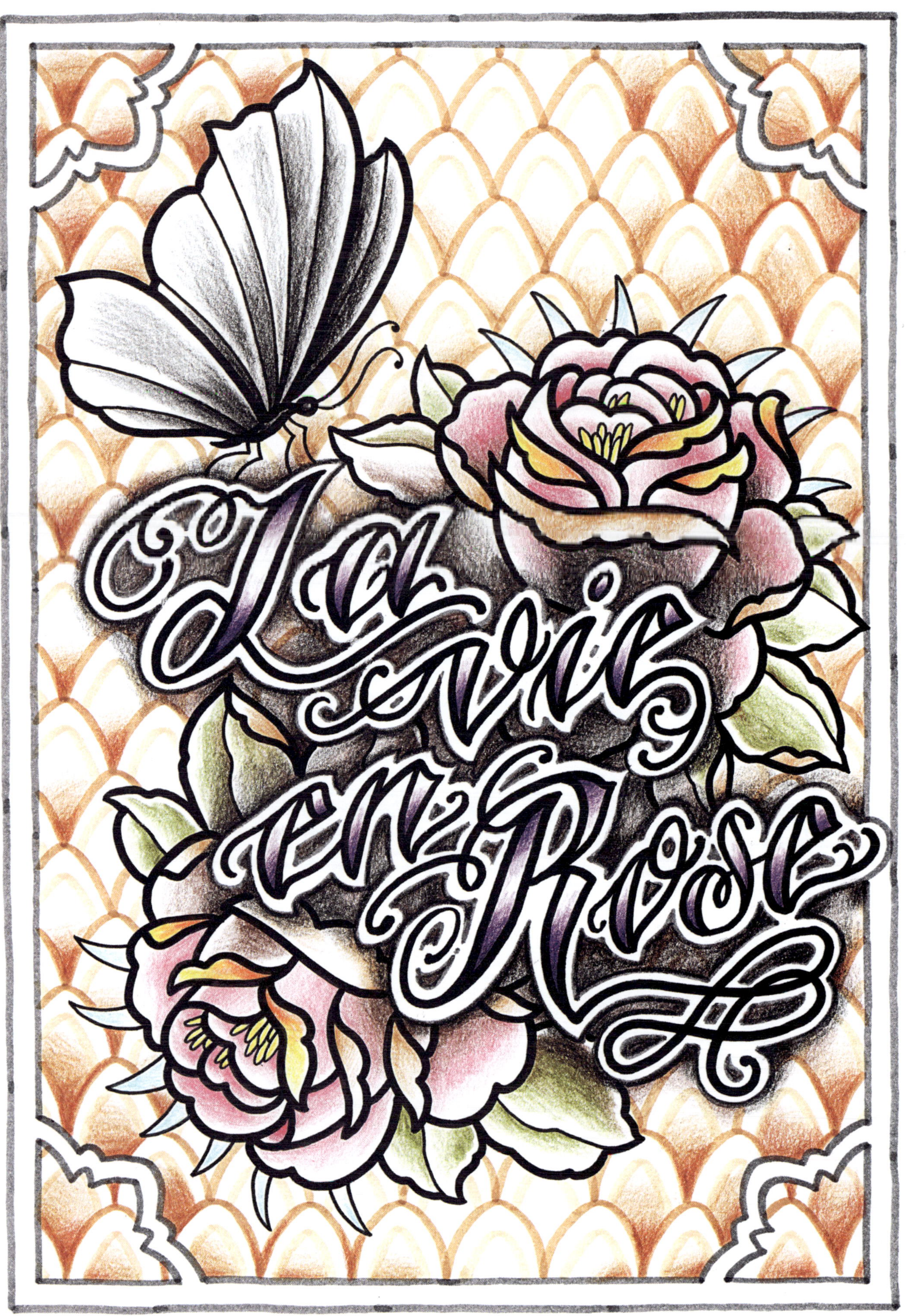
La vie en Rose

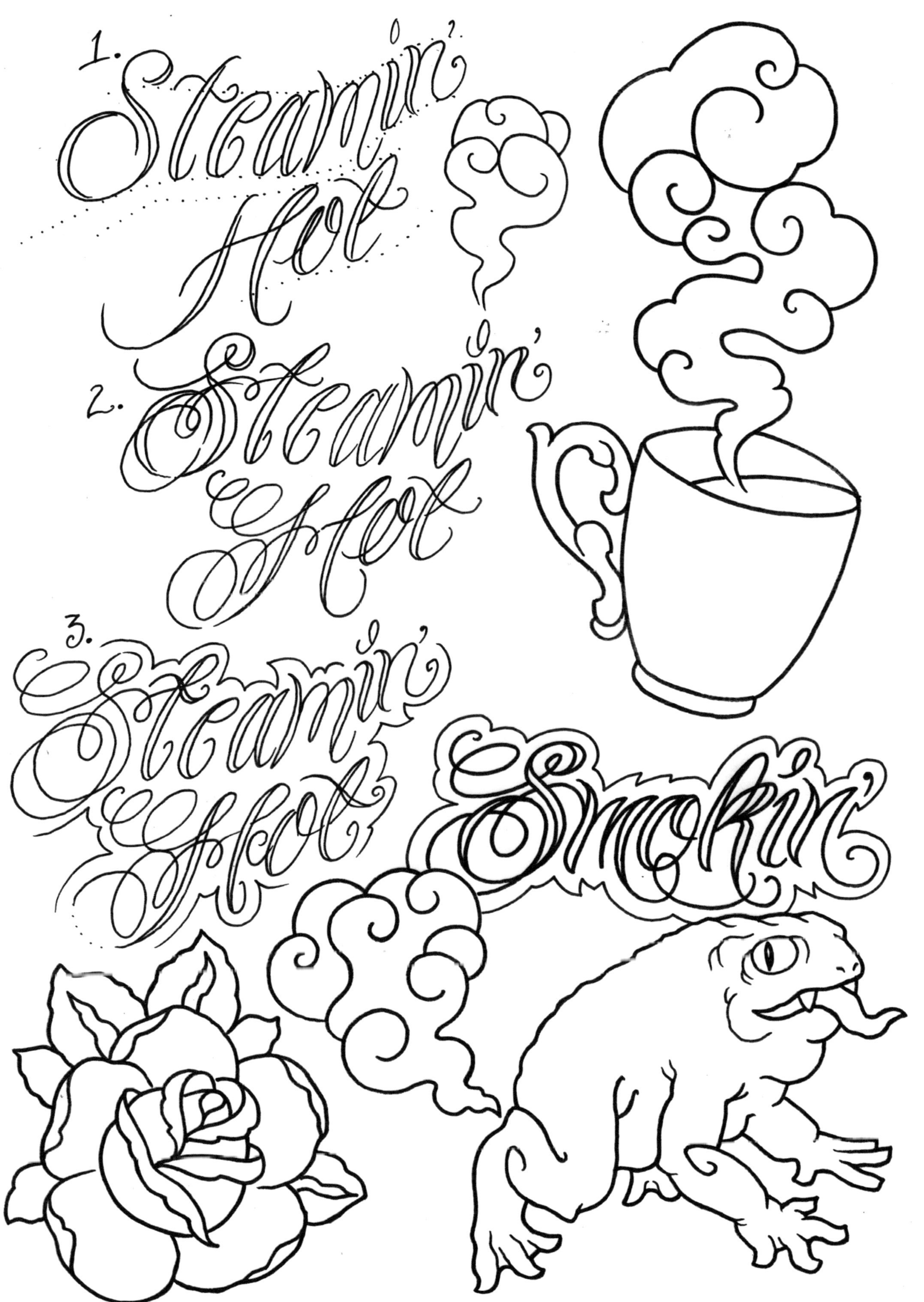
1. Steamin' Hot
2. Steamin' Hot
3. Steamin' Hot
Smokin'

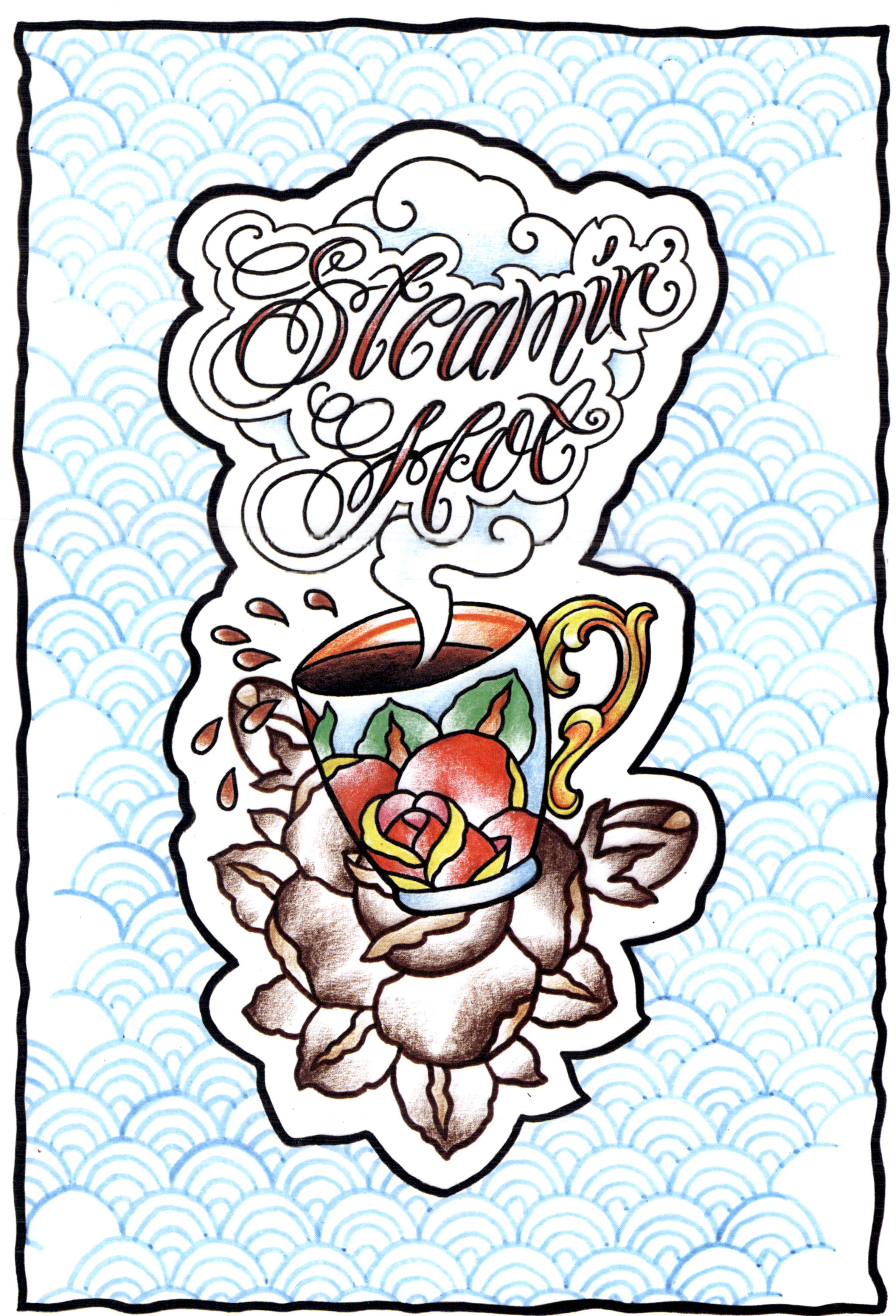
Steamin'
Hot

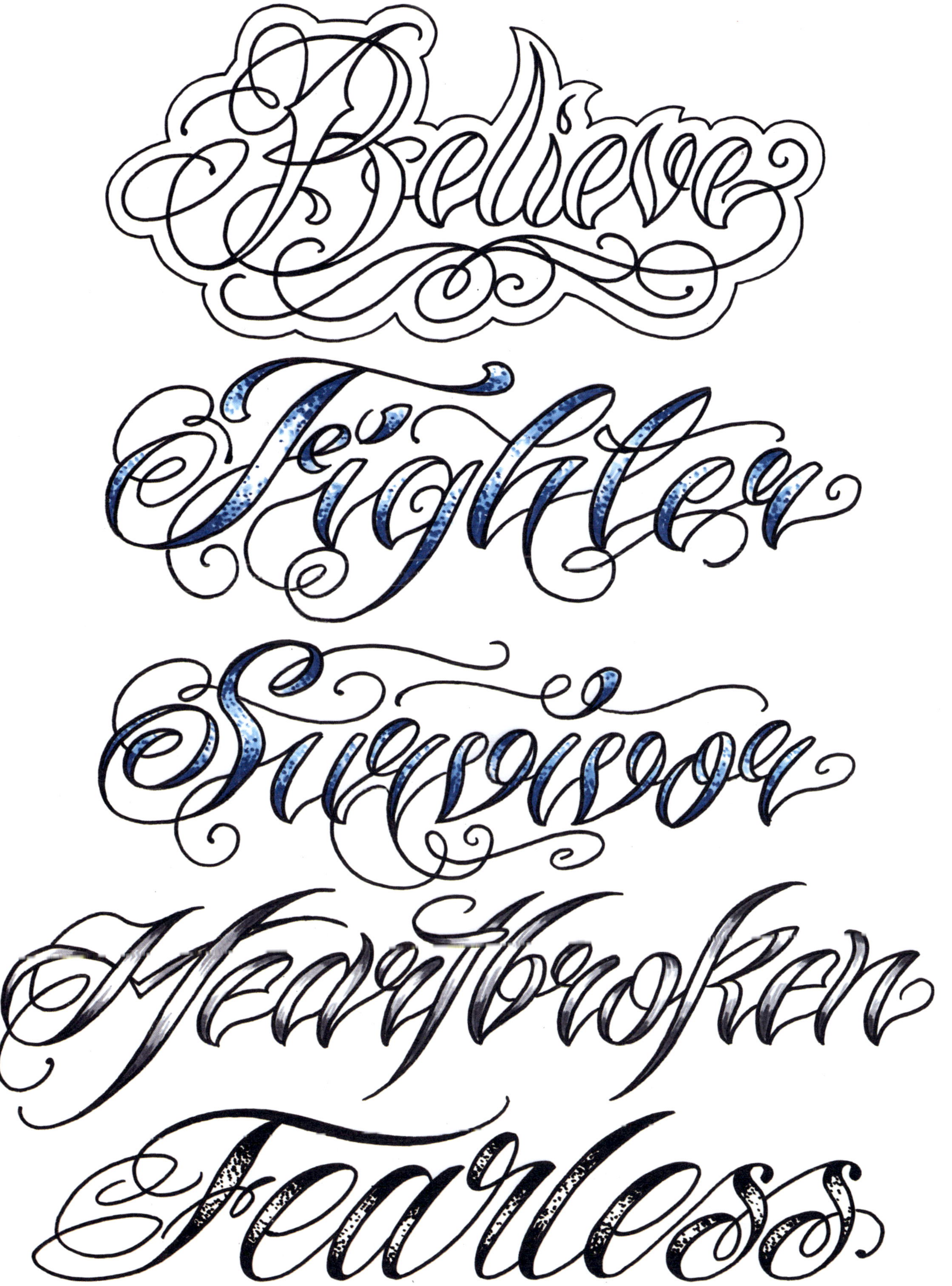
Believe
Fighter
Survivor
Heartbroken
Fearless

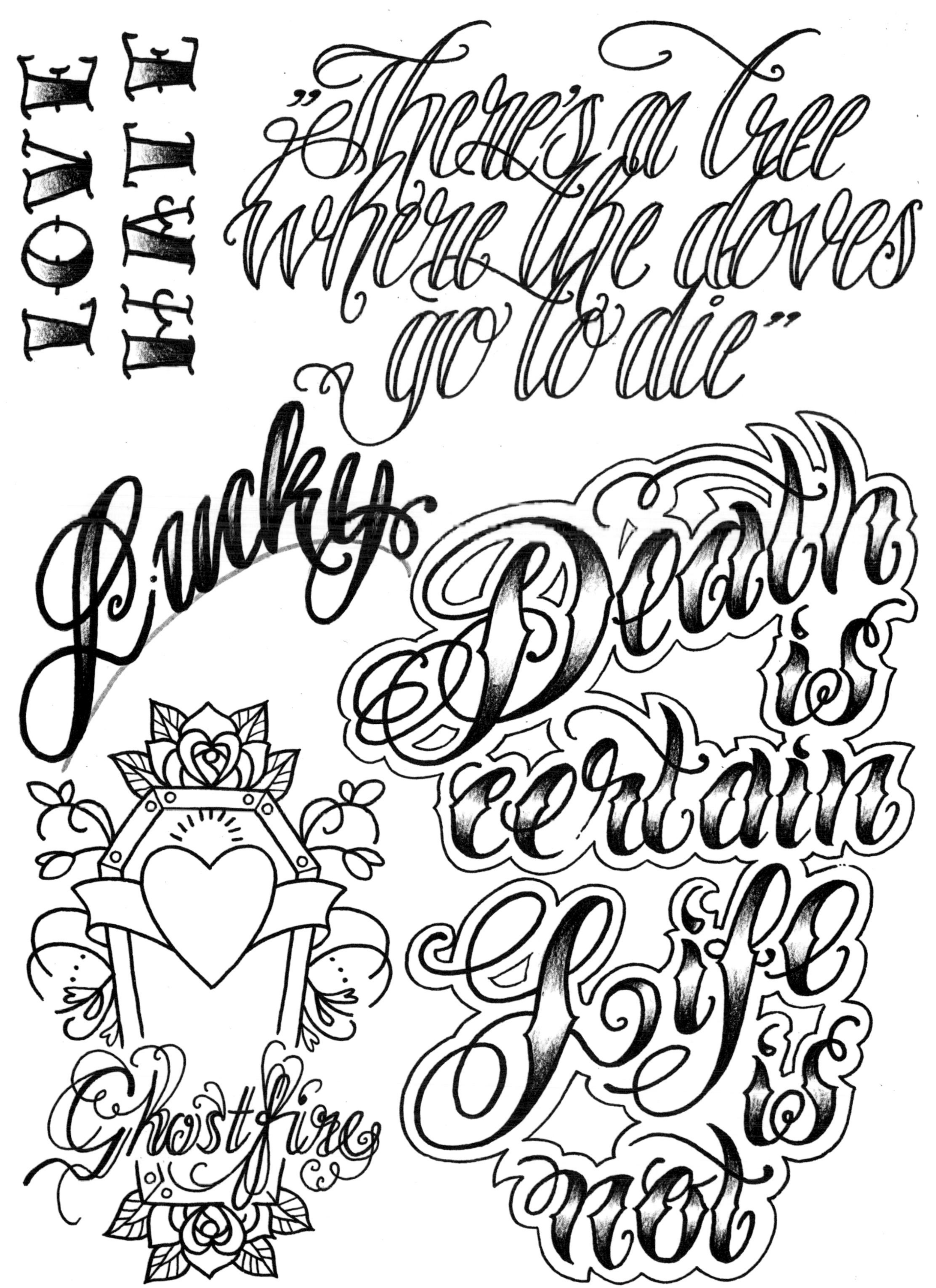
LOVE
HATE
"There's a tree where the doves go to die"
Lucky
Death is certain Life is not
Ghostfire

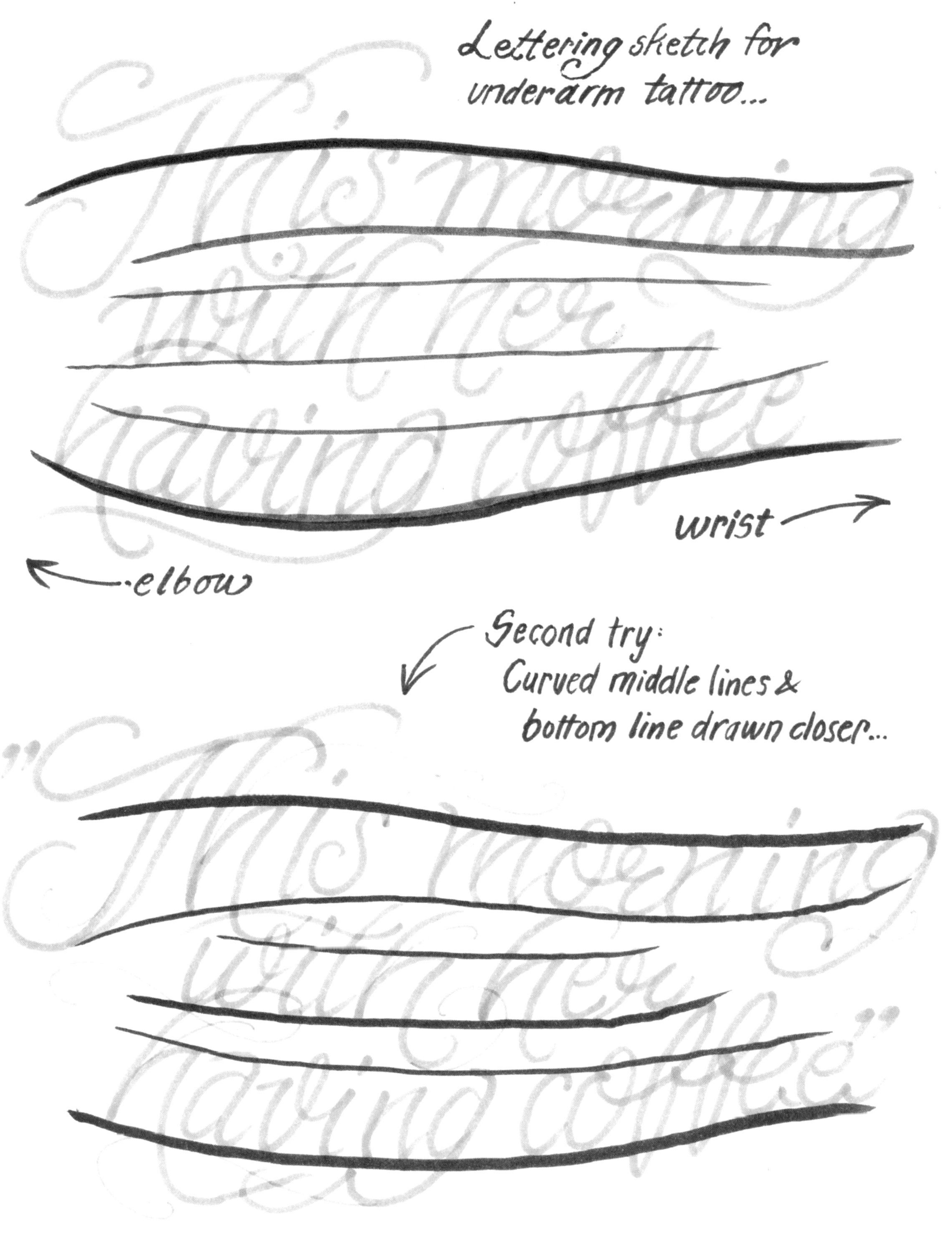

Lettering sketch for underarm tattoo...
This morning with her having coffee
wrist
elbow
Second try:
Curved middle lines & bottom line drawn closer...
"This morning with her having coffee"

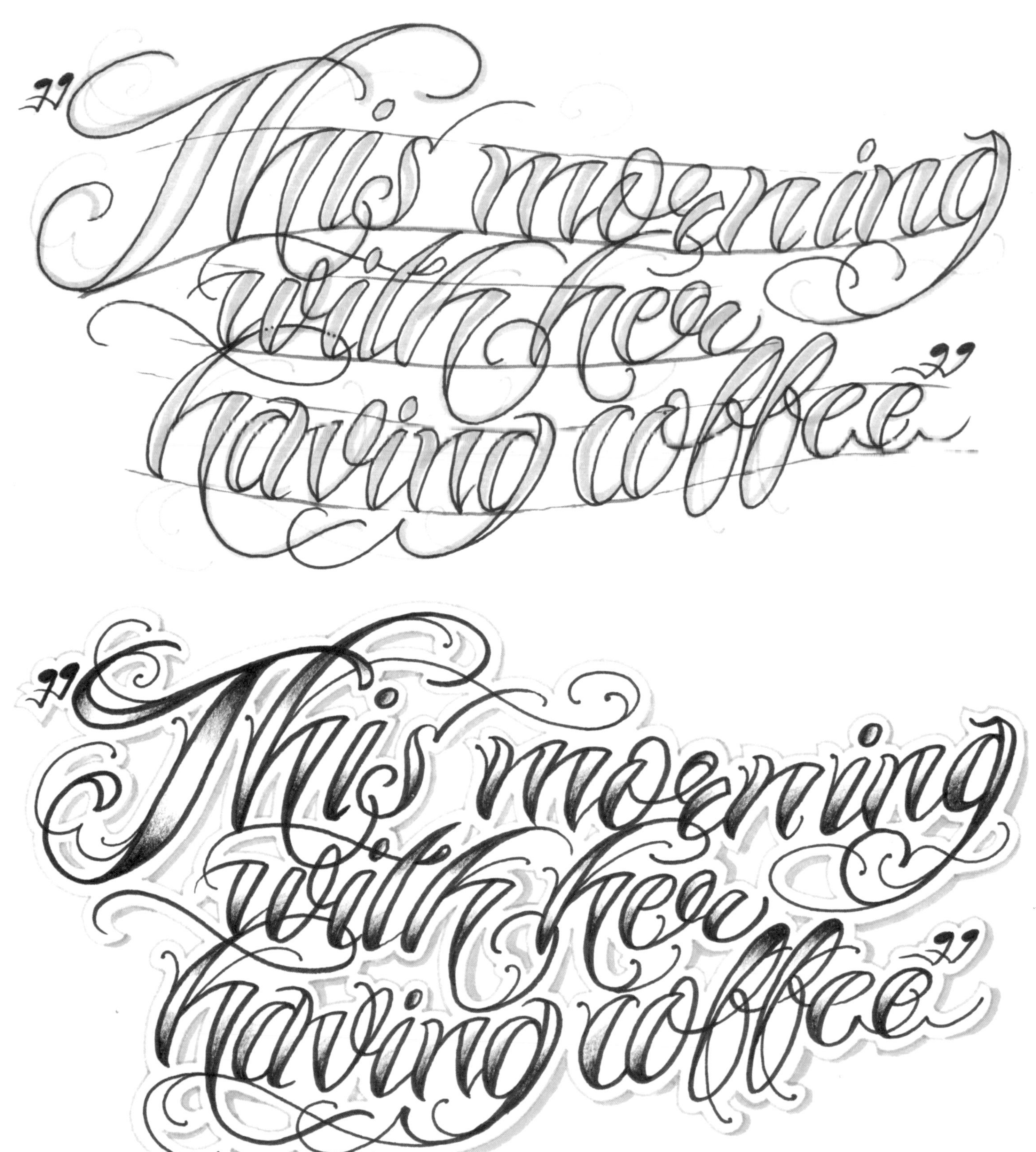
"This morning with her having coffee"
"This morning with her having coffee"

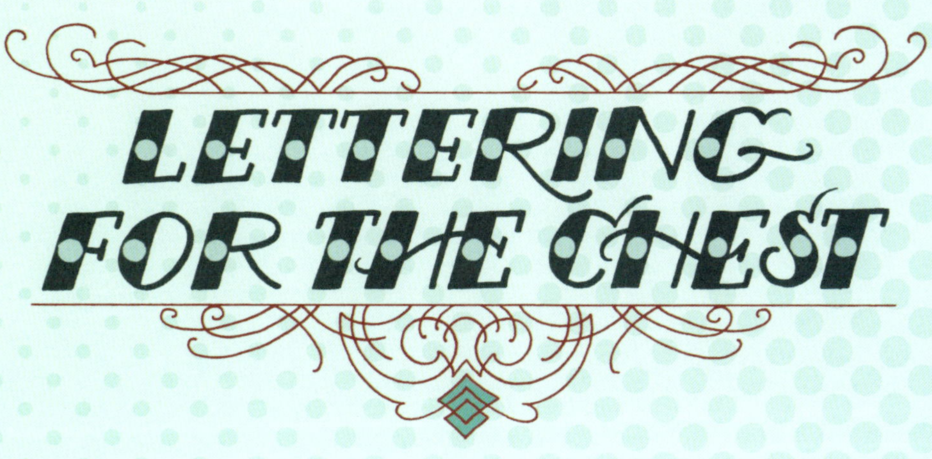

LETTERING FOR THE CHEST

Long Kiss Goodnight

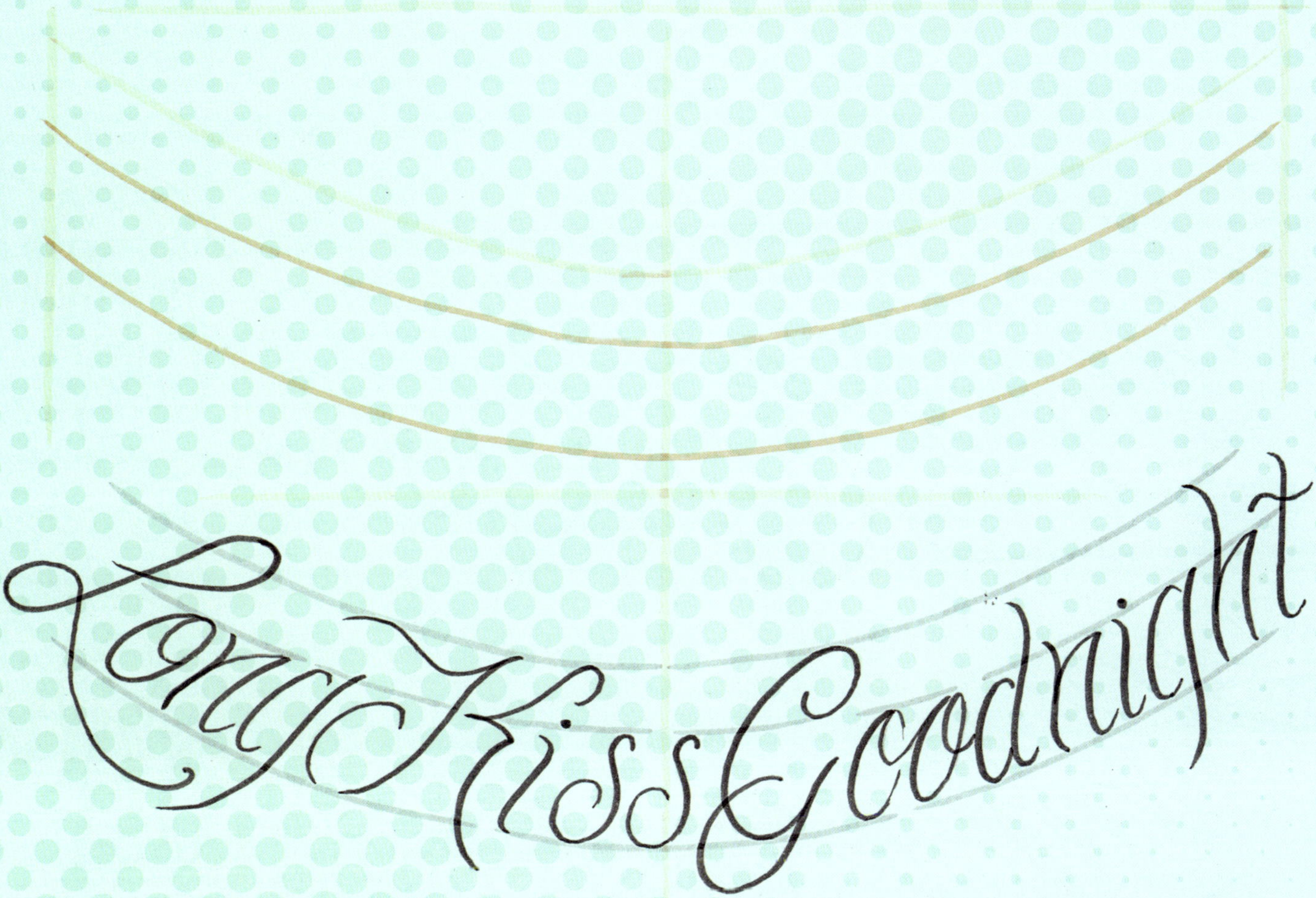

It is always good to have a plan. For tattoo artists executing curved lettering for the chest, the following sketches will show how I usually start drawing that sort of lettering. There are no wrongs or rights. I just think this is the easier way to go. Use transparent paper and fold it in the middle. This way you can produce a balanced sketch.

Size and placement does matter, and here is how I do it. Place the top of the text in the tract of the collarbones and not halfway down the chest. The tattoo should not extend to the front of the shoulders. This leaves the client room to get a sleeve tattoo that can follow the round shape of the shoulder.

On the front of the chest, the client may want to get more tattoos beneath the text, like a portrait, eagle, or whatever. Not everyone has a plan, but it's a good idea to do some thinking about future tattoos as you place the chest lettering.

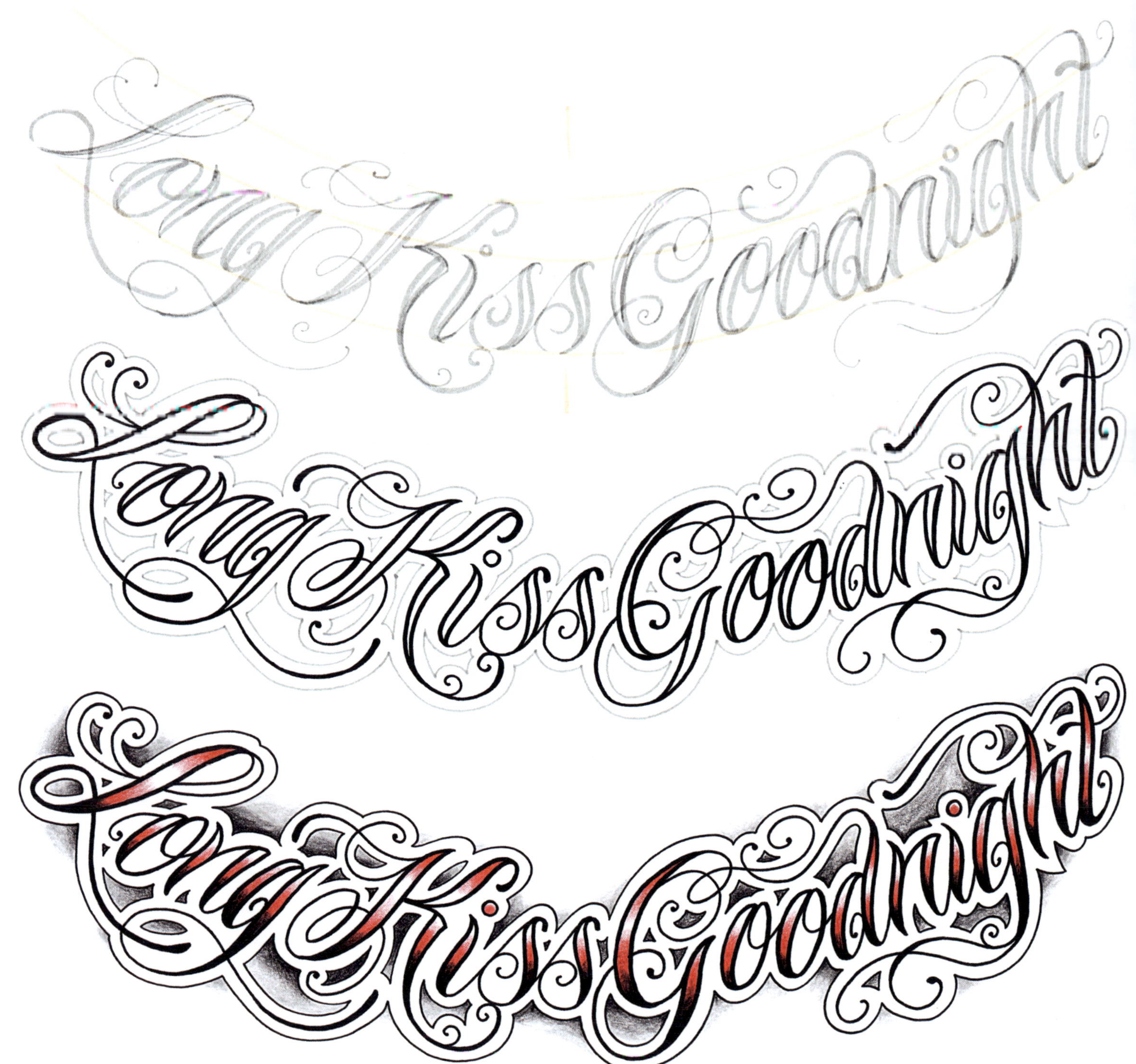
Long Kiss Goodnight
Long Kiss Goodnight
Long Kiss Goodnight

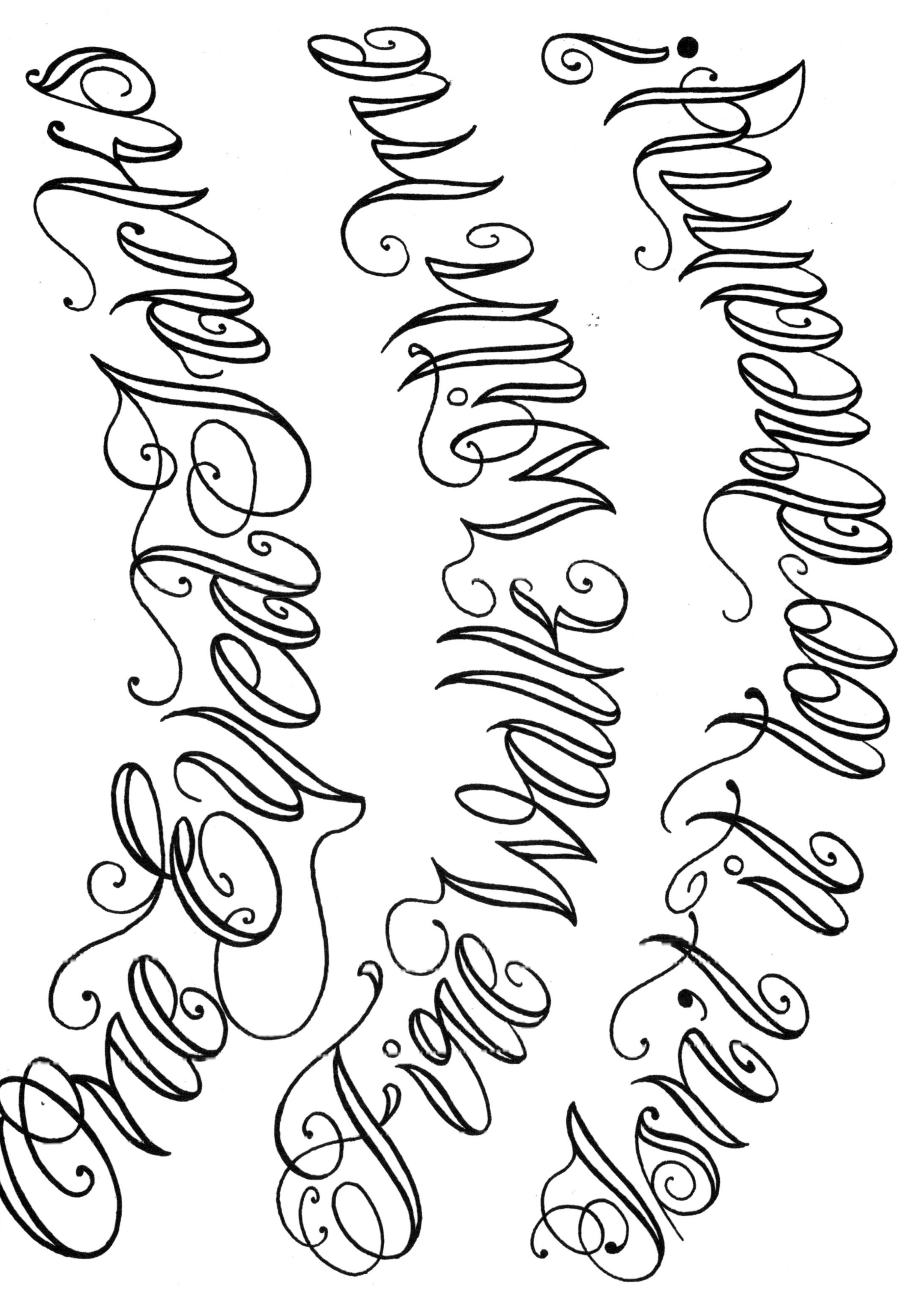

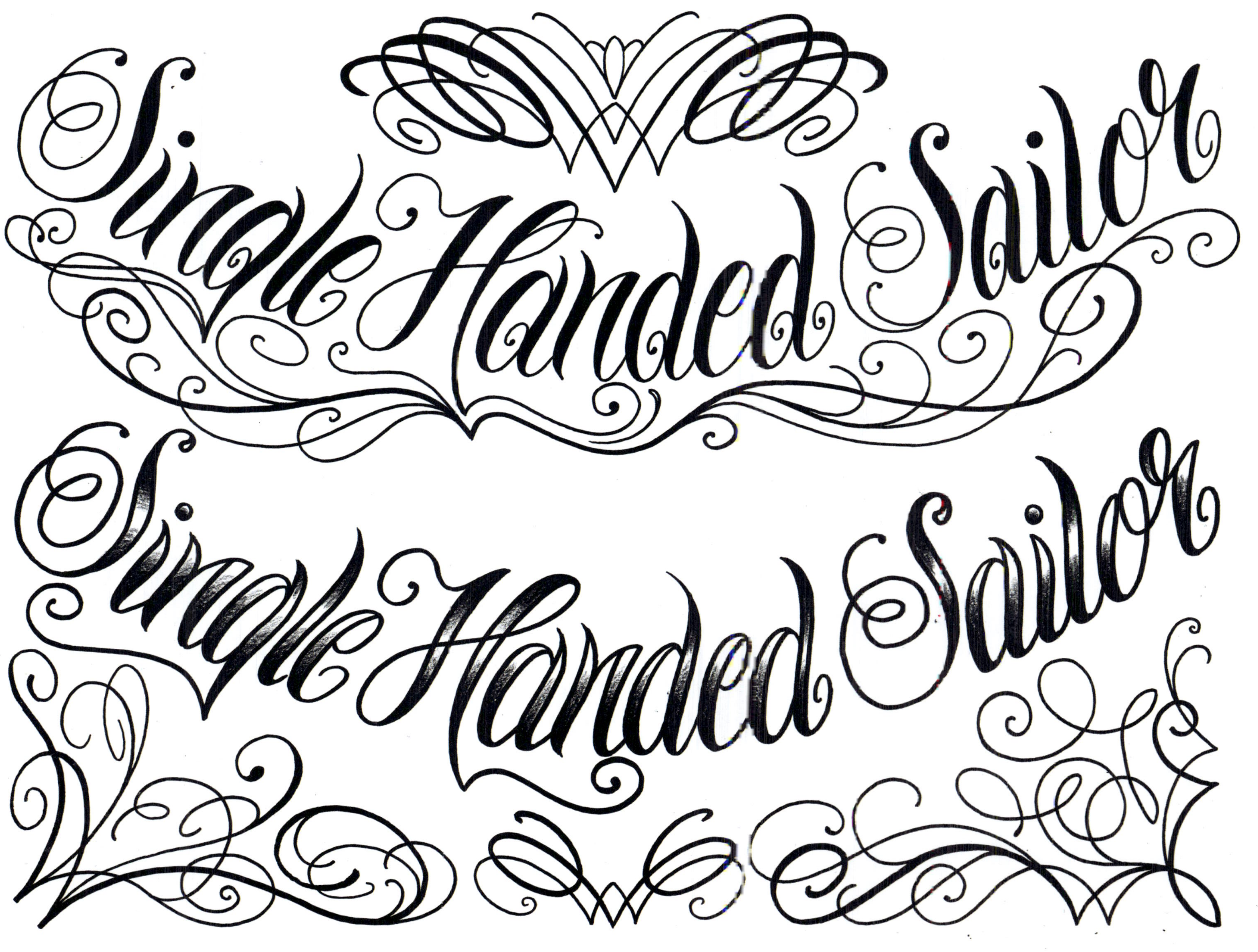
Single Handed Sailor
Single Handed Sailor

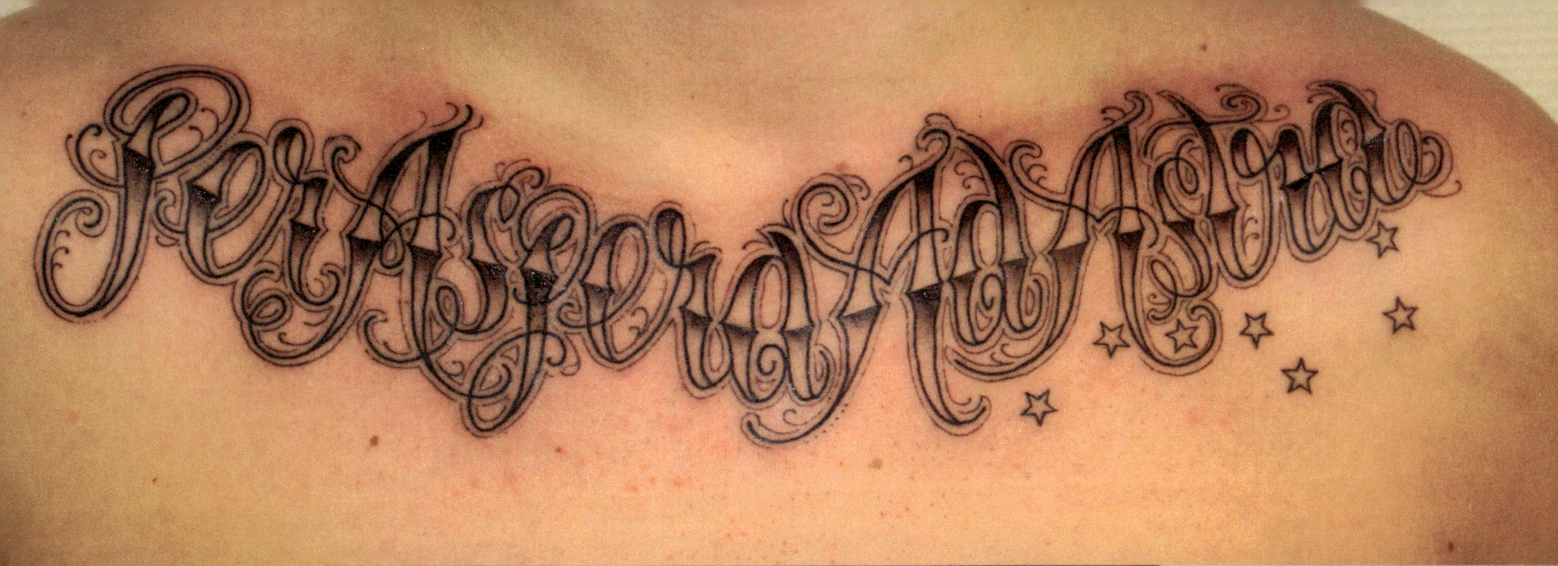
Per Aspera Ad Astra

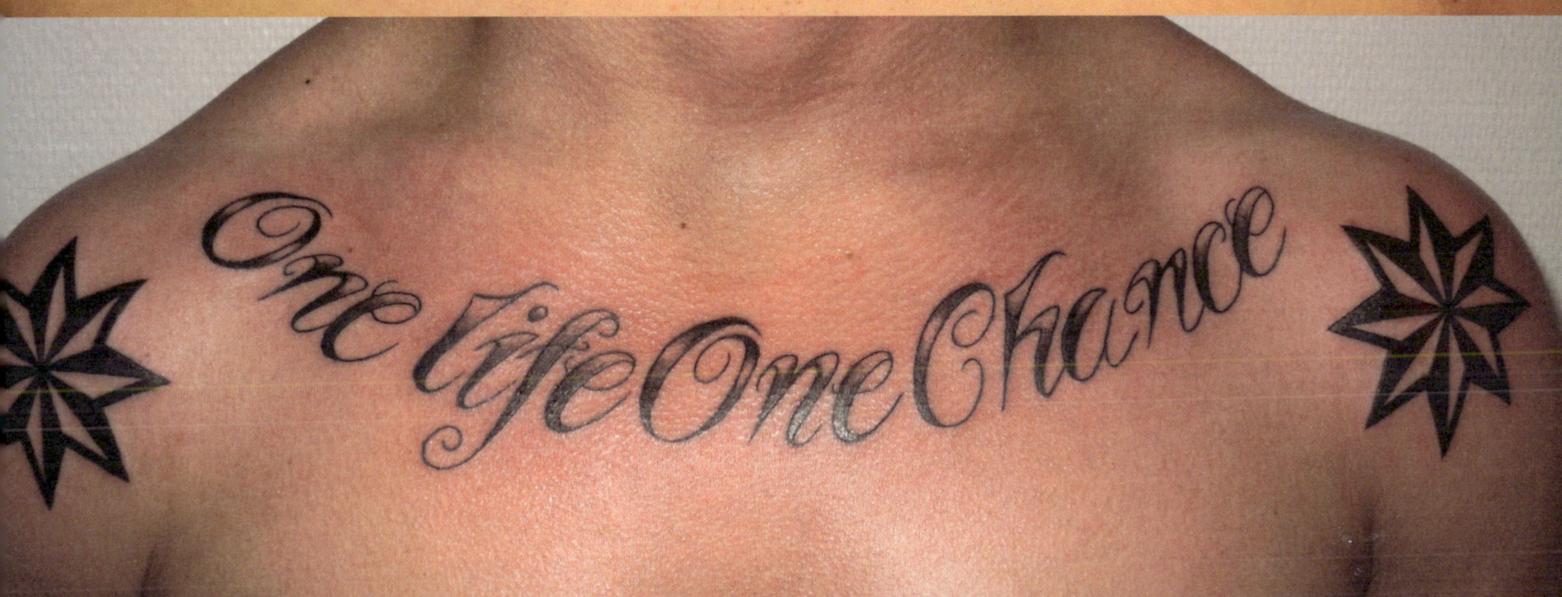
One Life One Chance

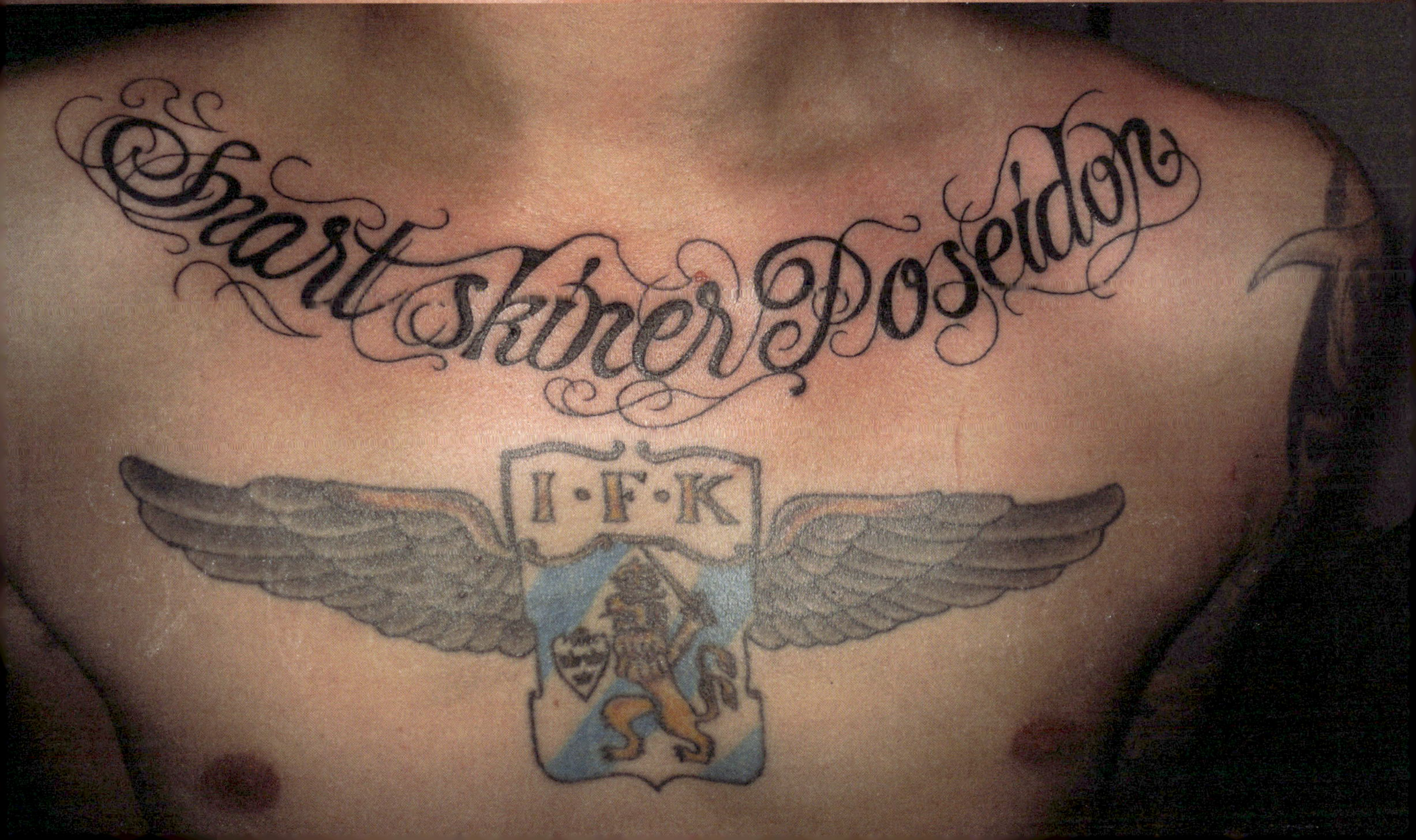

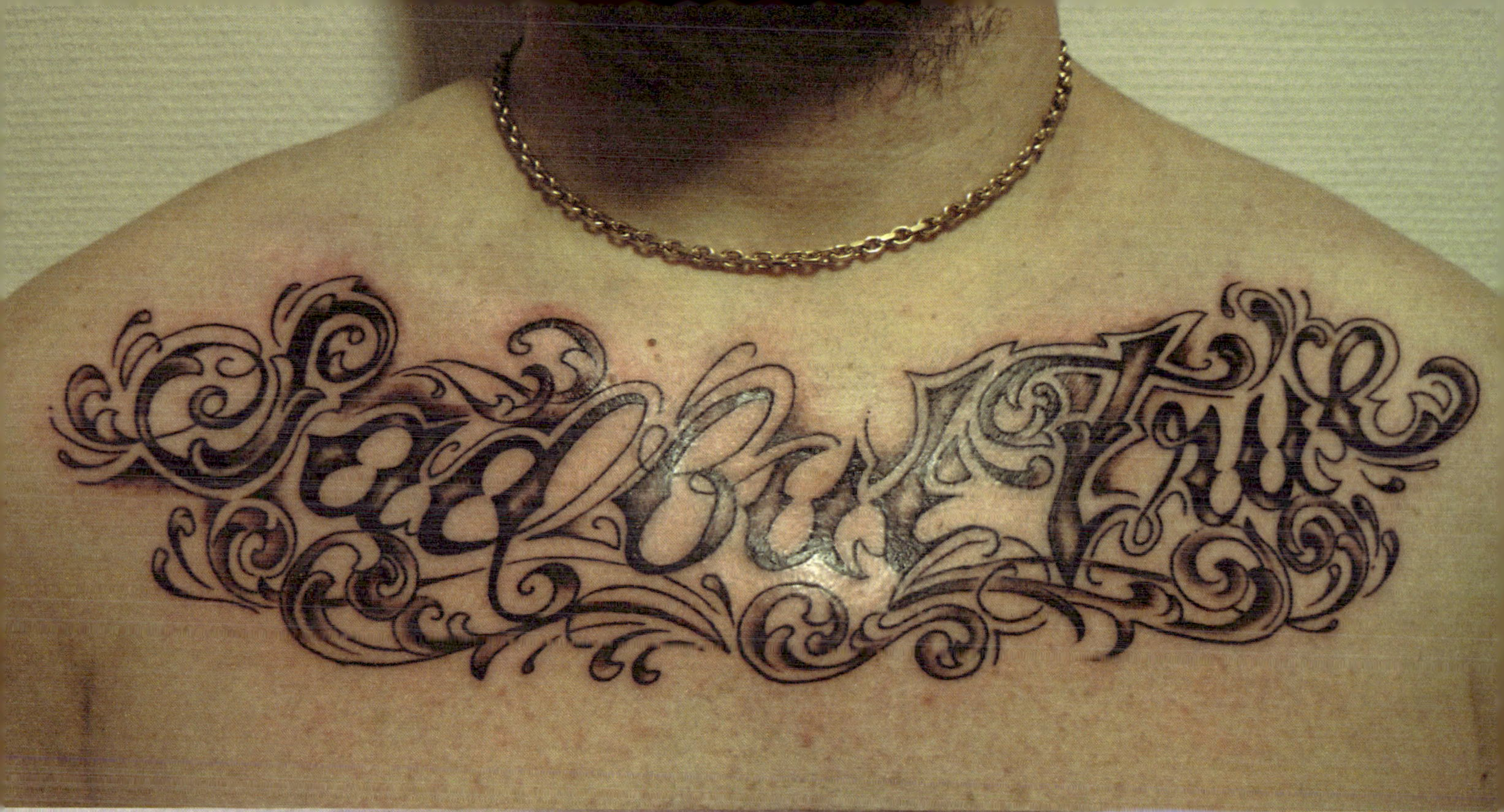

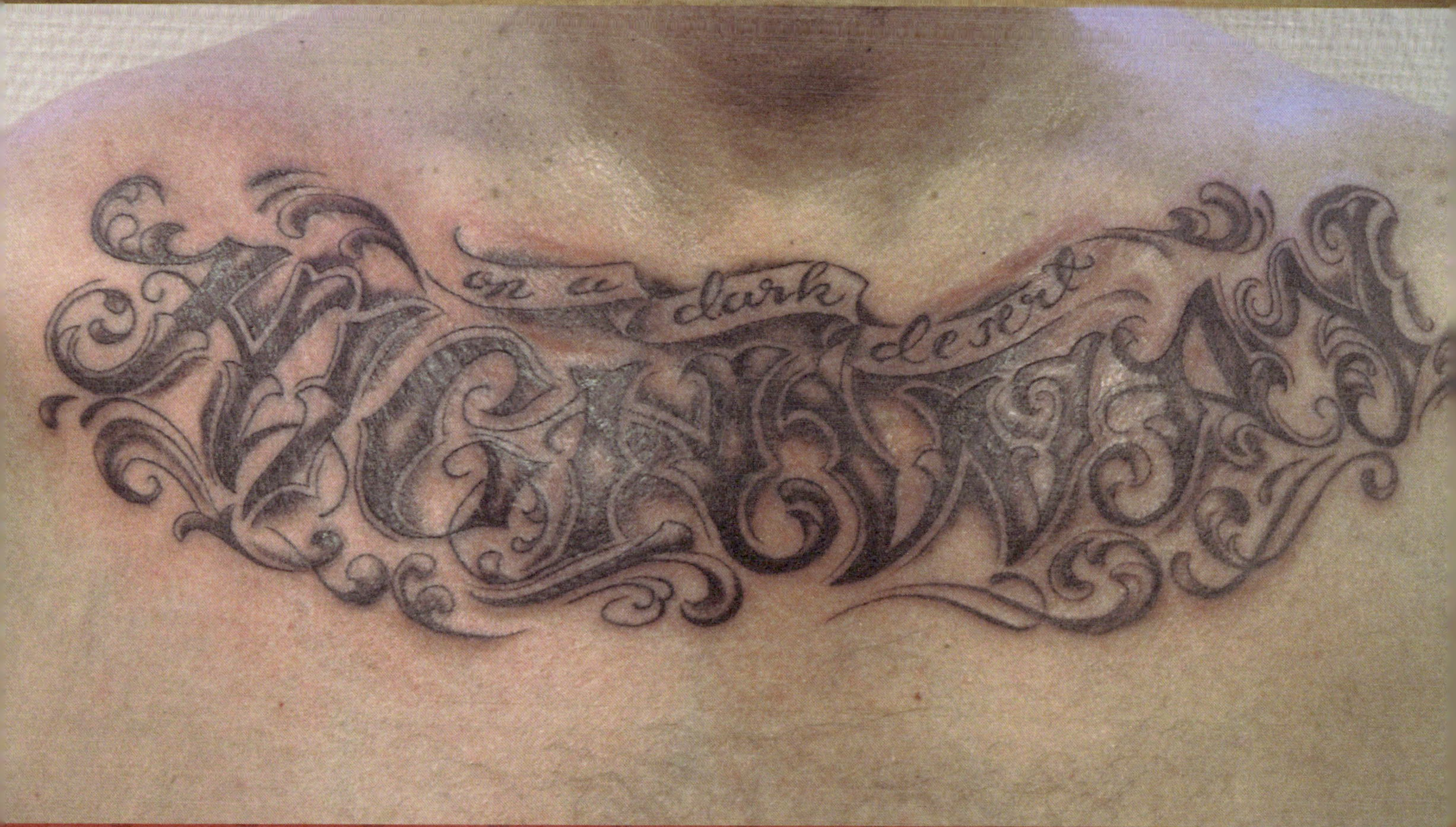

Olle Husberg's lettering tattoo reads "on a dark desert highway." I put a little banner on top of it to create more space for the big letters and filigree.

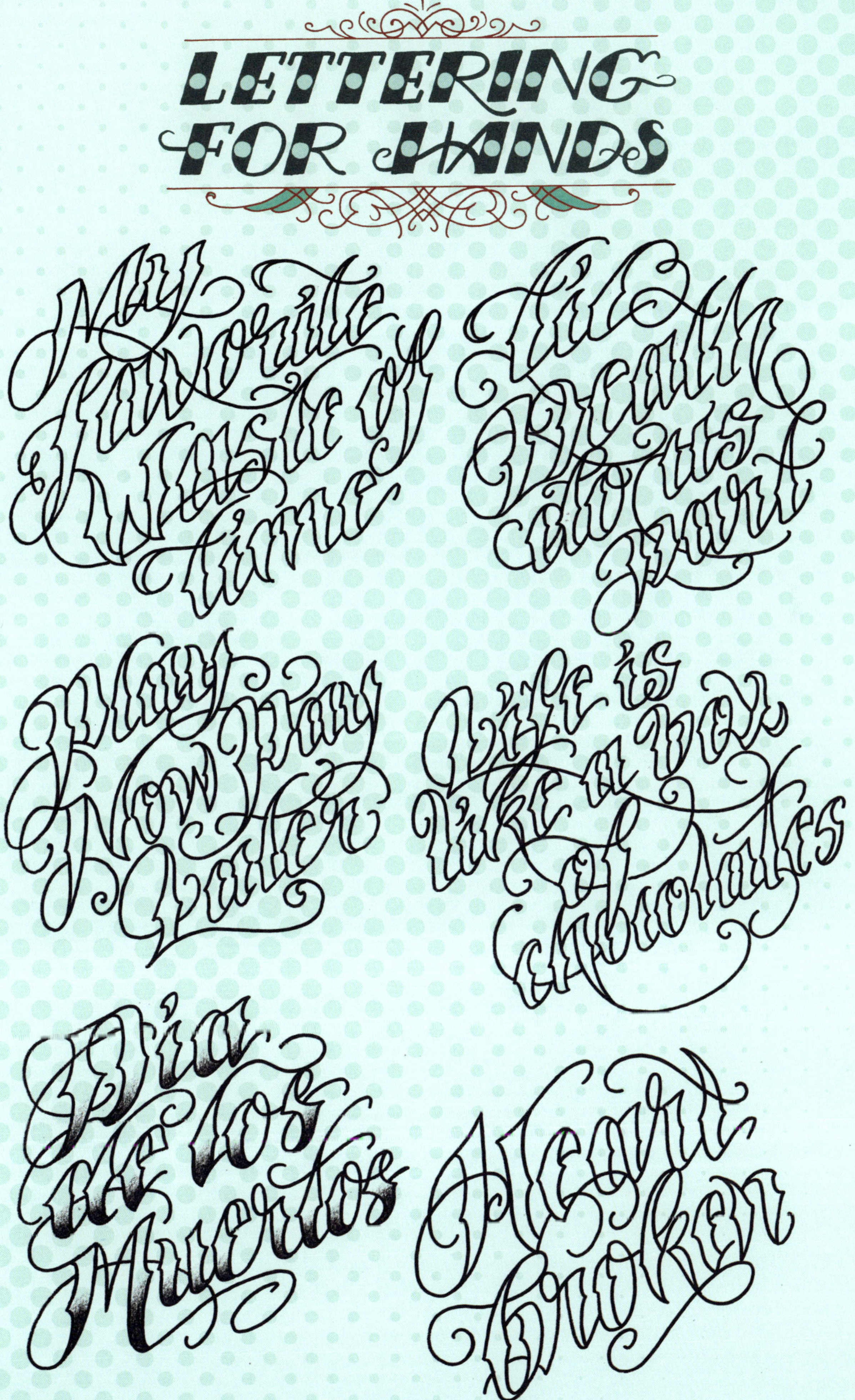
LETTERING FOR HANDS
My Favorite Waste of Time
Til Death do us part
Play Now Pay Later
Life is like a box of chocolates
Dia de los Muertos
Heart Broken

THICK AND THIN

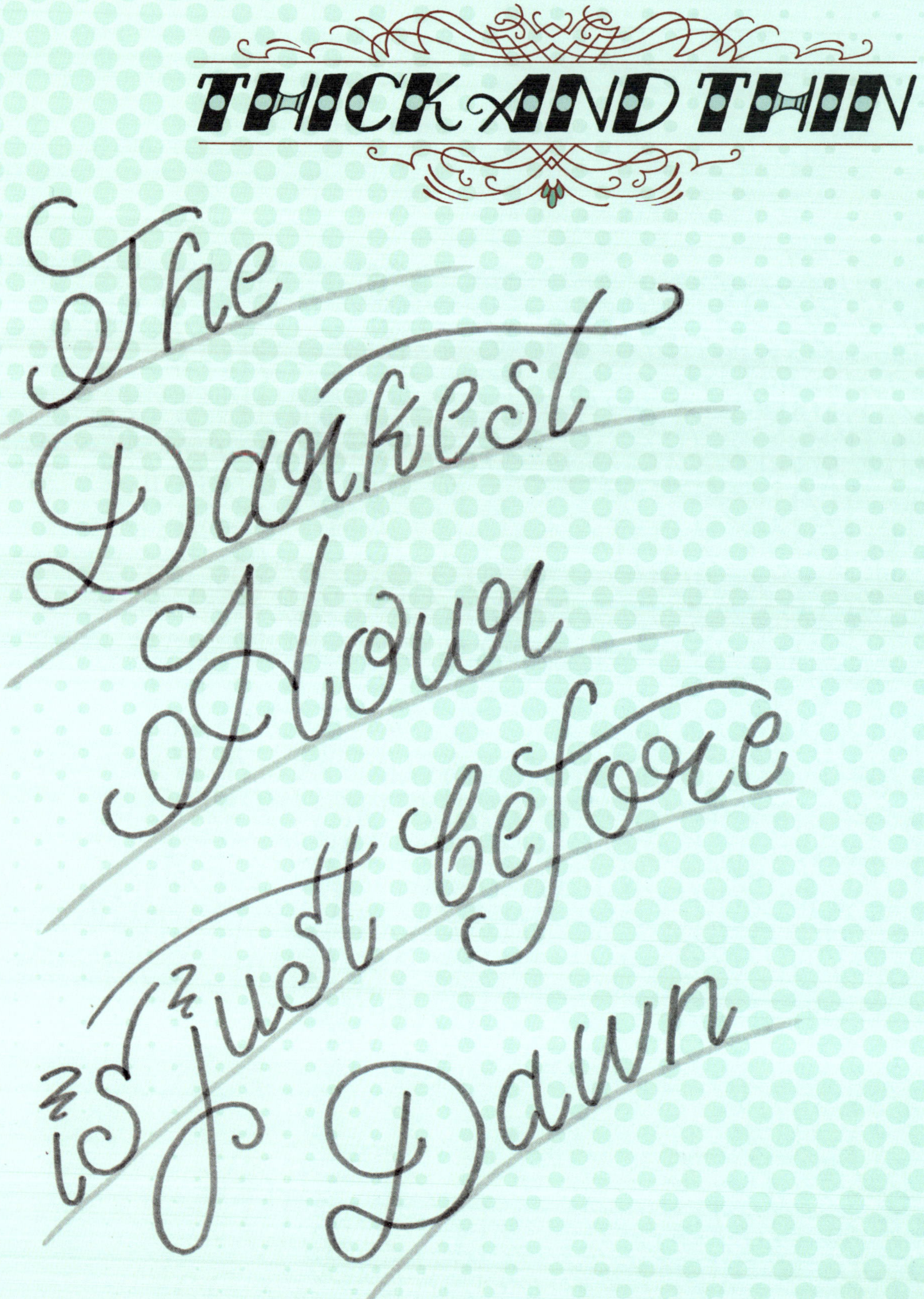

First quick sketch.

Drawing additional sets of thin lines around thick script creates dimension and is easy to do. Create a loose script sketch with enough space for the extra lines. Draw the original with a thicker marker pen. If you use a light table, simply move the tracing paper a little bit in the desired direction and switch to a thin line. To make an original and take a copy of it works, too. Put the copy under the original and move it slightly, then trace new thinner lines alongside the thicker ones.

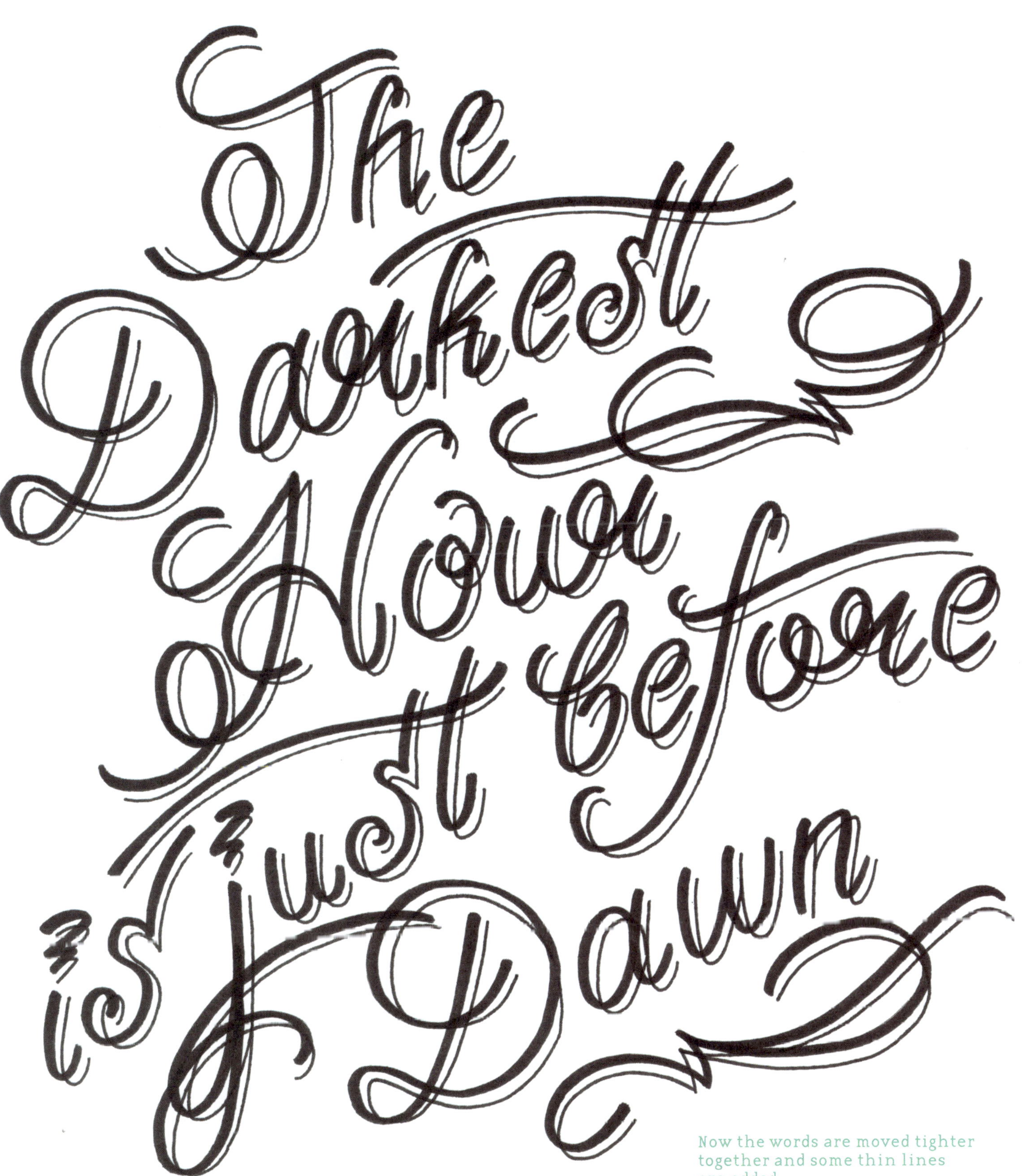

Now the words are moved tighter together and some thin lines are added.

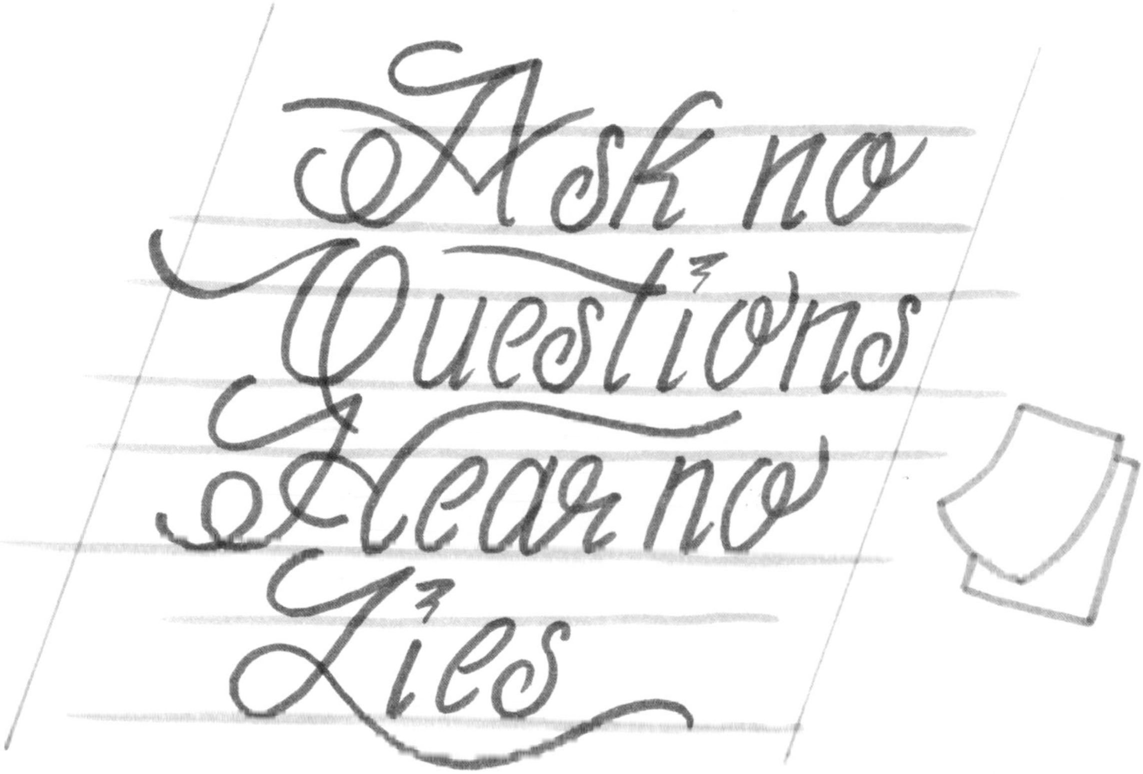

Ask no Questions Hear no Lies

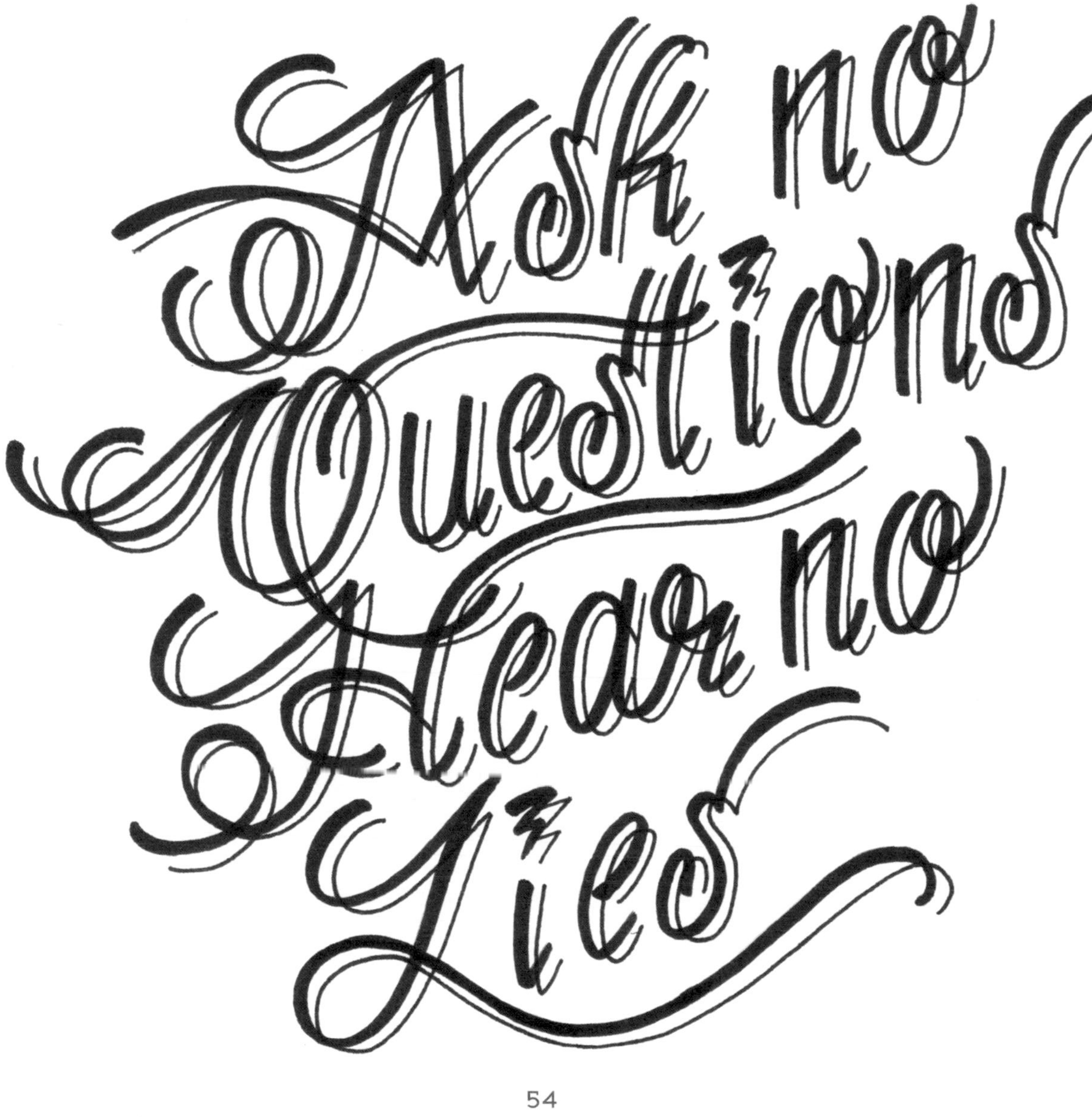

Ask no Questions Hear no Lies

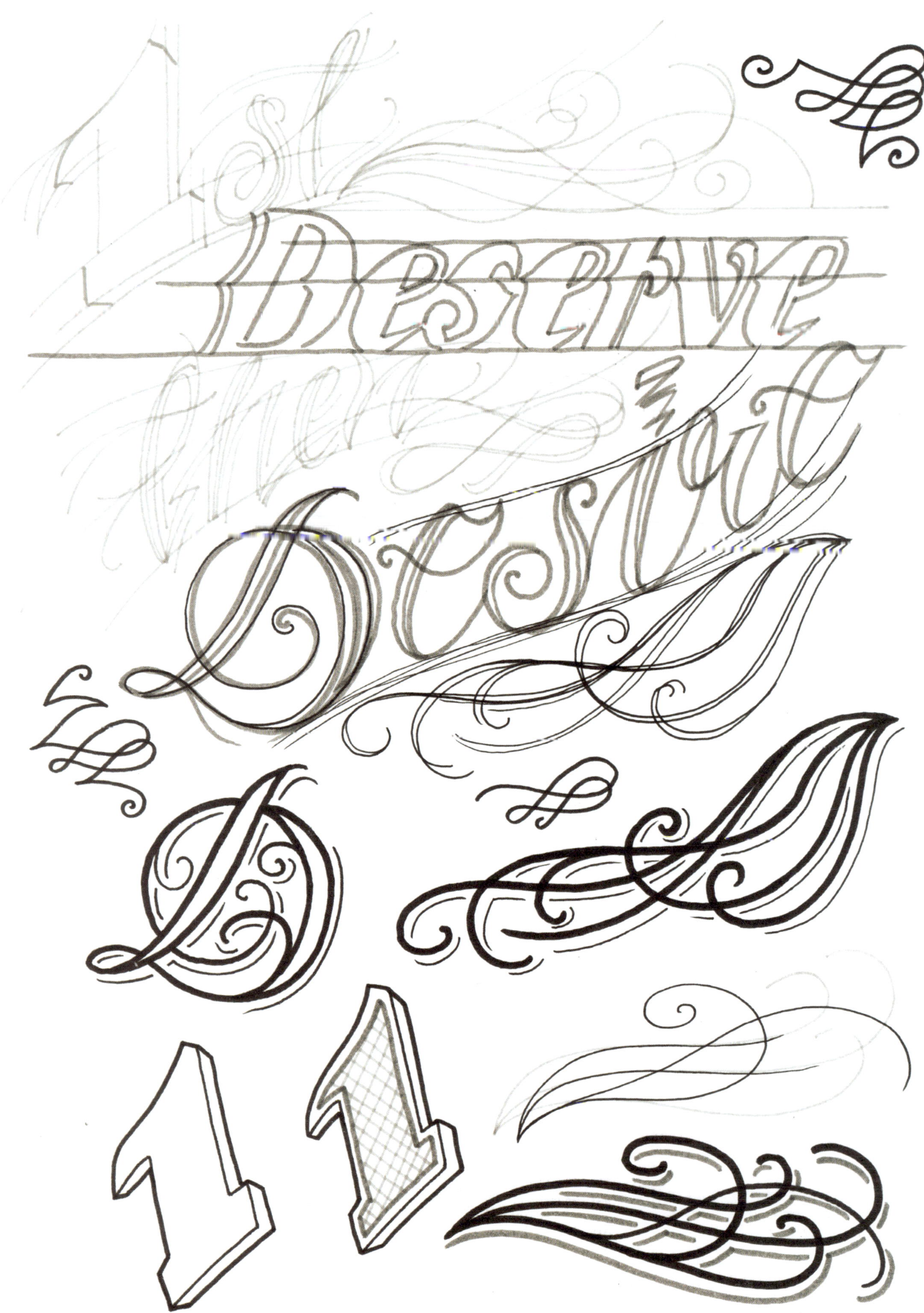
Deserve

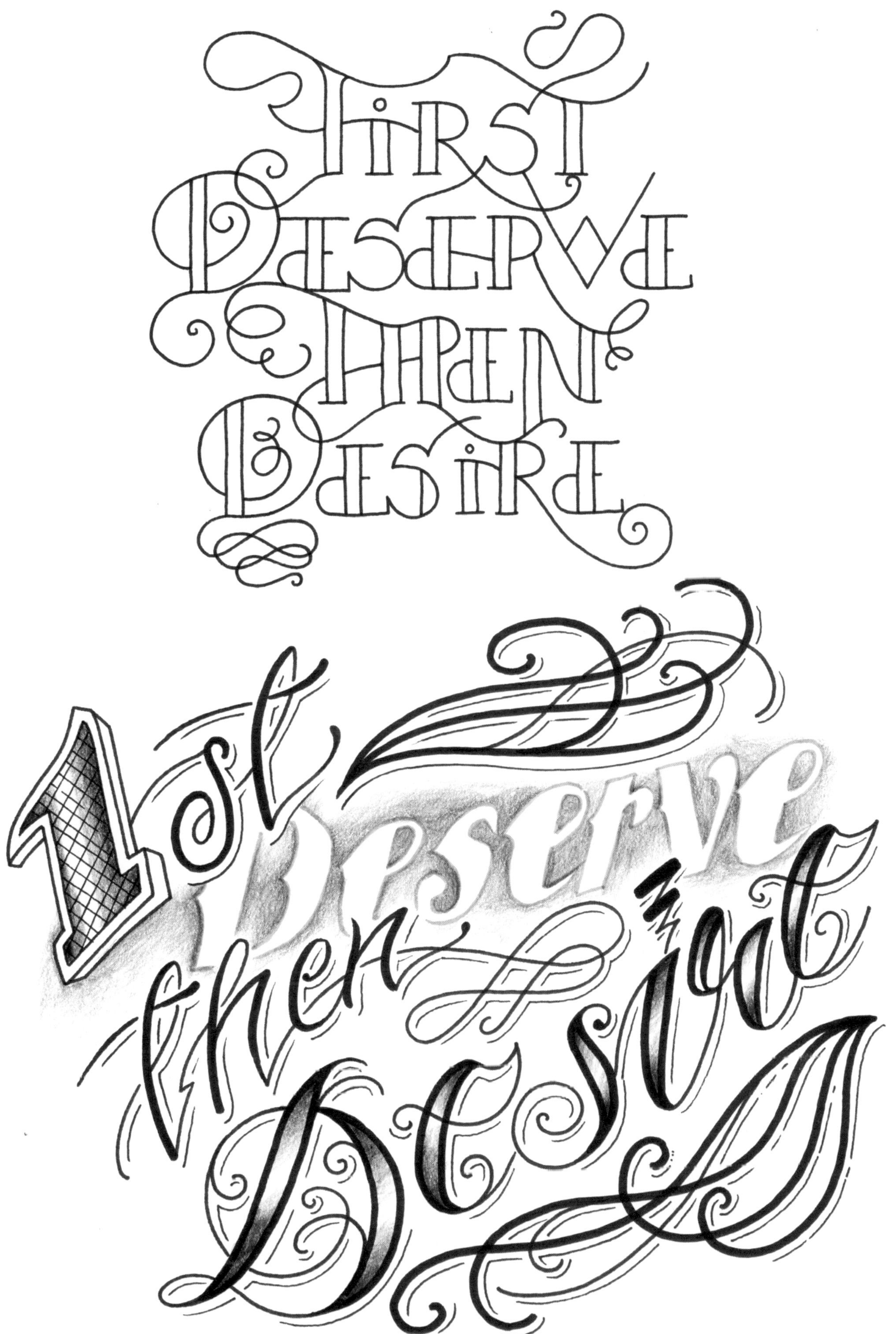
First
Deserve
Then
Desire
1st Deserve
then Desire

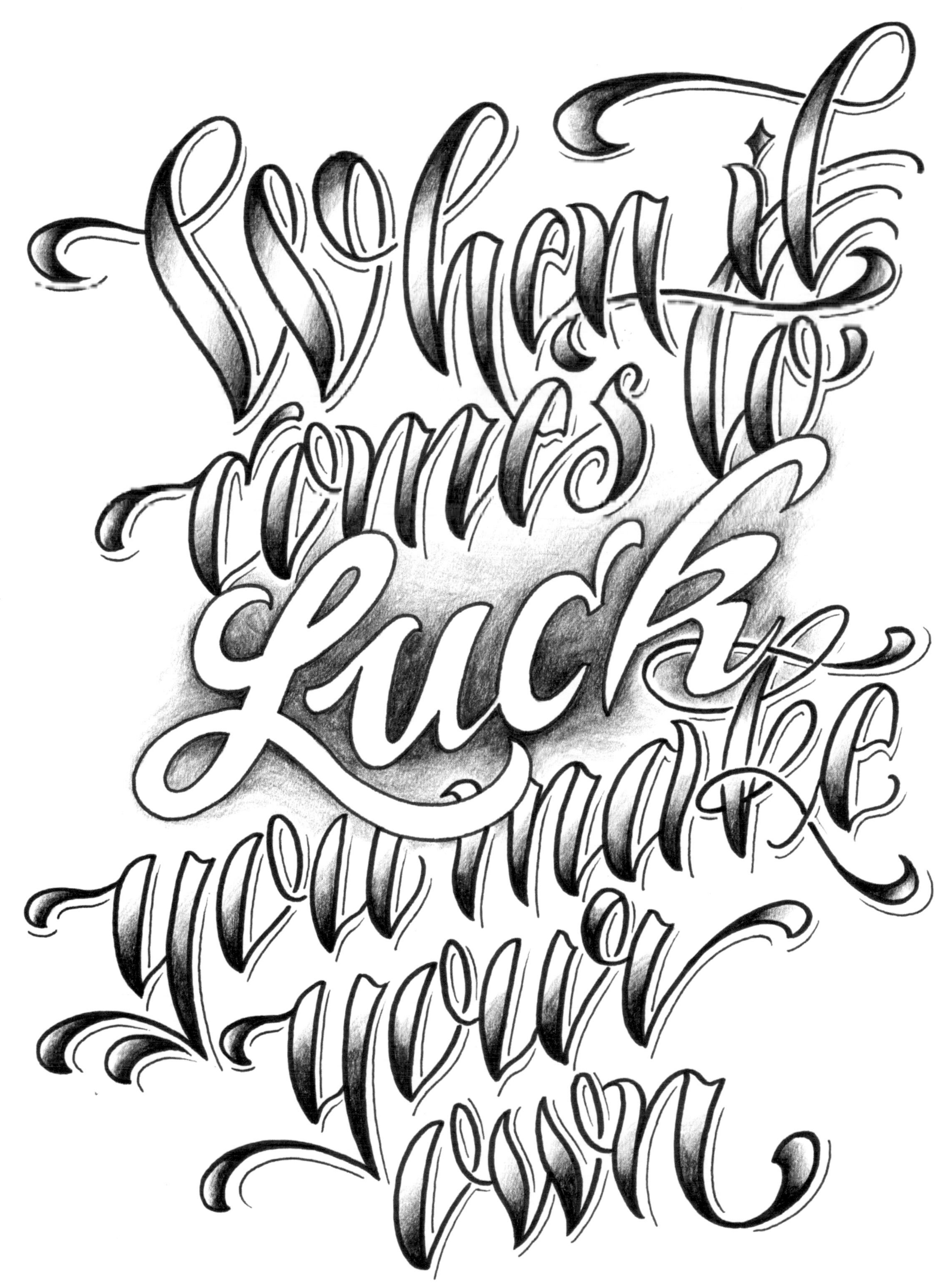
When it
comes to
Luck
you make
your
own

Chapter THREE

NAMES

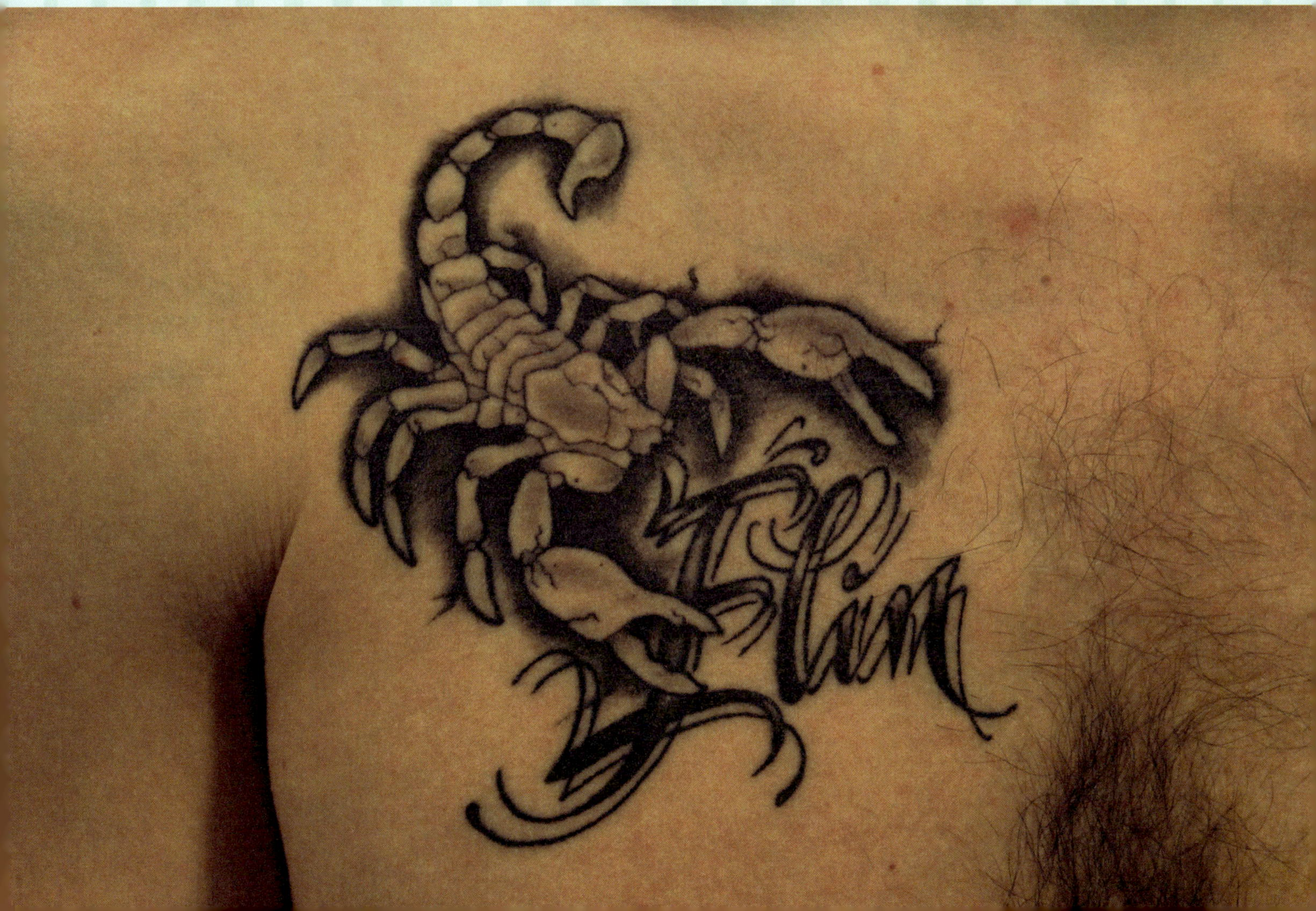

Angelica Alexander

ann Anders Algot

Alice

Amber

Arthur

Abigail

Alejandro

Alexandra

Al Alison Anton

Alex Anna

alanna Alicia

Beth
Betty
baby
Benjamin
Barbara
Bozo
BROOKLYN
Belinda
billy
Barbie
Britney
Bob
Bobby
Bella
Bea
Barney

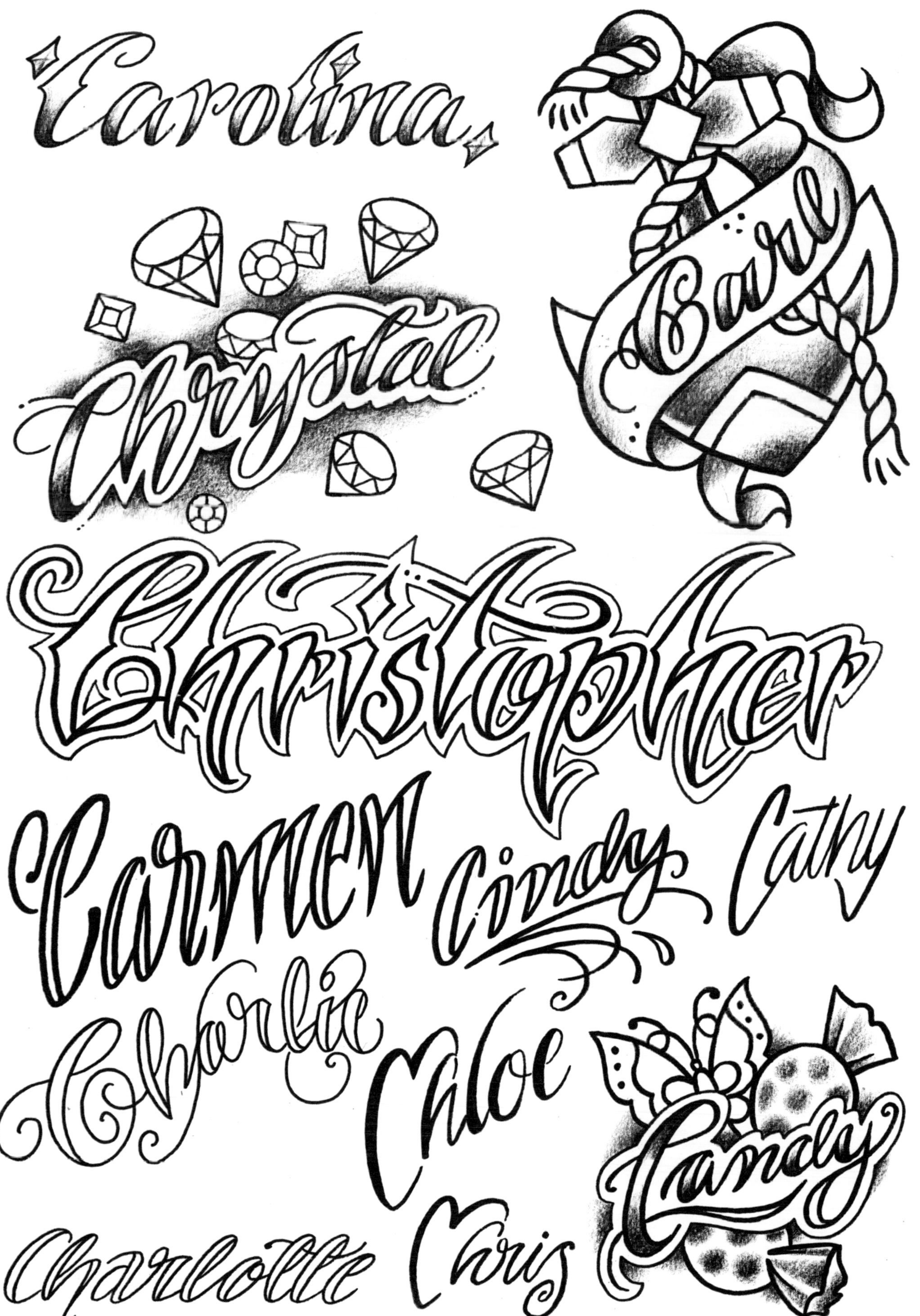
Carolina
Carl
Chrystal
Christopher
Carmen
Cindy
Cathy
Charlie
Chloe
Candy
Charlotte
Chris

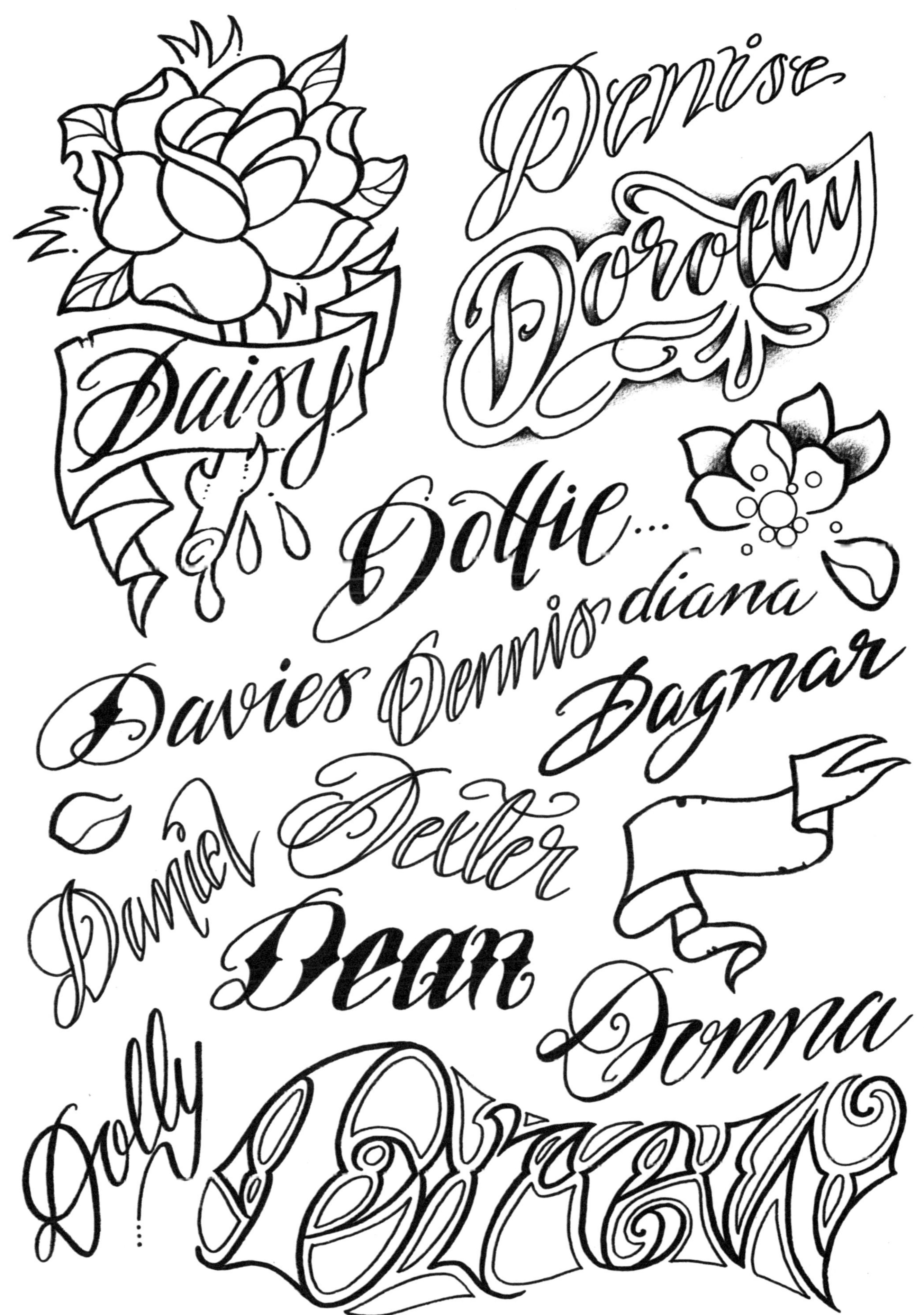
Denise
Dorothy
Daisy
Dottie...
Dennis
diana
Davies
Dagmar
Daniel
Dexter
Dean
Donna
Dolly

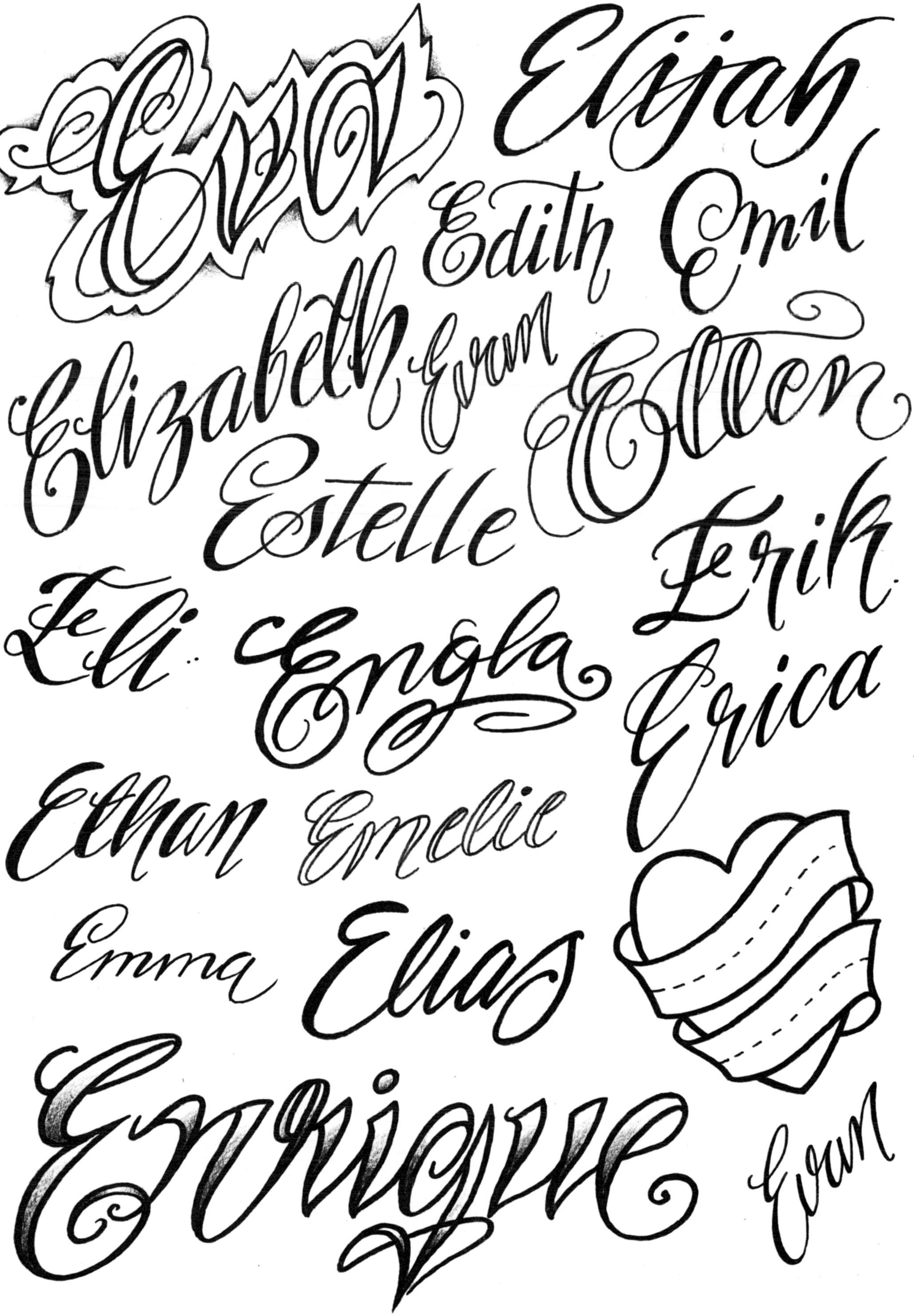

Eva

Elijah

Edith

Emil

Elizabeth

Evan

Ellen

Estelle

Erik

Eli

Engla

Erica

Ethan

Emelie

Emma

Elias

Enrique

Evan

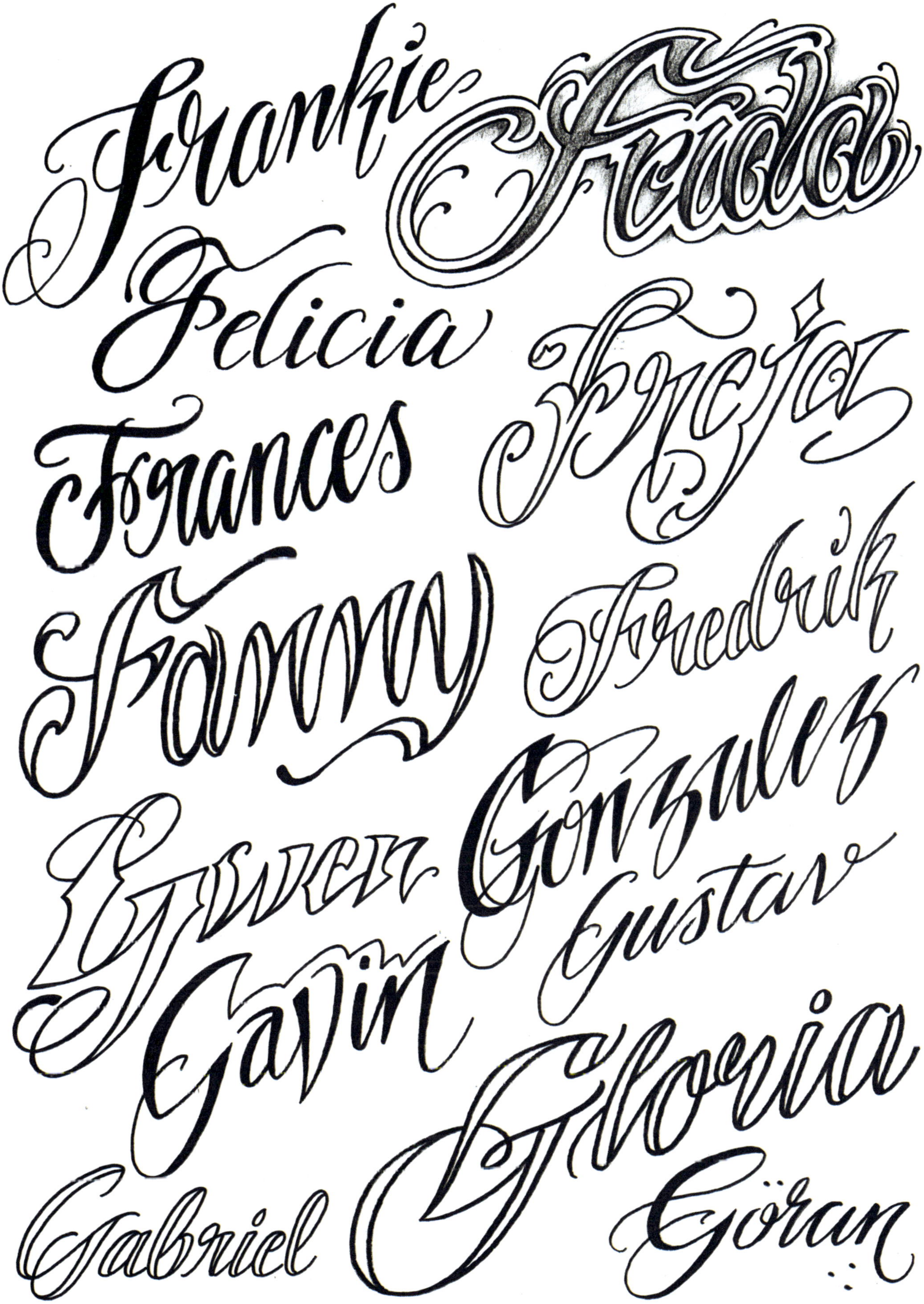

Frankie

Frida

Felicia

Freja

Frances

Fanny

Fredrik

Gwen

Gonzalez

Gustav

Gavin

Gloria

Gabriel

Göran

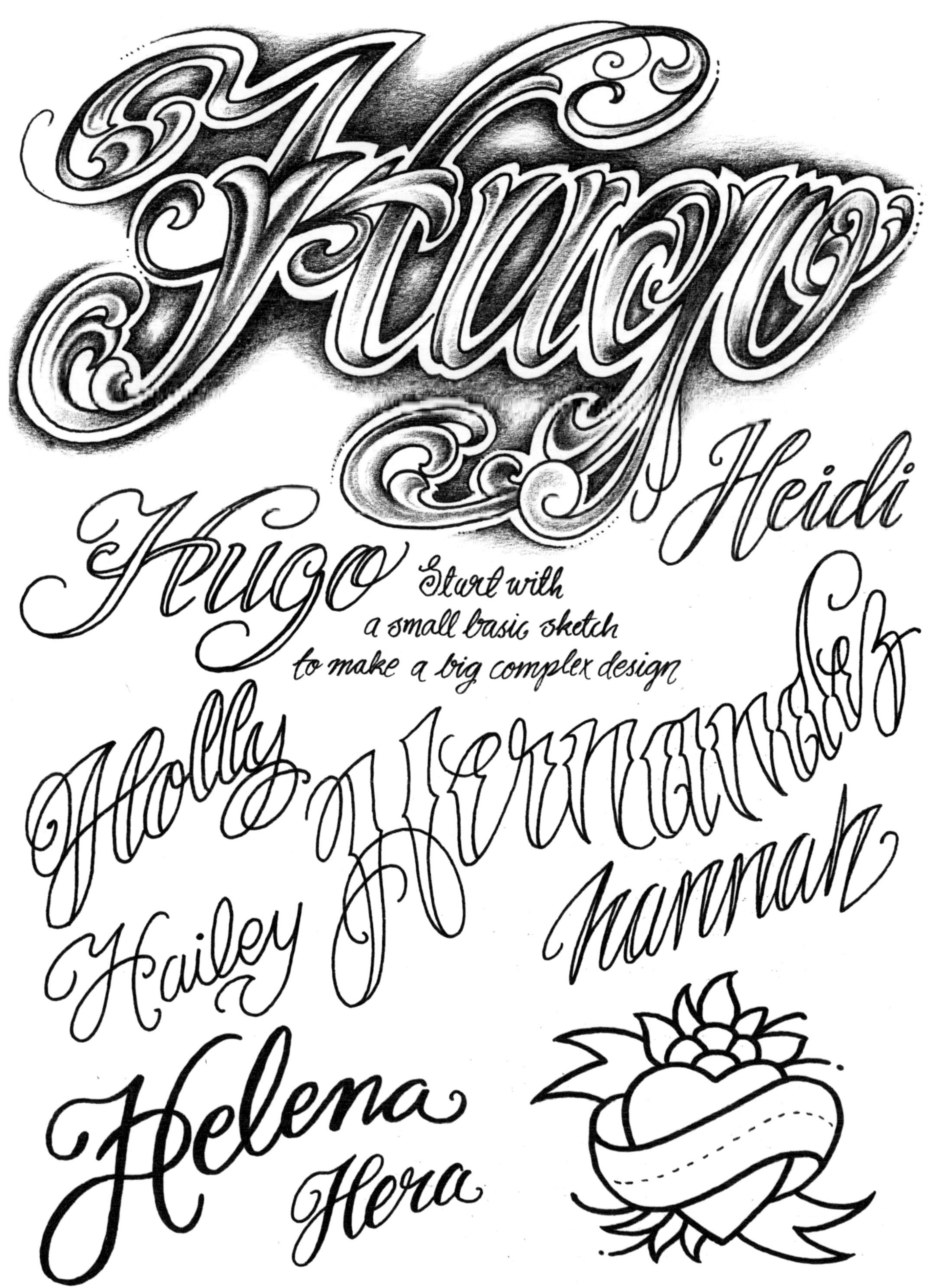
Hugo
Hugo
Heidi
Start with
a small basic sketch
to make a big complex design
Holly
Hernandez
Hailey
Hannah
Helena
Hera

Isaac Isabella

Ichabod Igor Iris

Ida Irene Isaiah

JONAS

Jenny

June

Jane Jules

Judd

Jesus Jose Jennifer

Julie Jovo Jacob

Kim Kevin Kate

Kerstin Karl Kelly

Karen Kimberly

Lea

Konstantin Lee

Keith

Leijla

Lucy Lemmy Lois

Laurel Lisa

Melvin

Molly

Maria

Magnus

Marc

Malin

Marija

Mary

MORGAN

Marina

Nellie

Martin

Michael

Natalie

Mandy

Noah

Nina

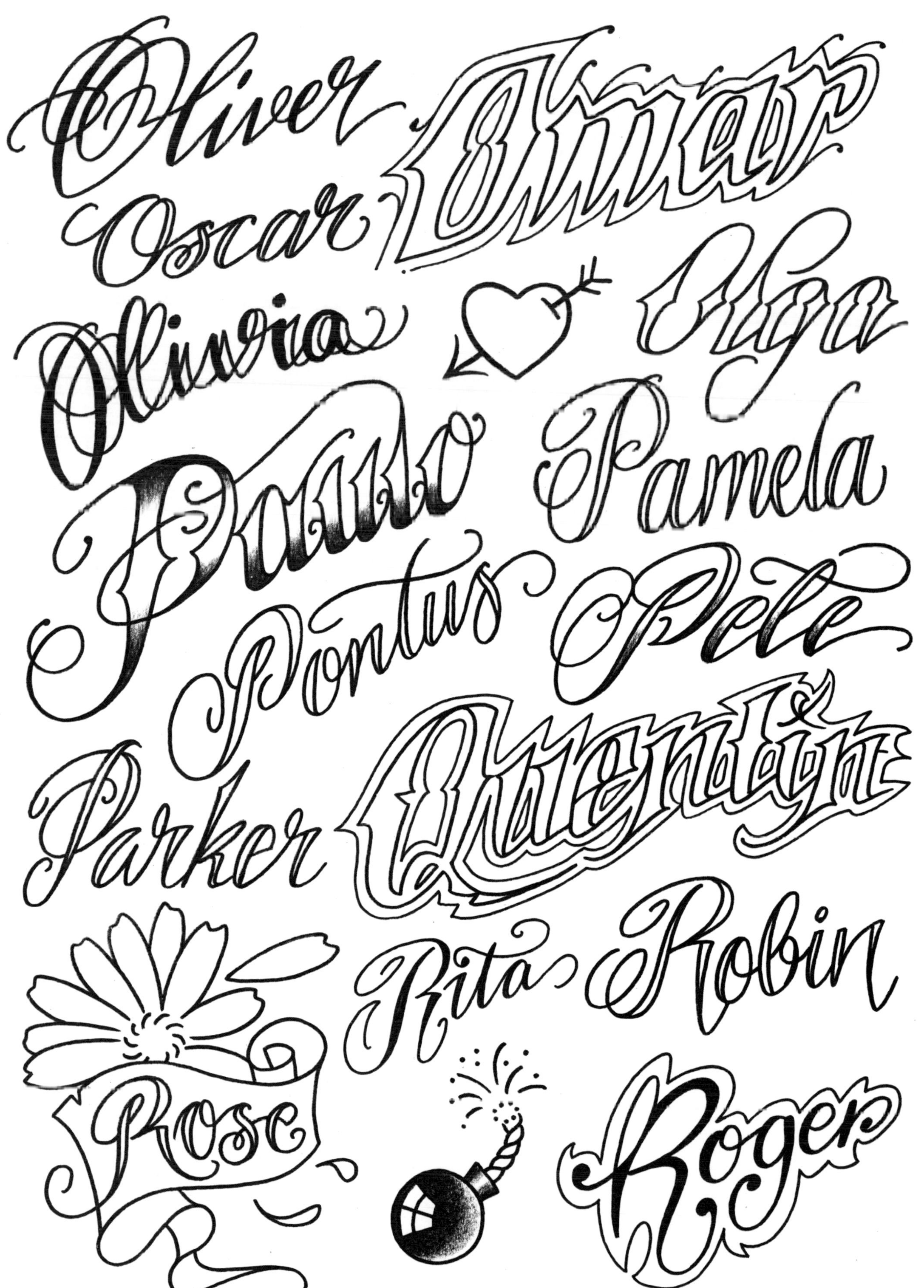
Oliver
Omar
Oscar
Olivia
Olga
Pablo
Pamela
Pontus
Pete
Parker
Quentin
Rita
Robin
Rose
Roger

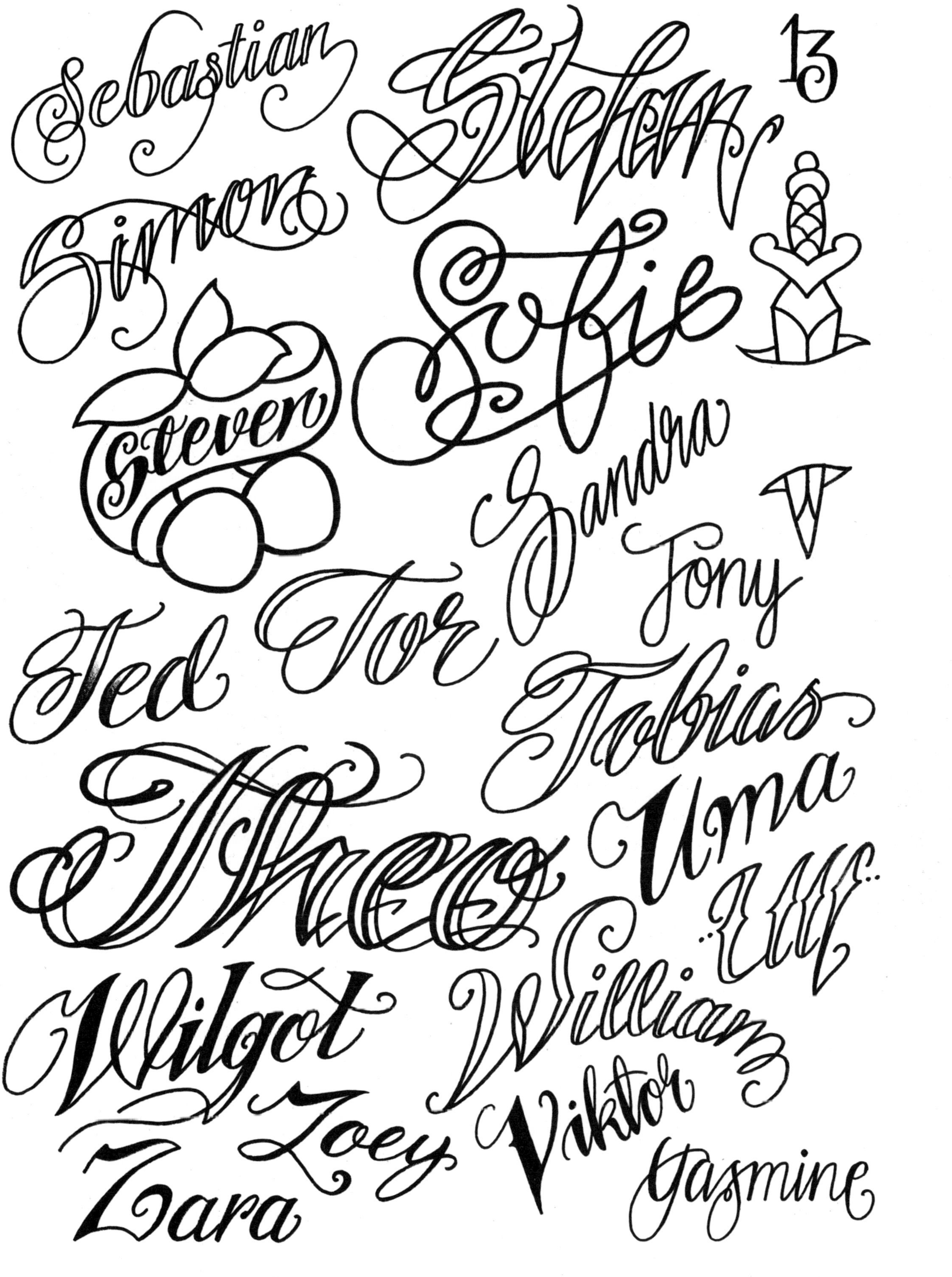

Sebastian

Stefan

13

Simon

Sofie

Steven

Sandra

Tony

Ted

Tor

Tobias

Theo

Uma

Ulf

Wilgot

William

Viktor

Zoey

Zara

Yasmine

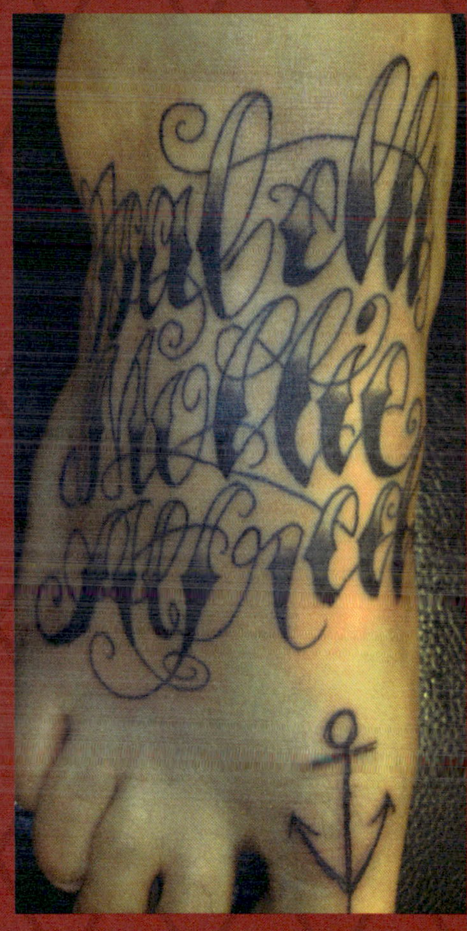

Big Foot tattoo on Jonas Strömberg.

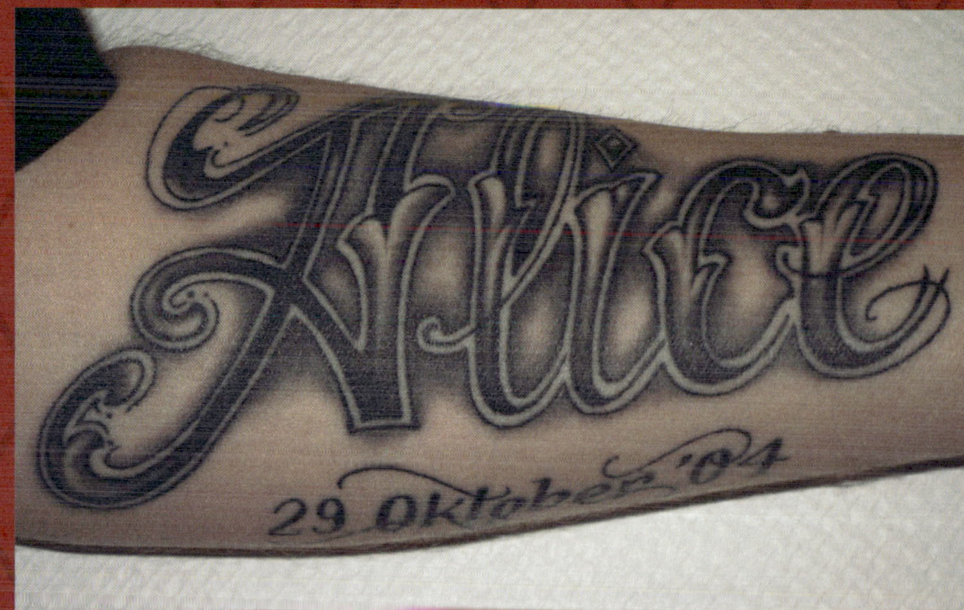

Mikael Fogelqvist

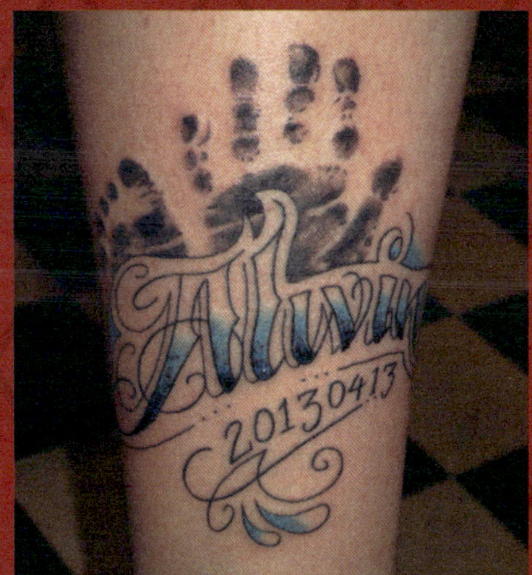

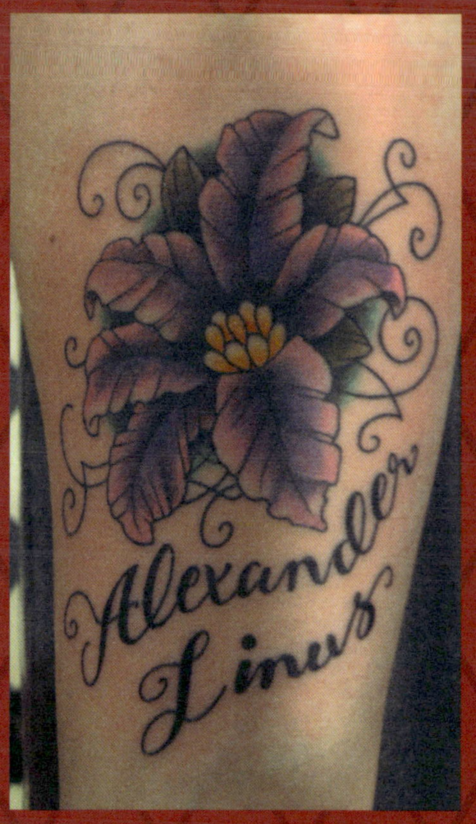

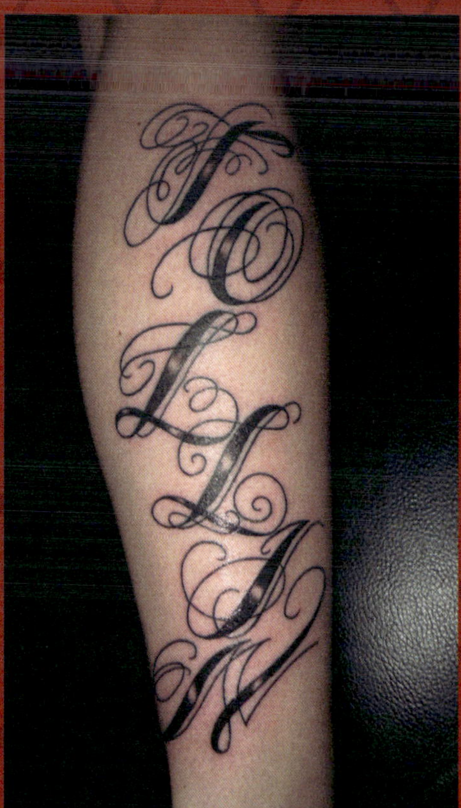

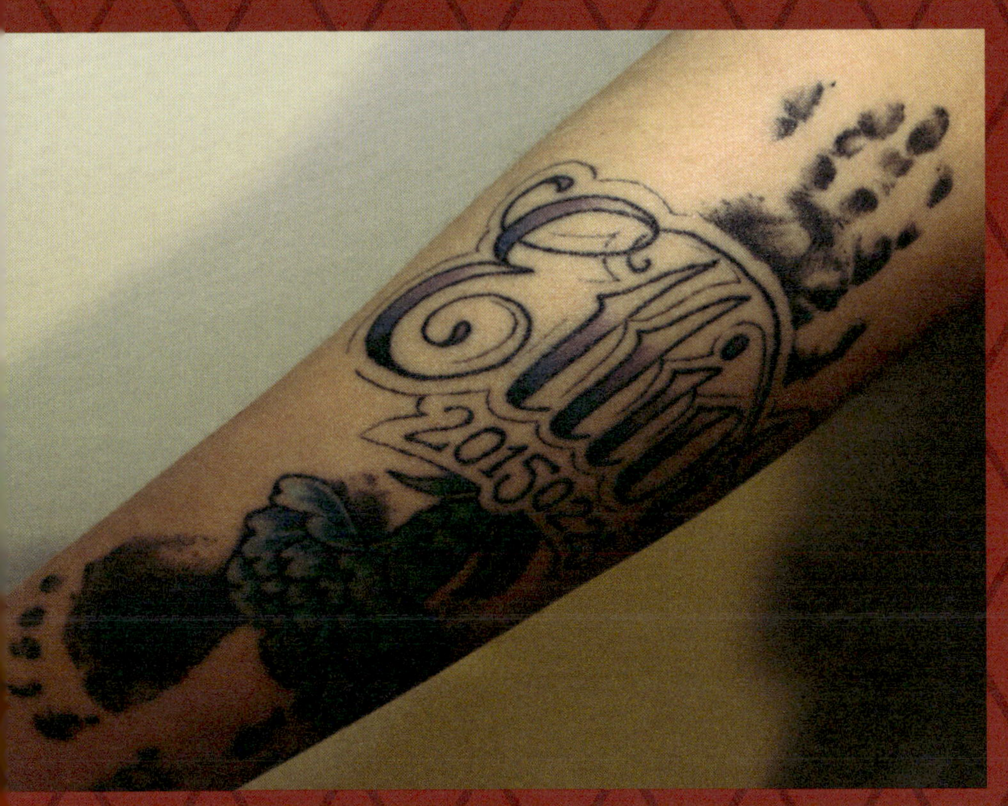

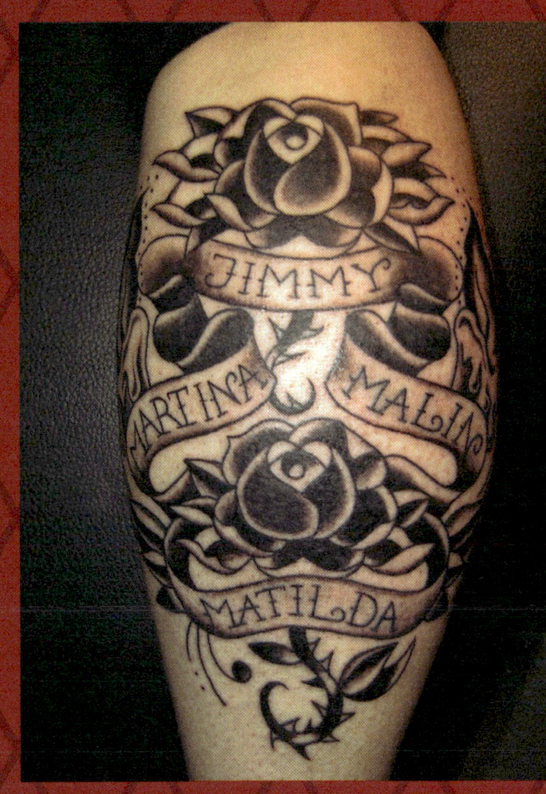

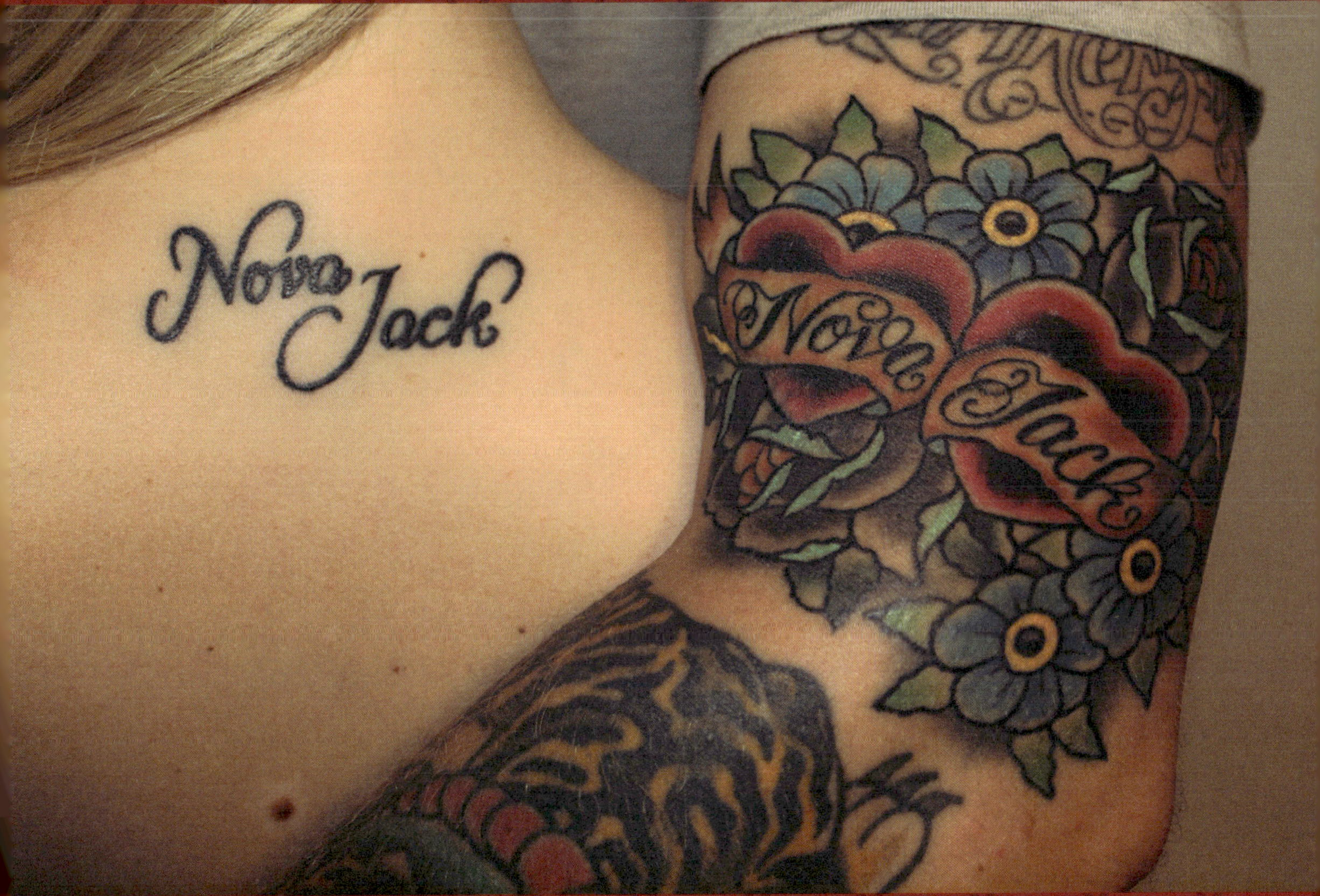

Amanda and Emil

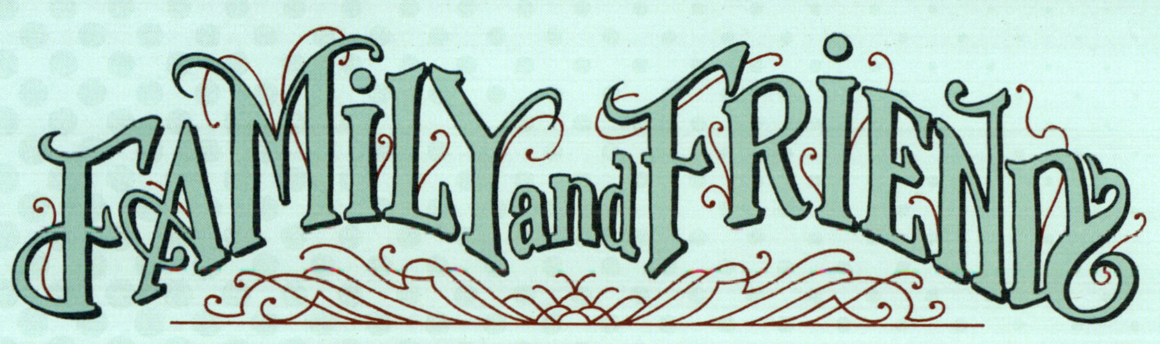

Friends..
are relatives..
..you make..
..for yourself

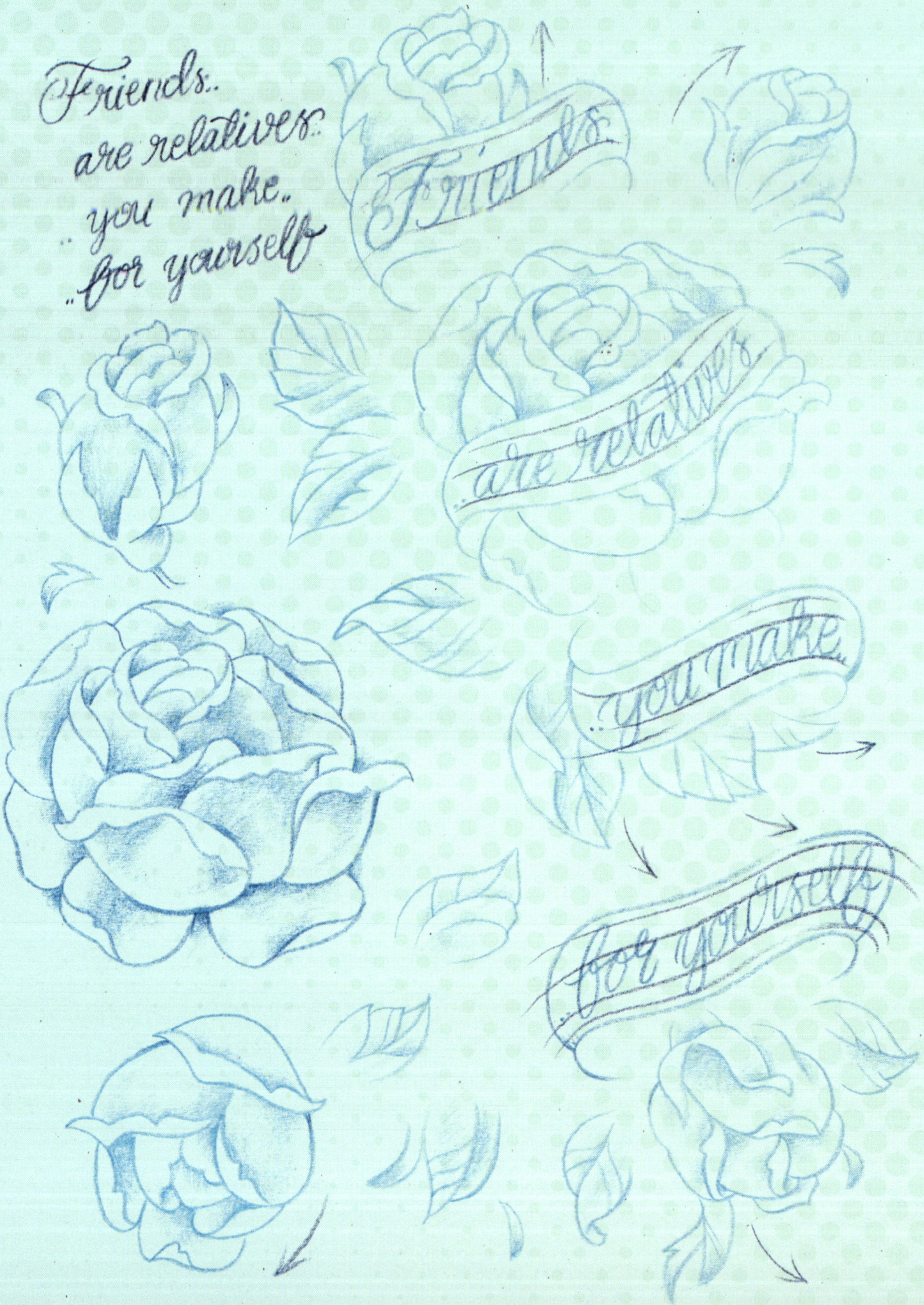

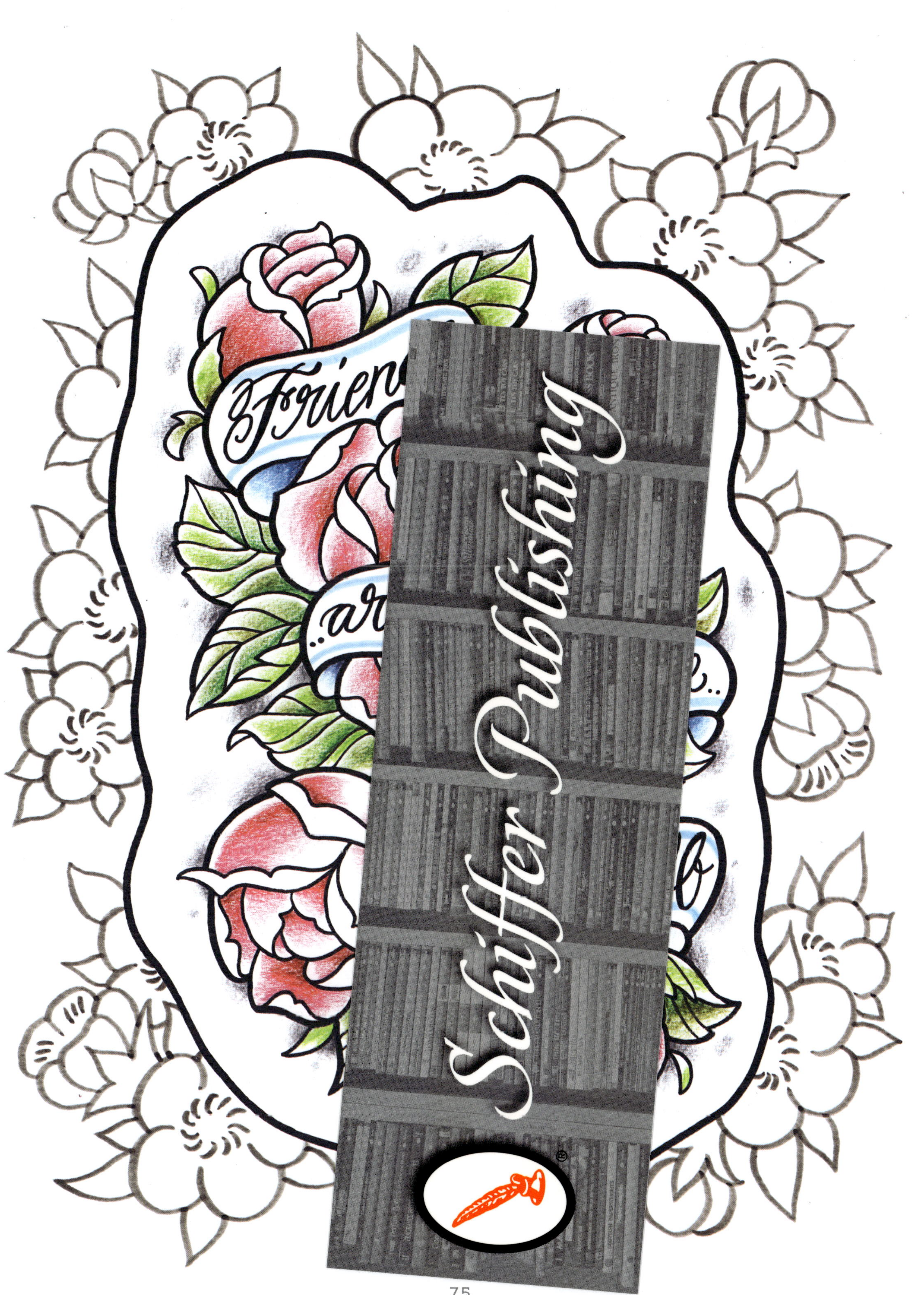
Schiffer Publishing

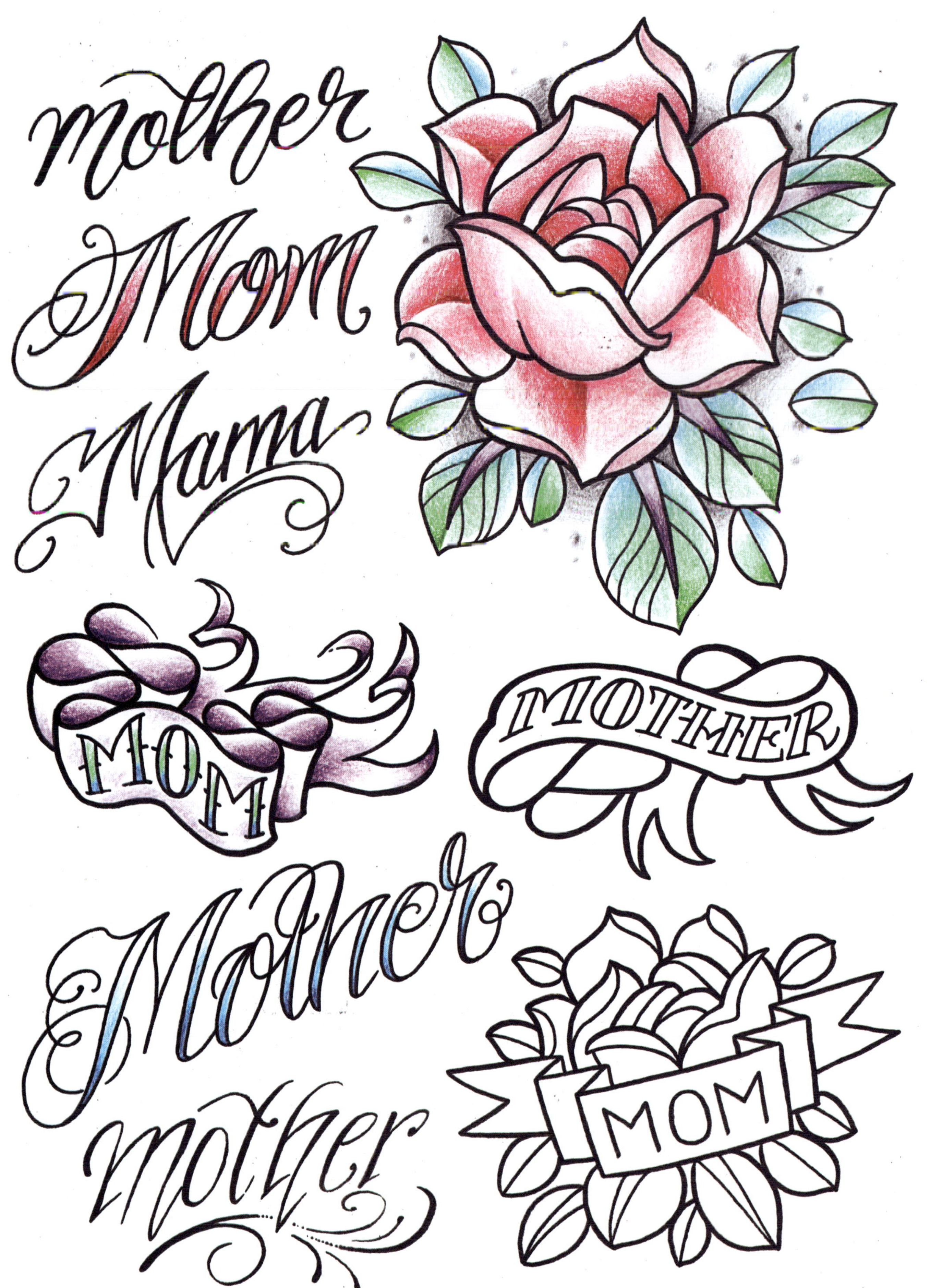
mother
Mom
Mama
MOM
MOTHER
Mother
mother
MOM

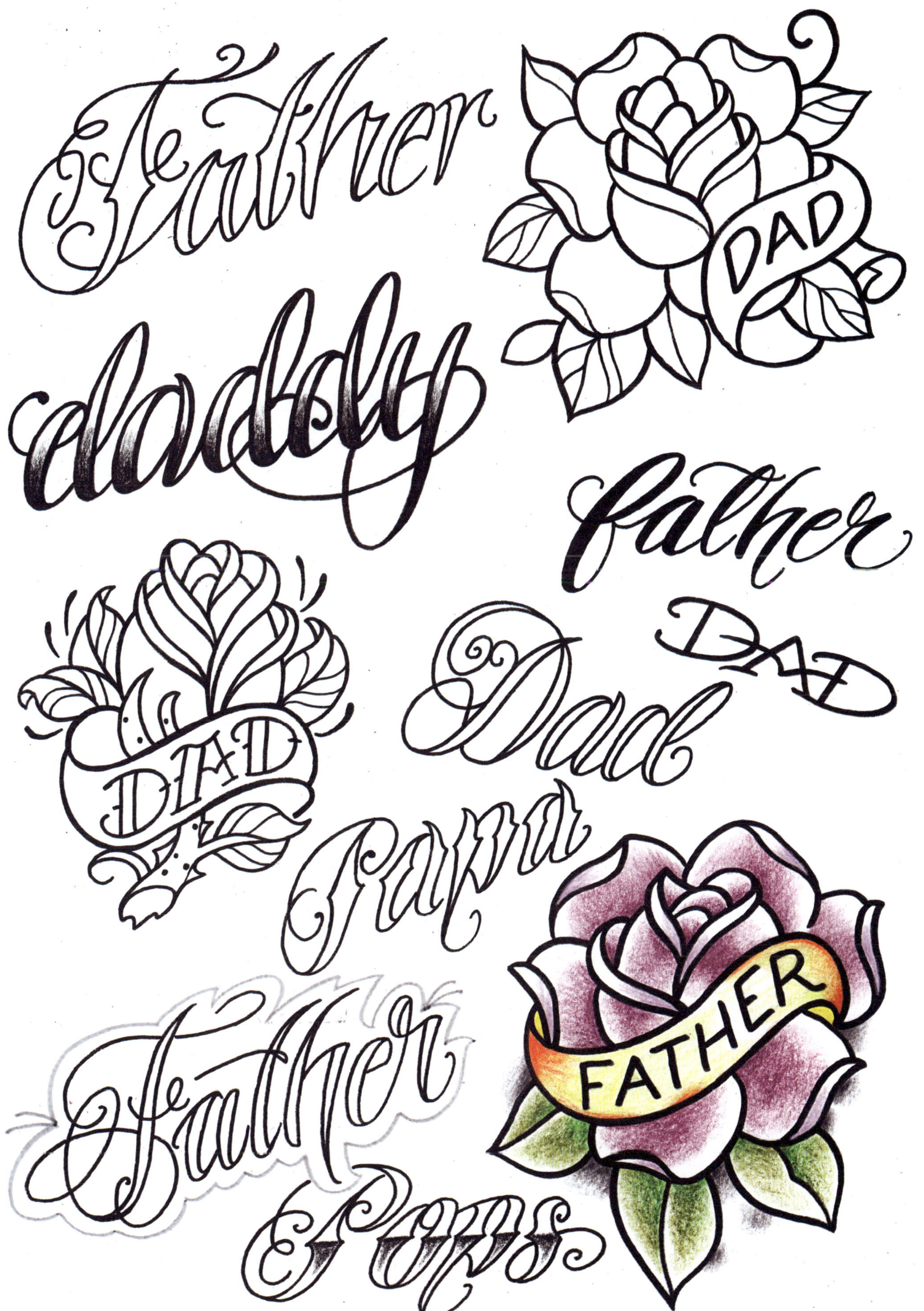

Father
DAD
daddy
father
DAD
DAD
Dad
Papa
FATHER
Father
Pops

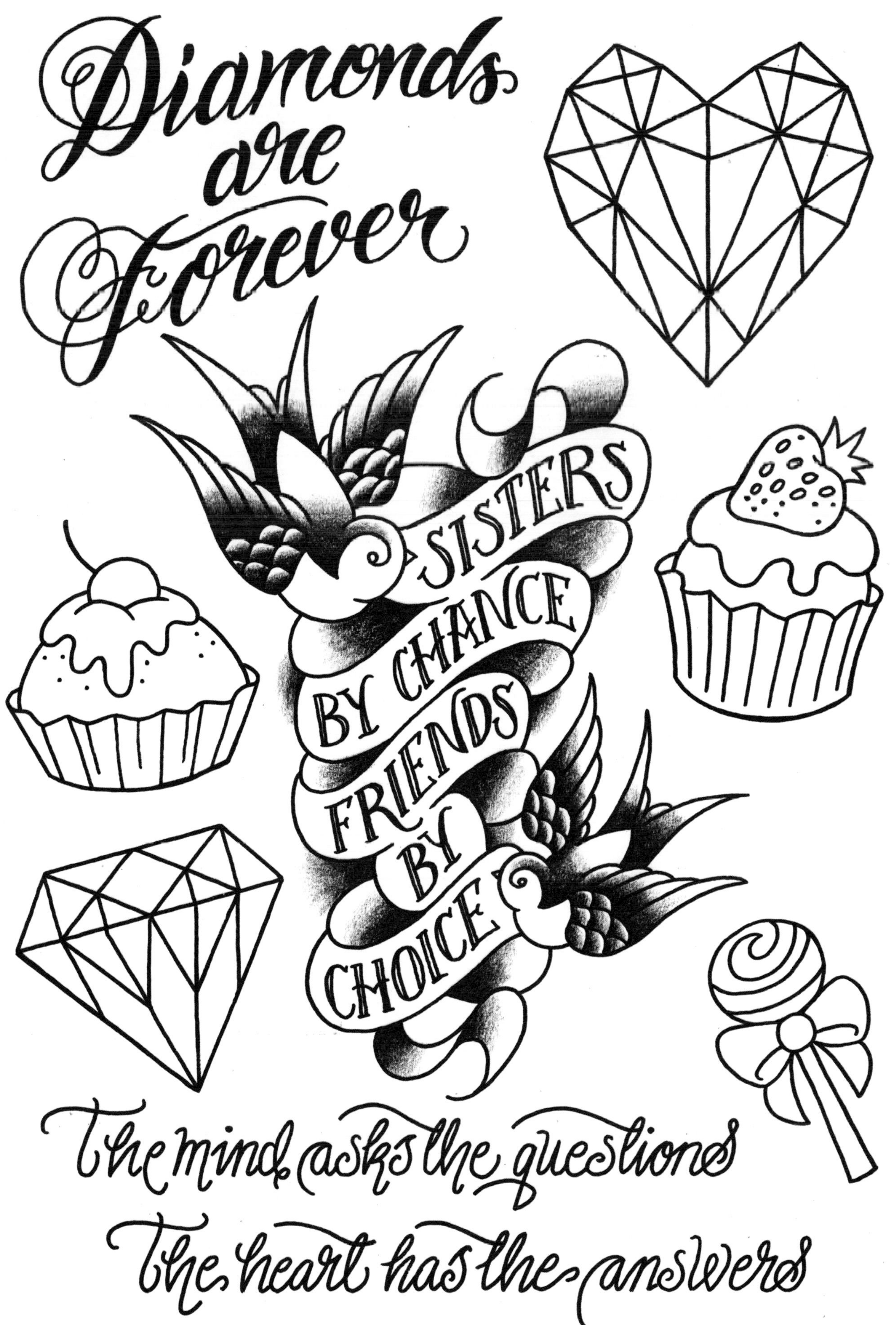
Diamonds are Forever
SISTERS BY CHANCE FRIENDS BY CHOICE
The mind asks the questions
The heart has the answers

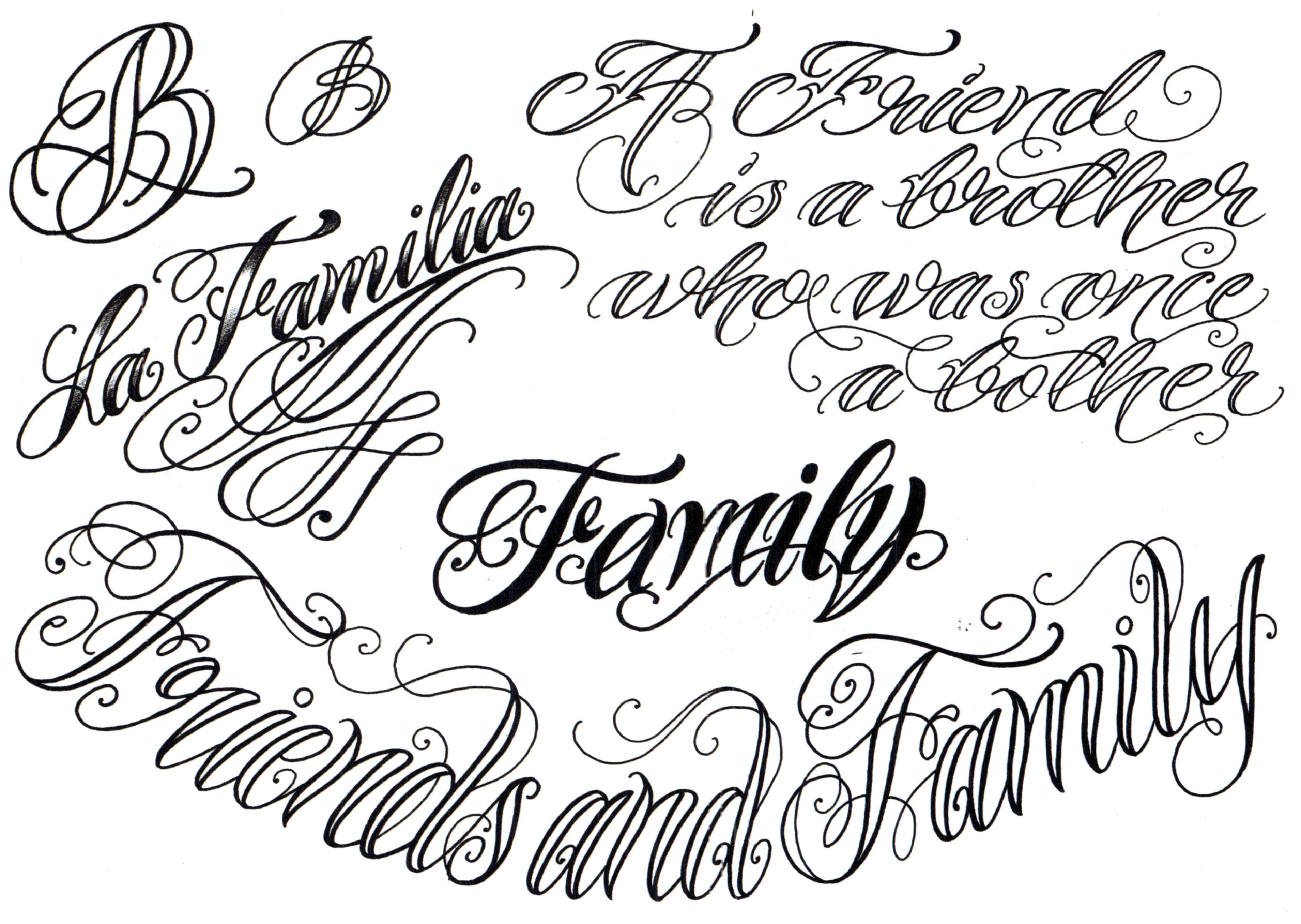
B
B
A Friend
is a brother
who was once
a bother
La Familia
Family
Friends and Family

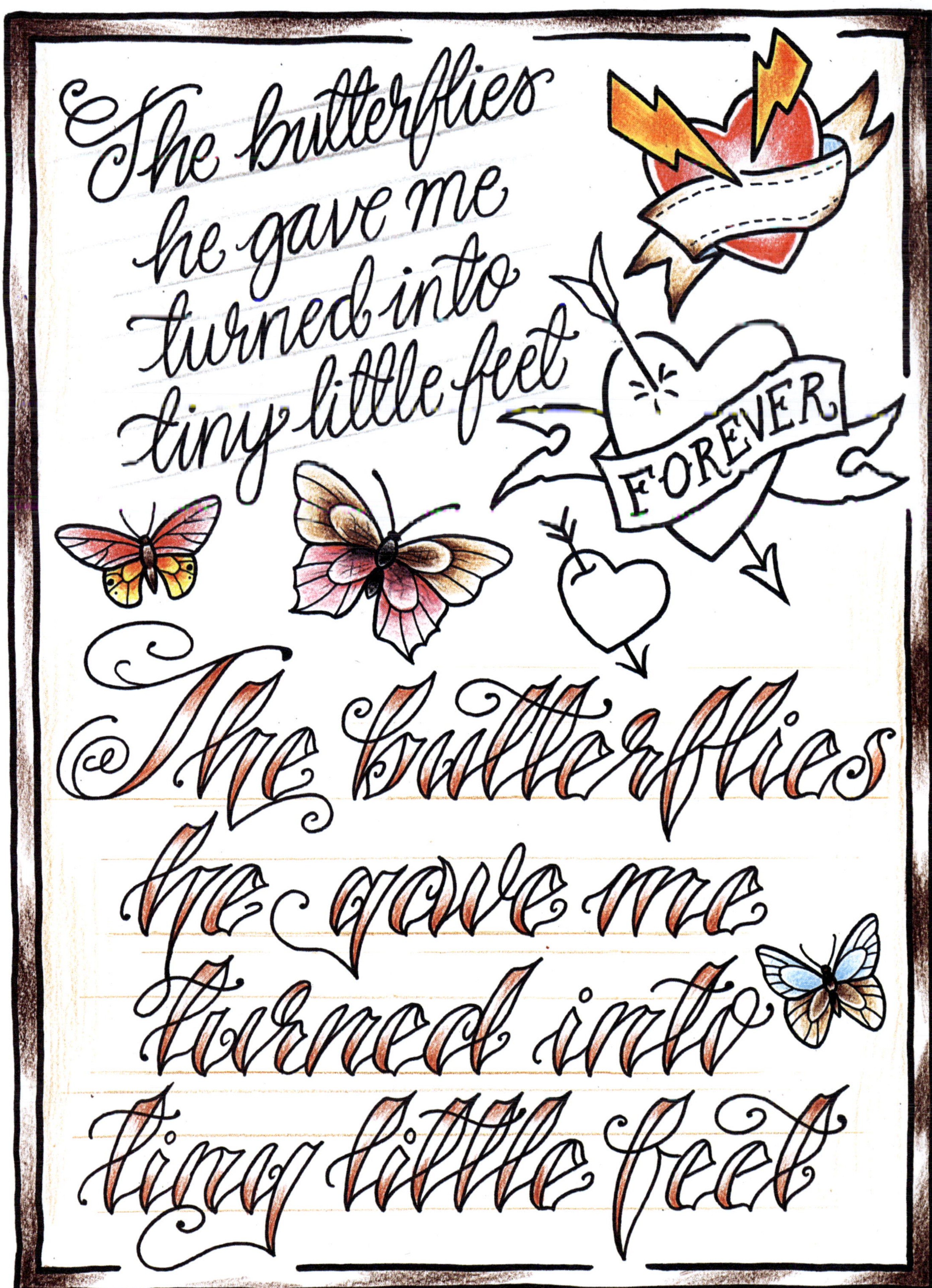
The butterflies
he gave me
turned into
tiny little feet
FOREVER
The butterflies
he gave me
turned into
tiny little feet

Chapter Four

The Day of the Dead

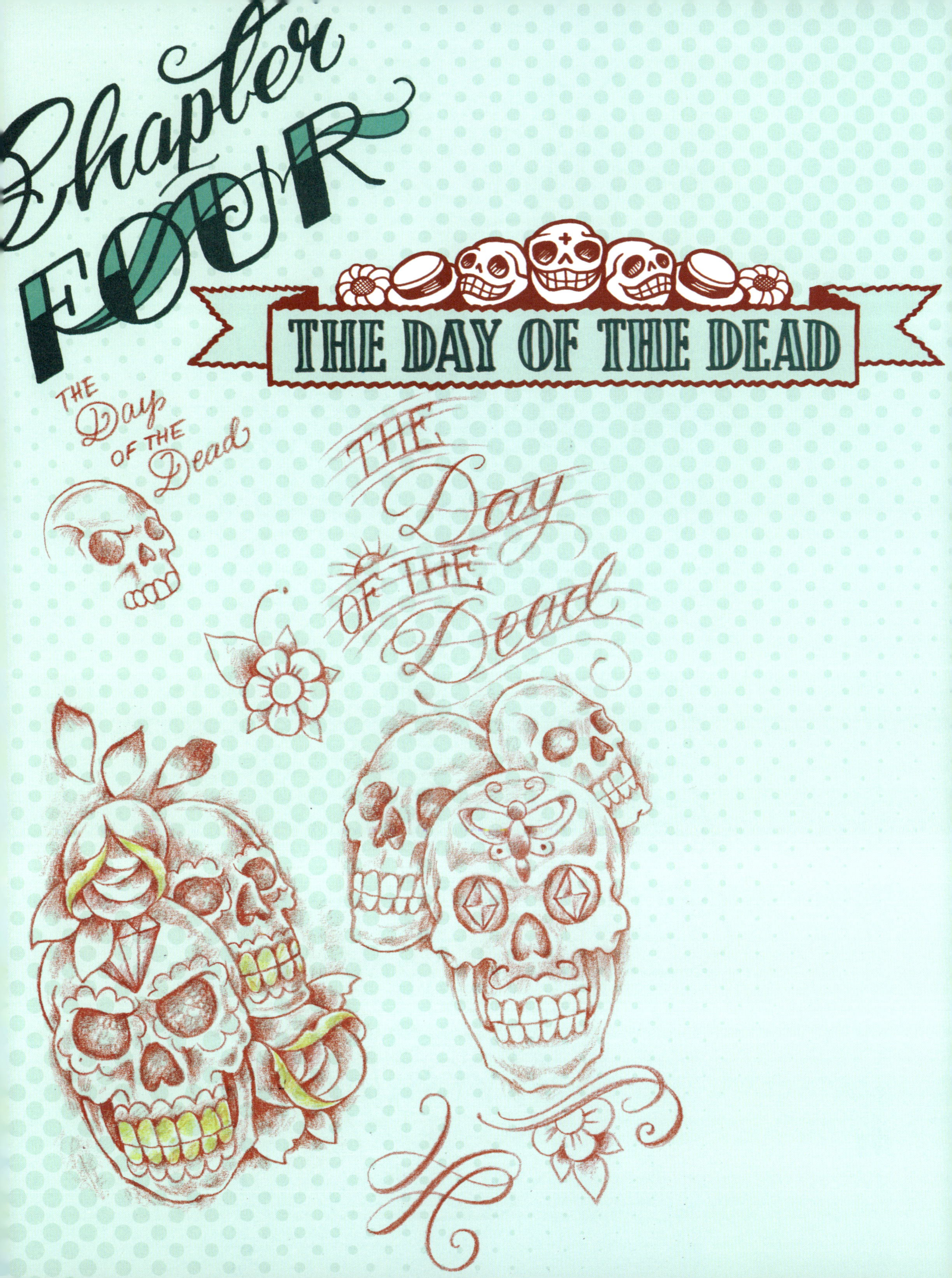

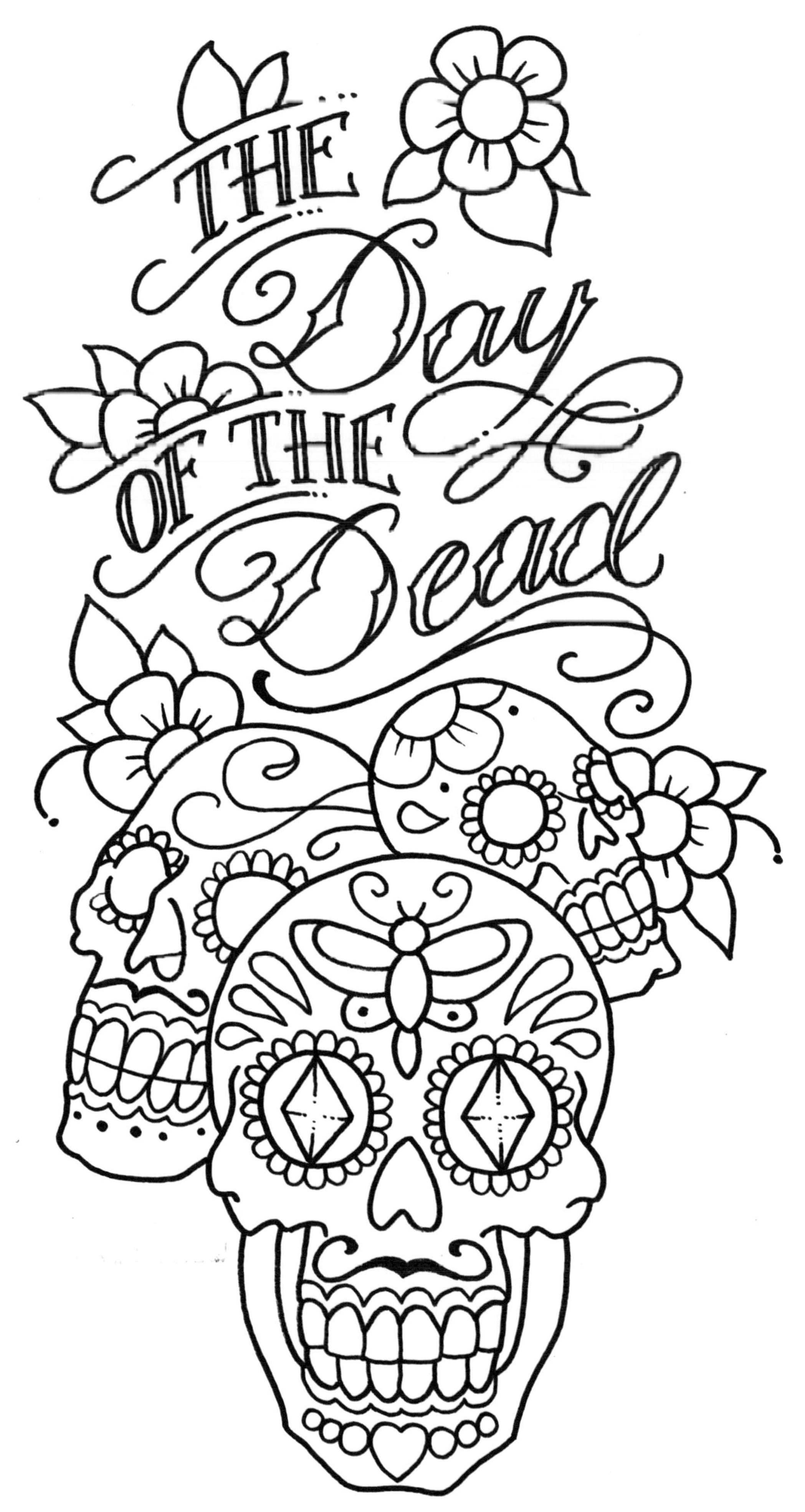
THE
Day
OF THE
Dead

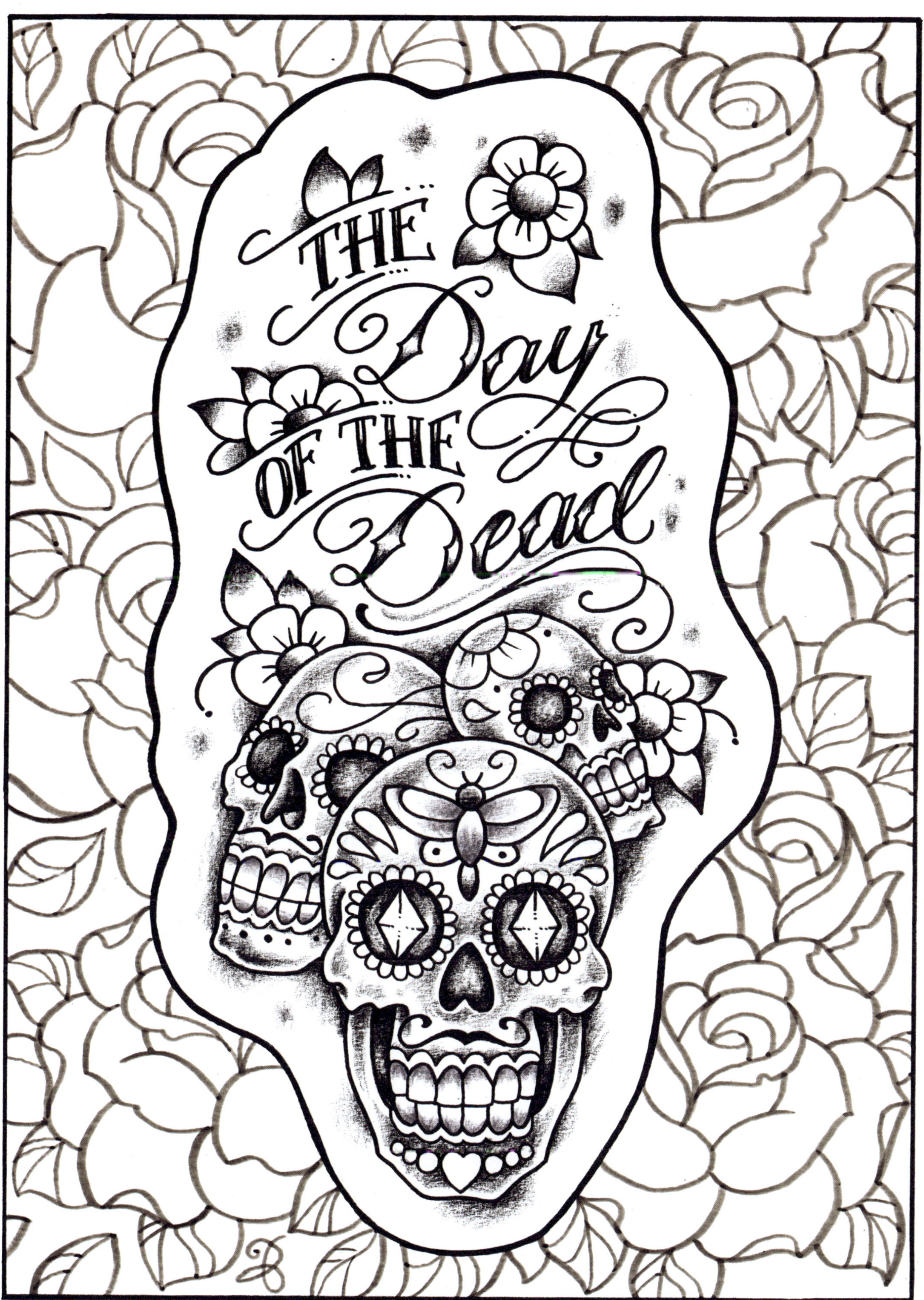
THE
Day
OF THE
Dead

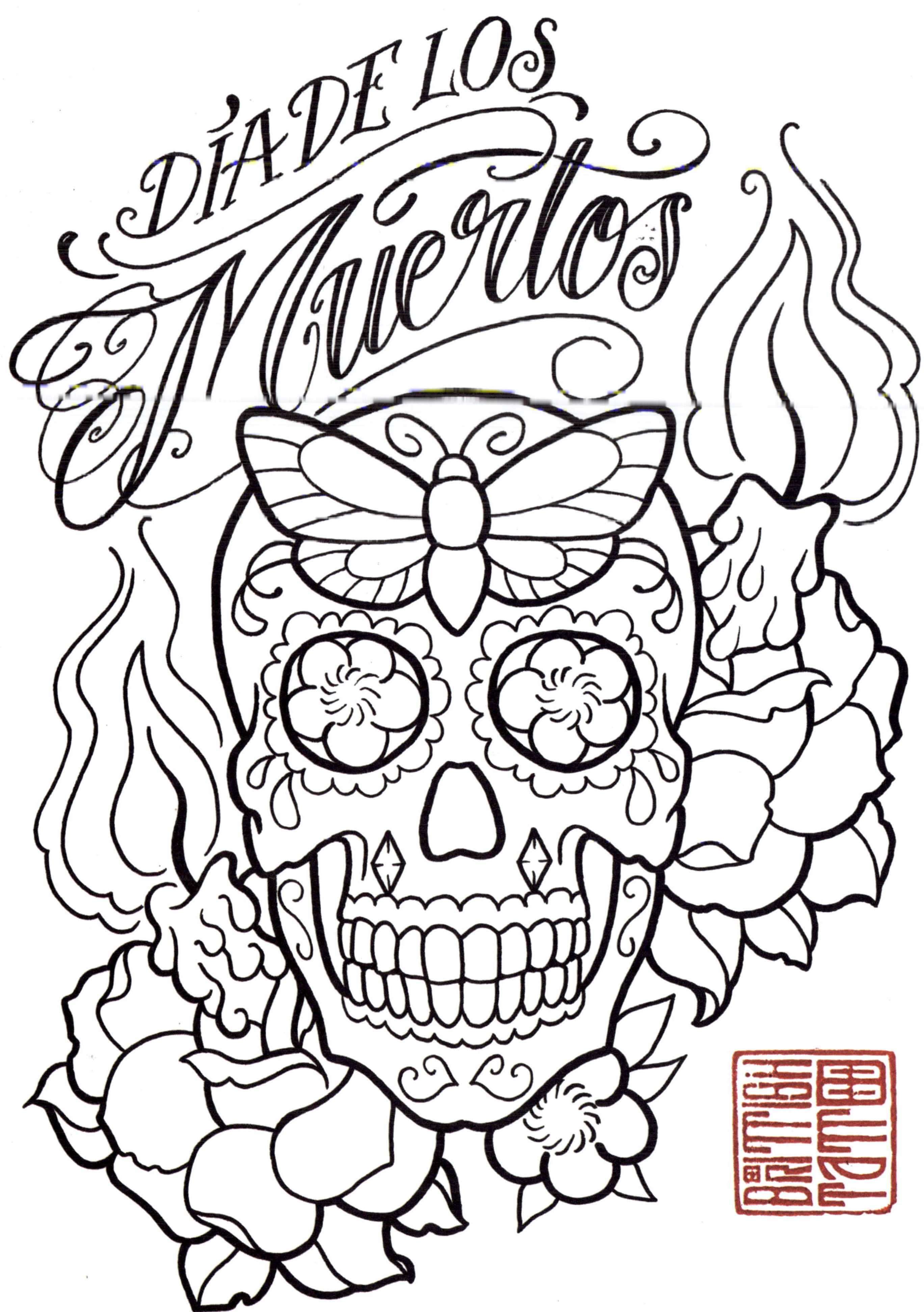
DÍA DE LOS
Muertos

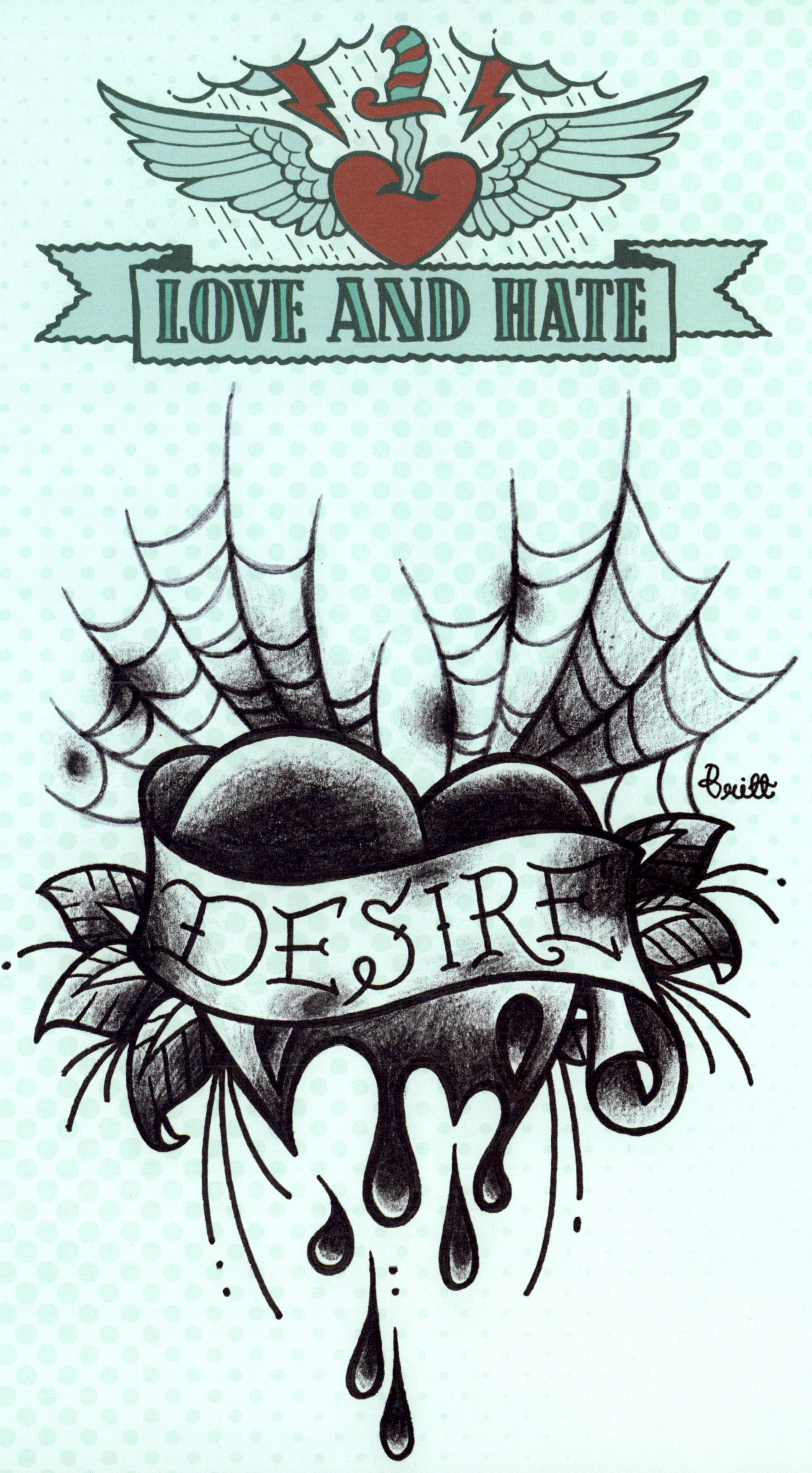
LOVE AND HATE
DESIRE
Britt

Simon Bladh

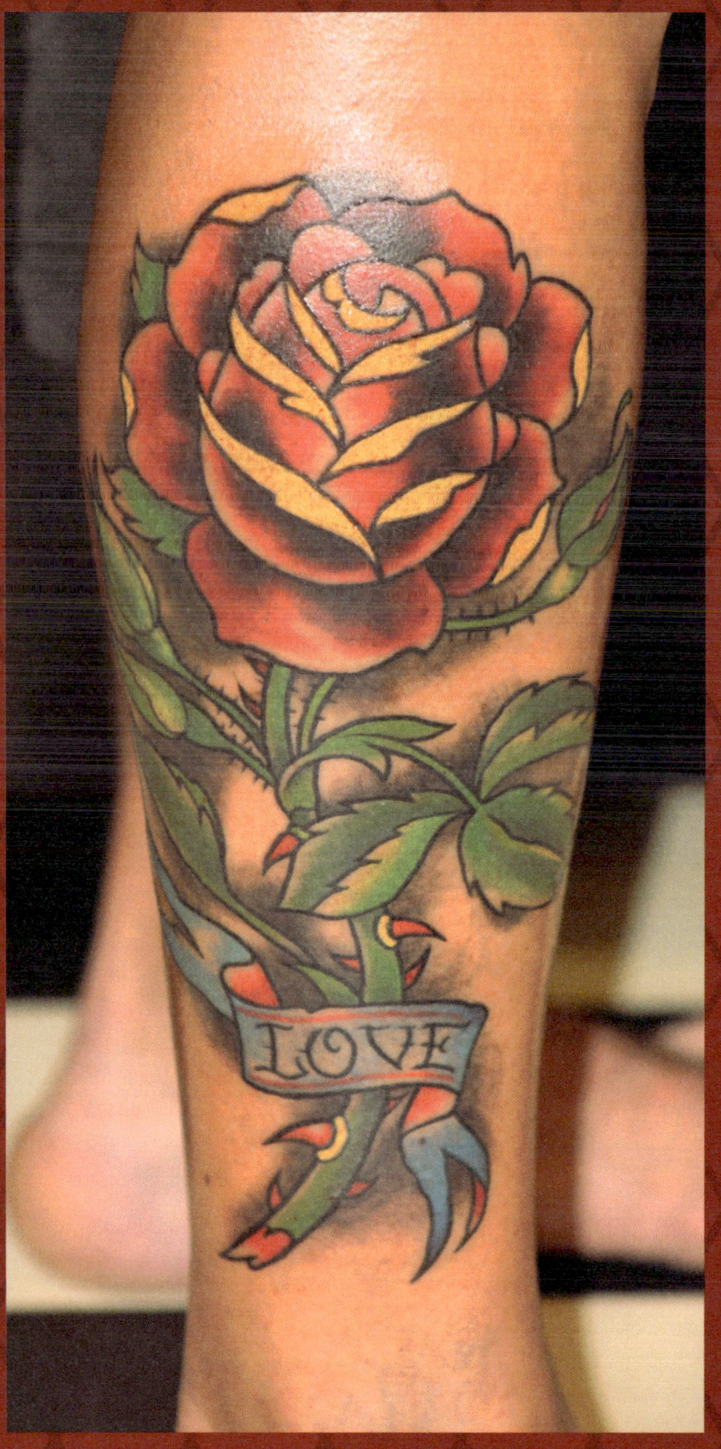

Villy Fridelind

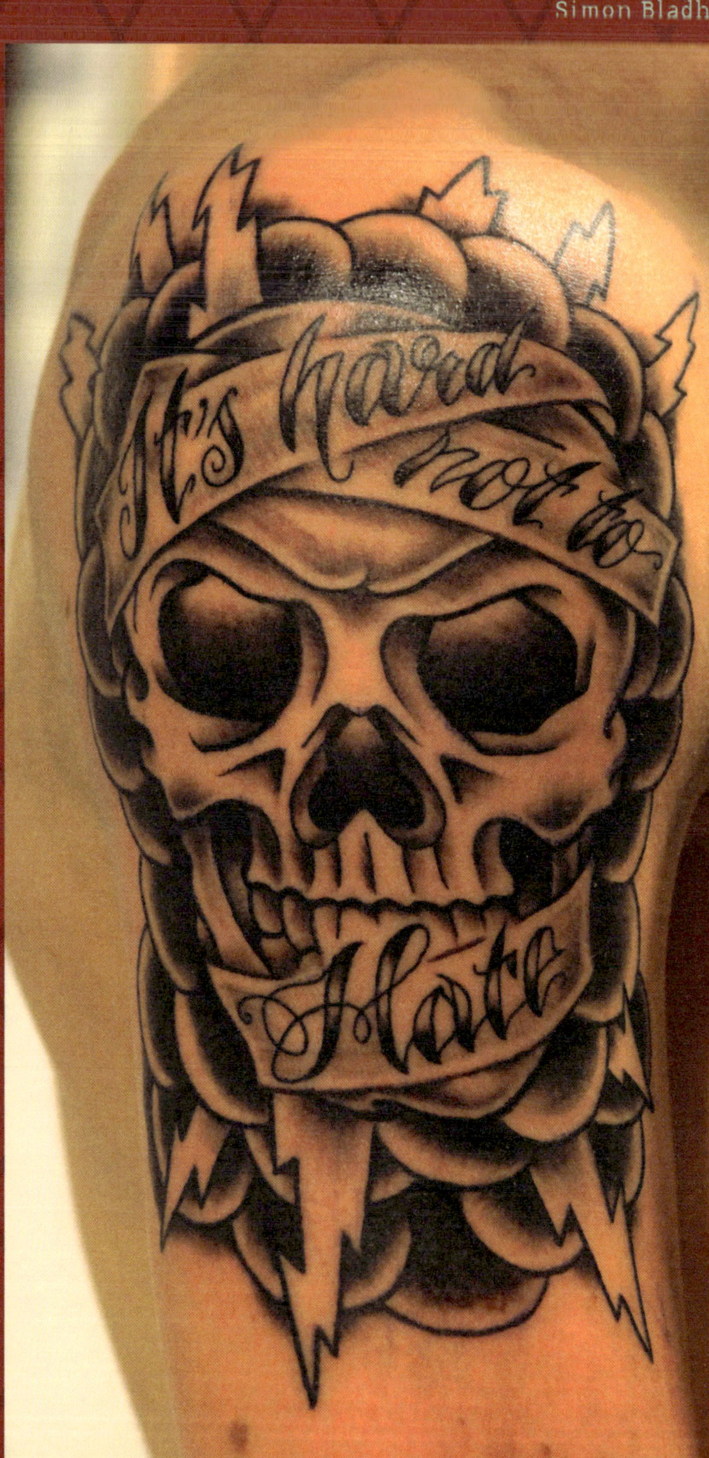

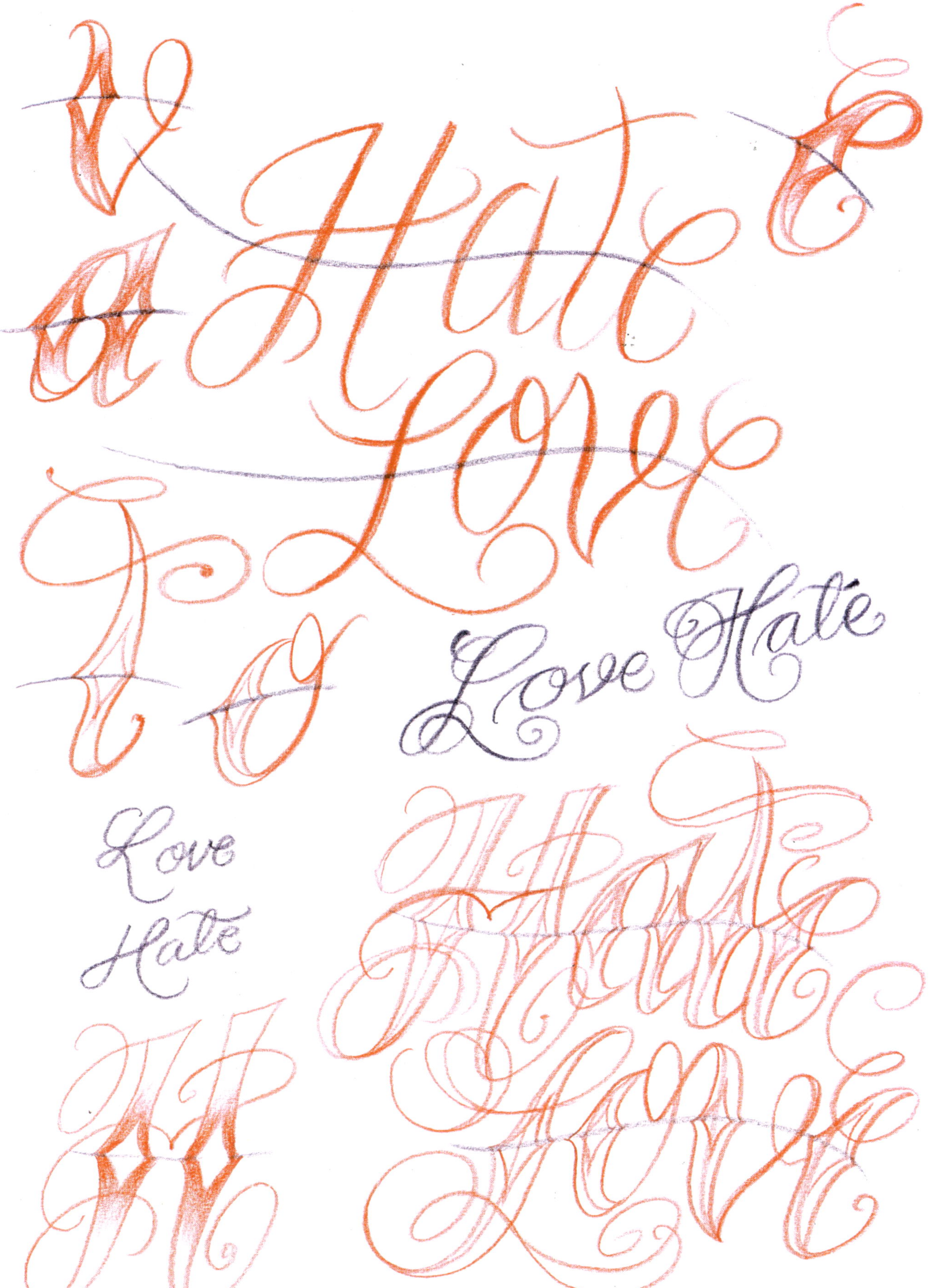

Hate

Love

Love Hate

Love

Hate

Hate

Love

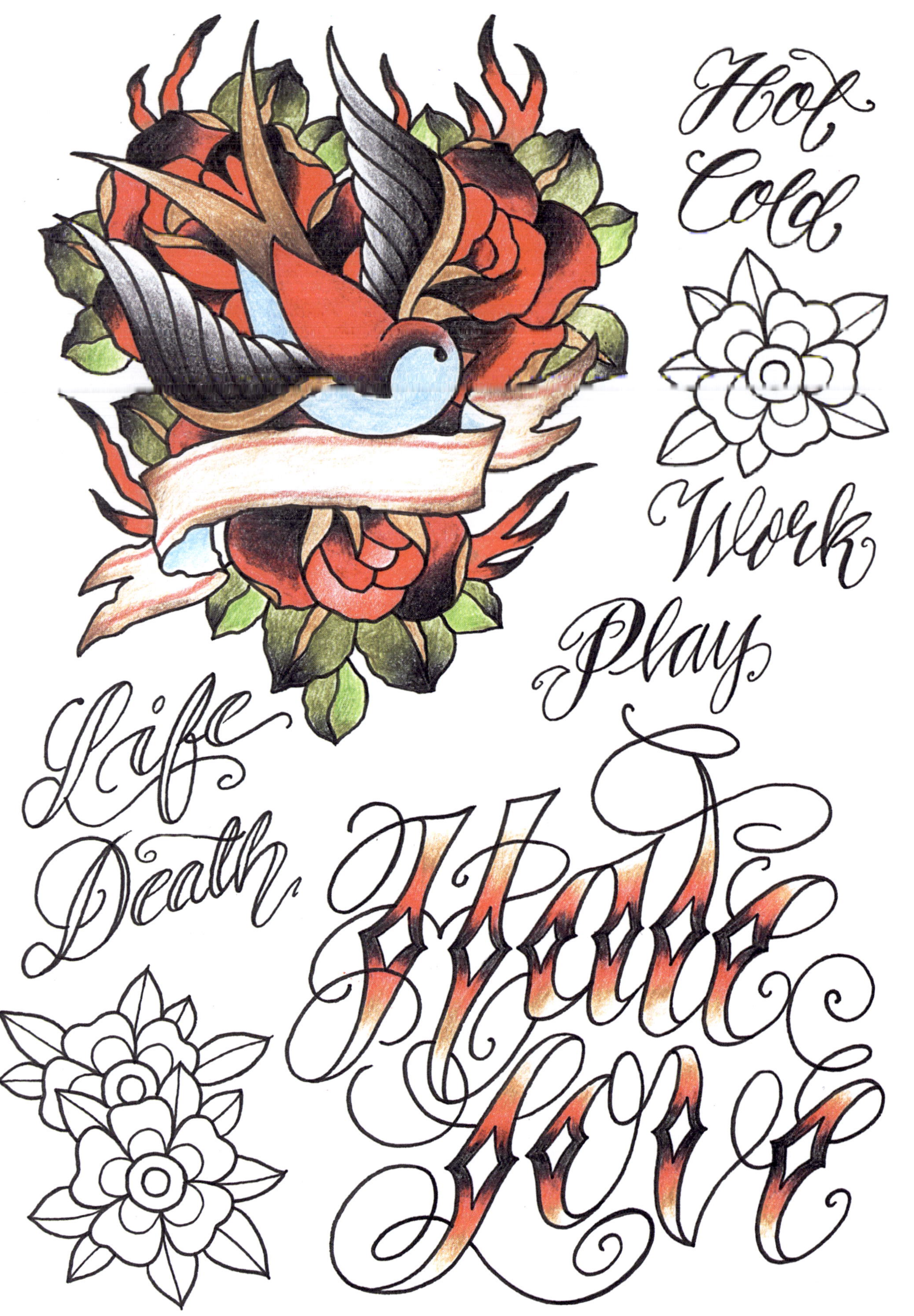
Hot
Cold
Work
Play
Life
Death
Hate
Love

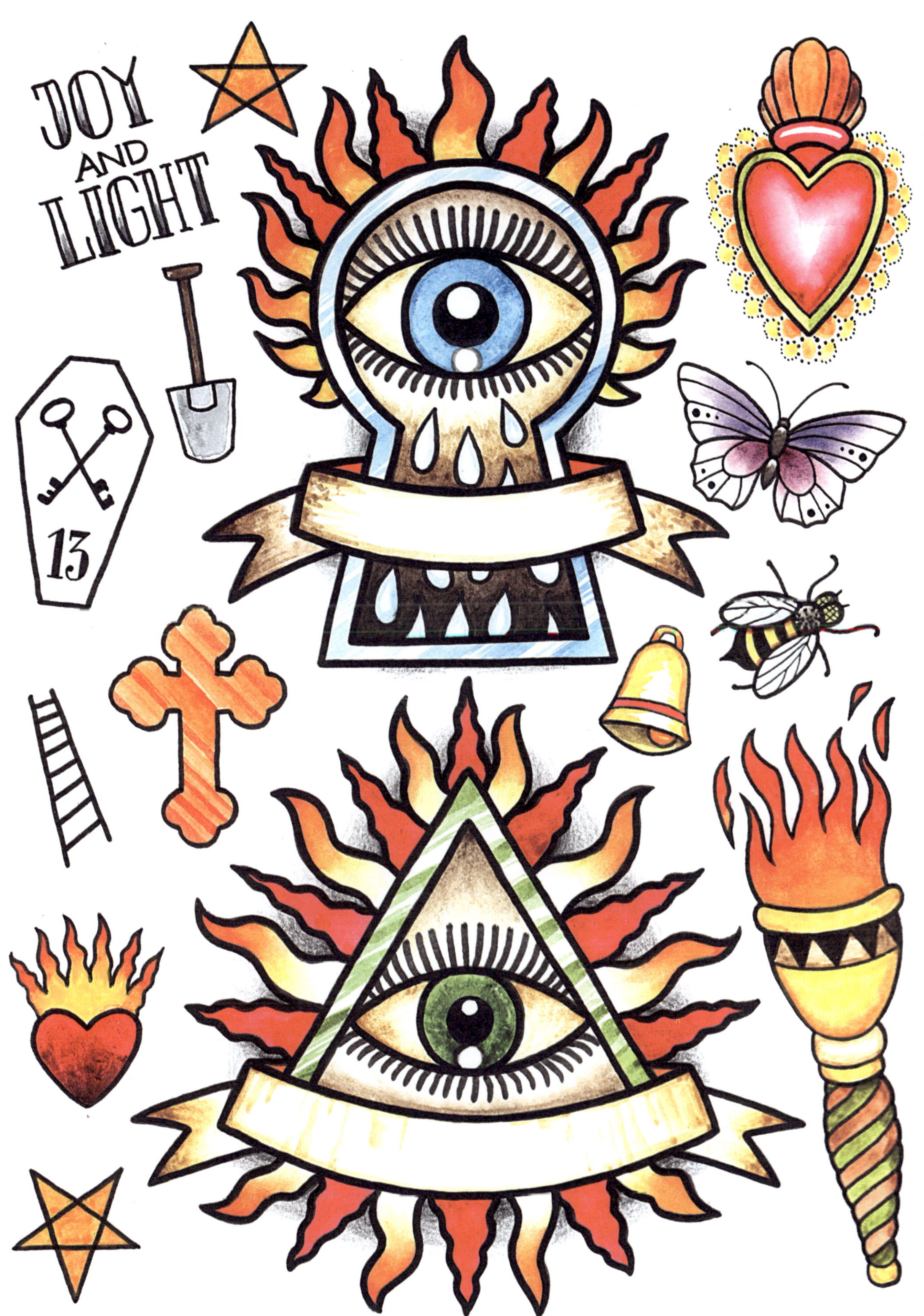

Freemasonry flash, 2015. Pigment ink and watercolor: 21 × 30 cm (8" × 12").

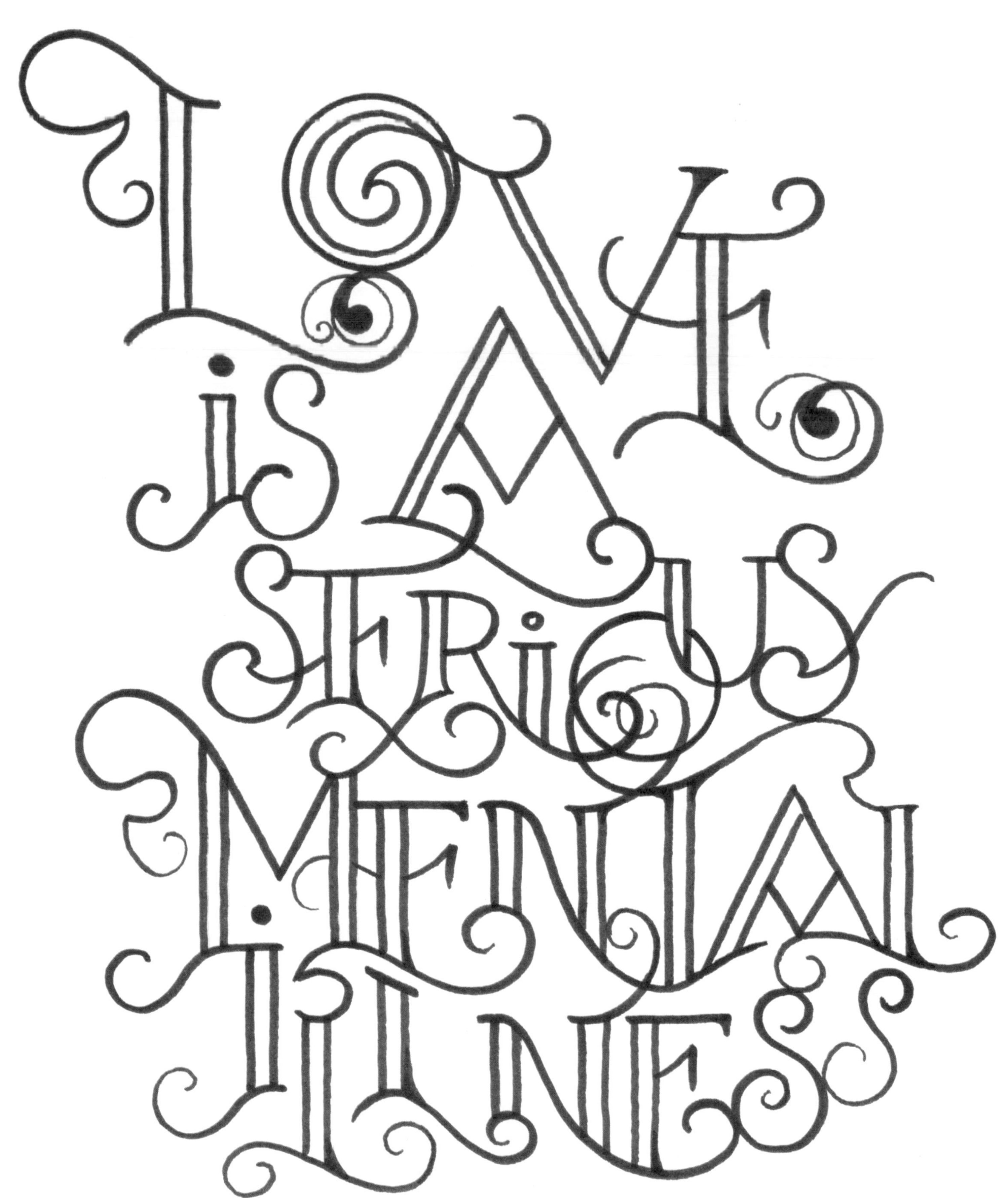
Love
is a
serious
mental
illness

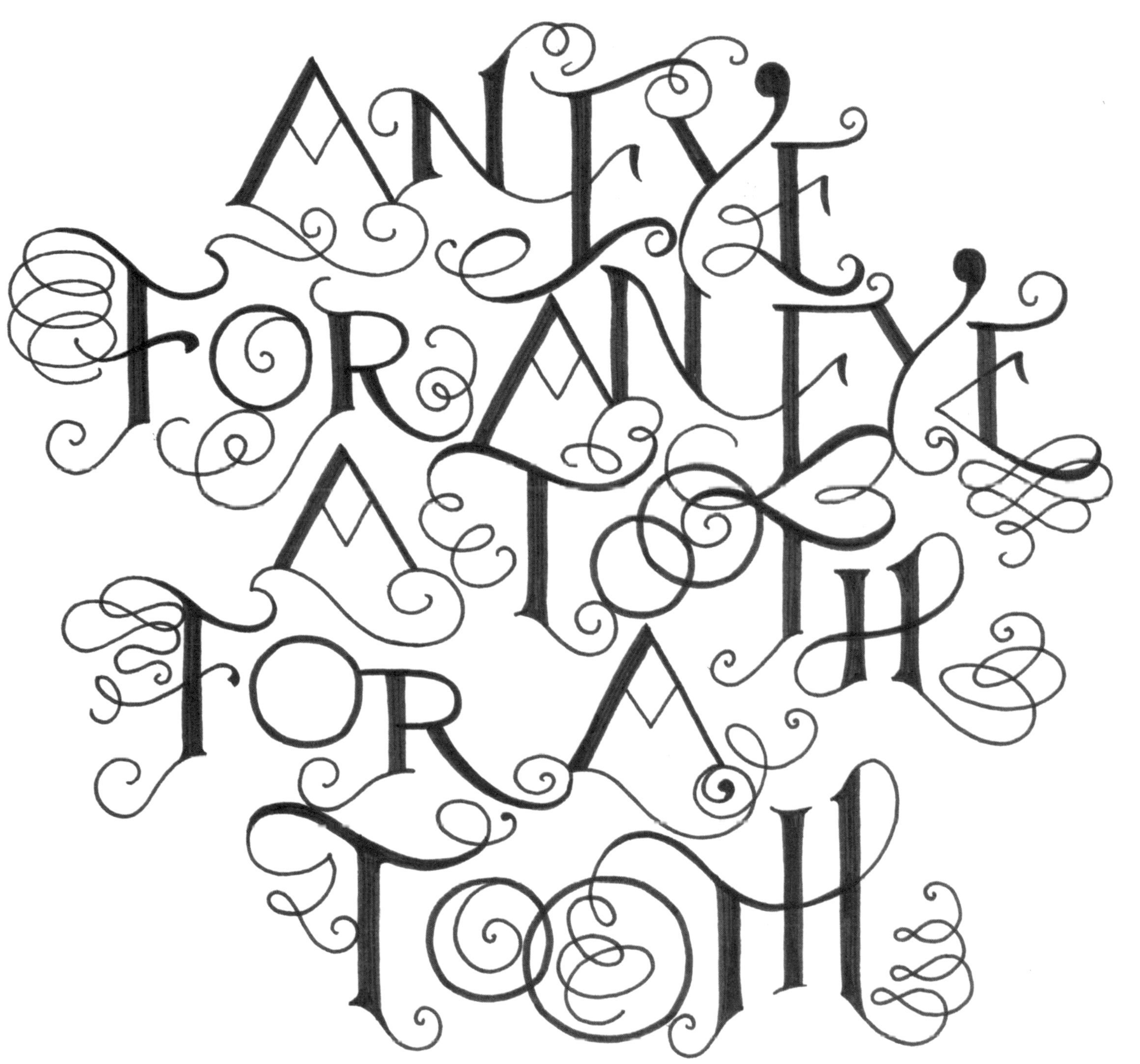
AN EYE
FOR AN EYE
A TOOTH
FOR A
TOOTH

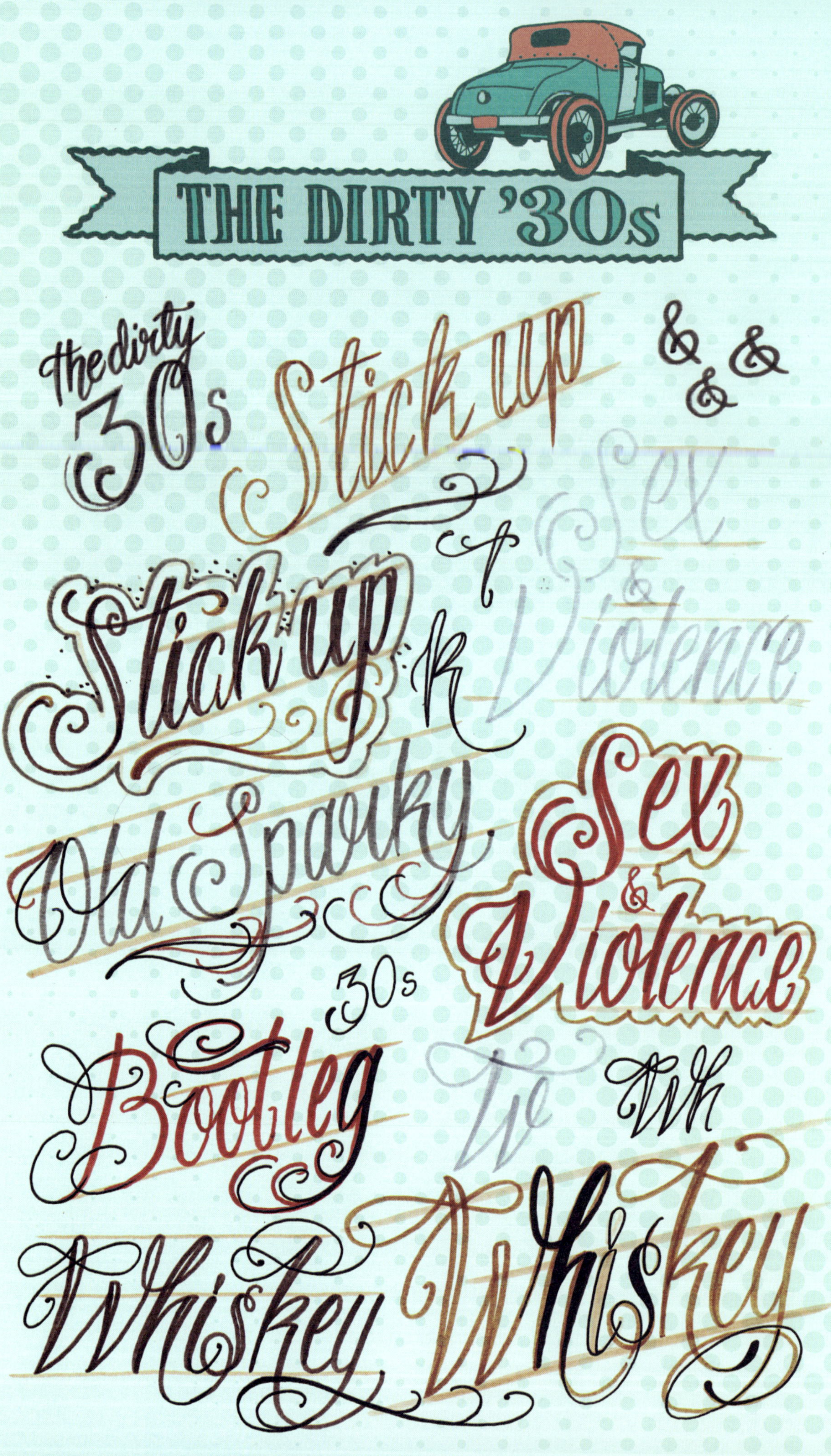
THE DIRTY '30s
the dirty 30s
Stick up
Stick up
Sex & Violence
Old Sparky
Sex & Violence
30s
Bootleg
Whiskey
Whiskey

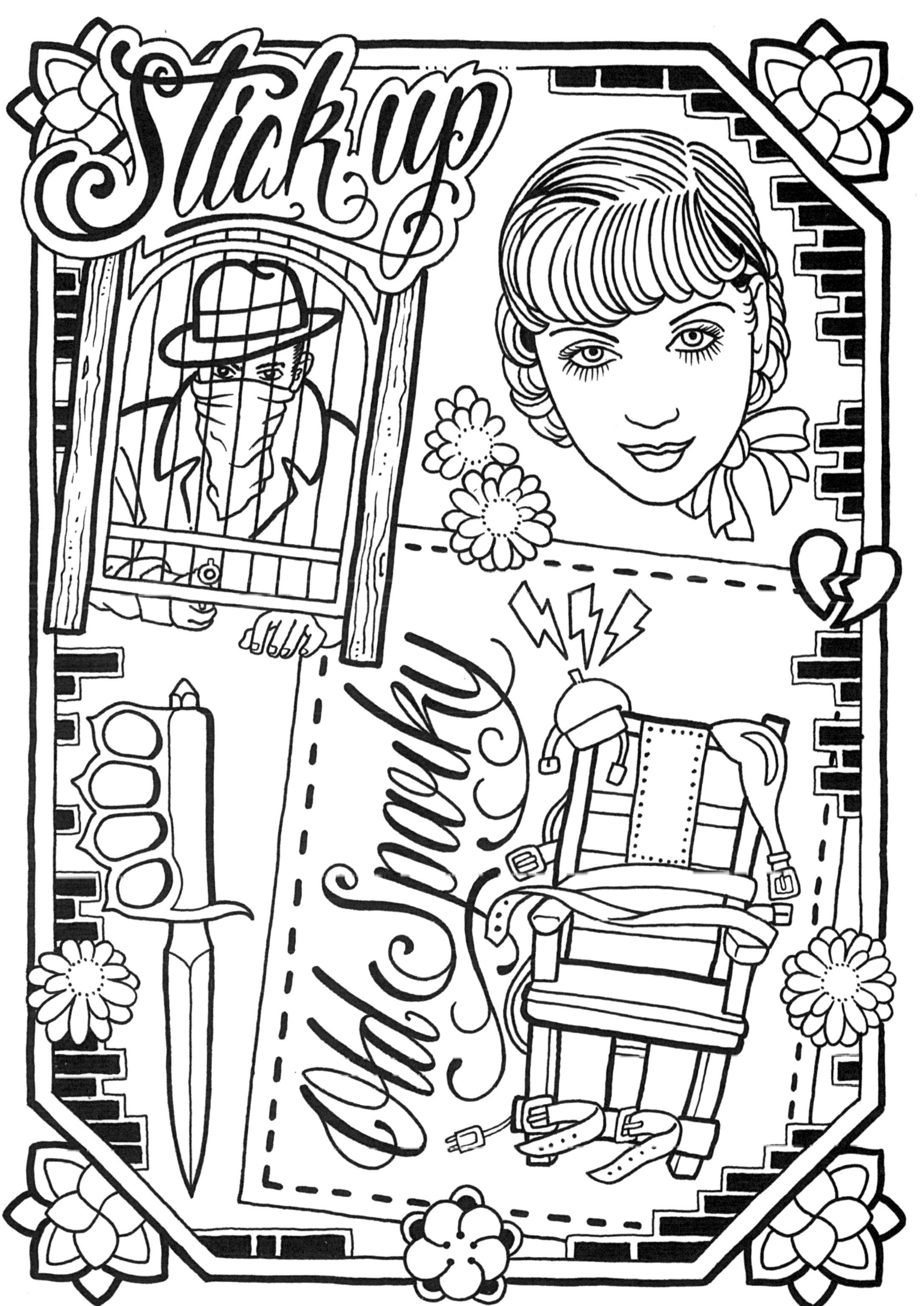
Stick up
Old Sparky

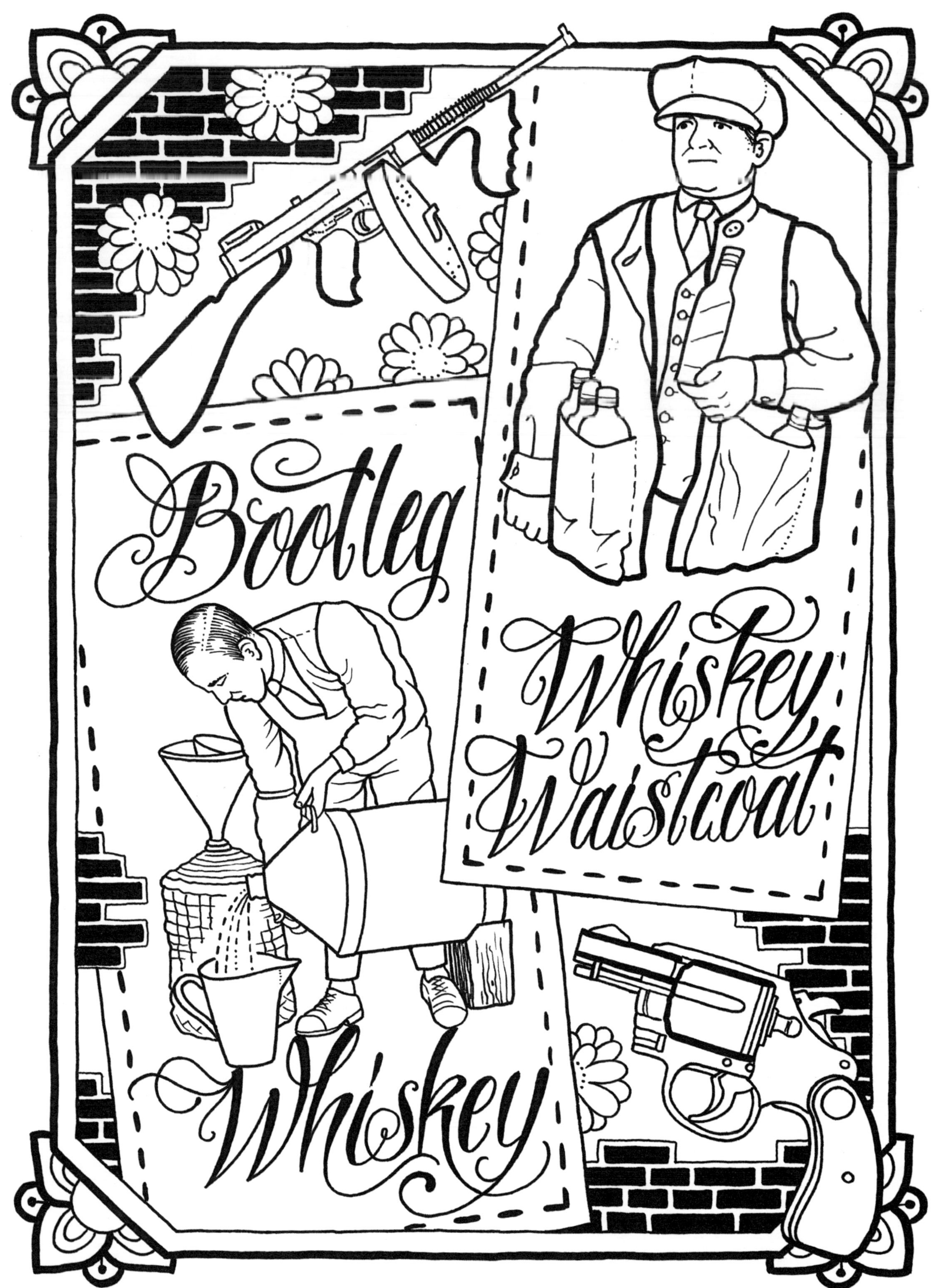
Bootleg
Whiskey
Whiskey
Waistcoat

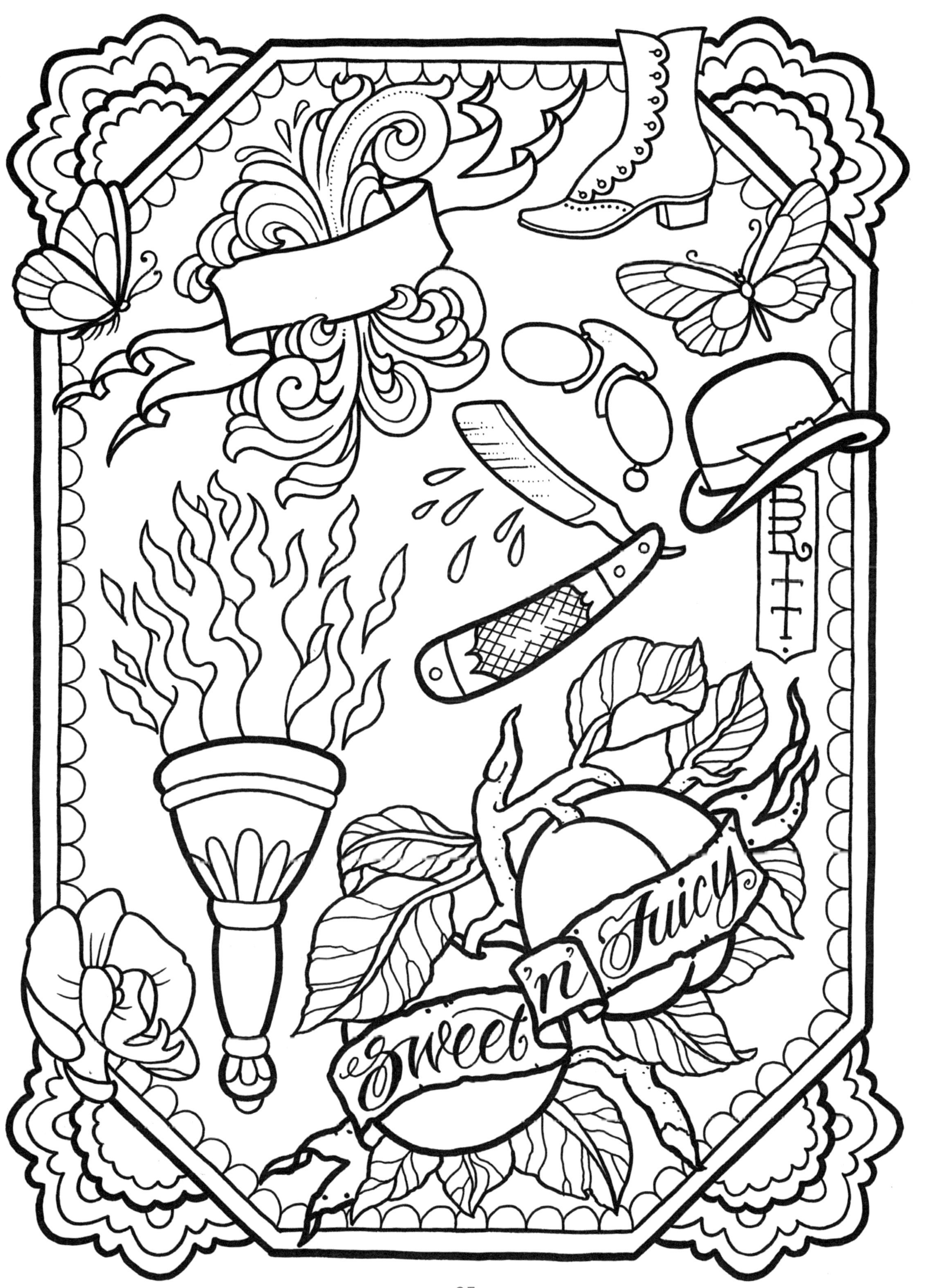
Sweet n' Juicy

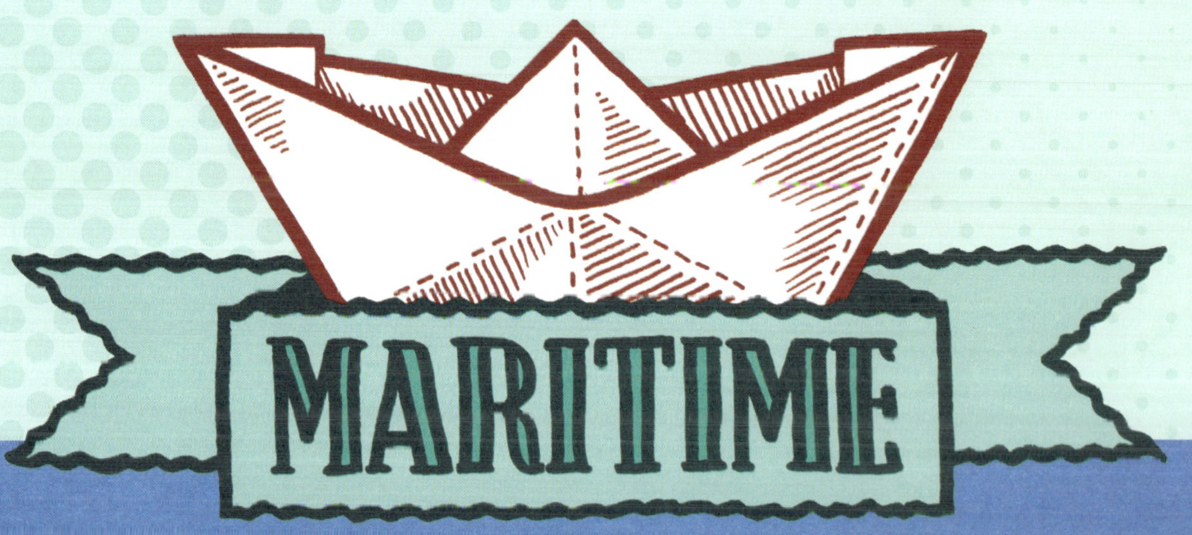
MARITIME

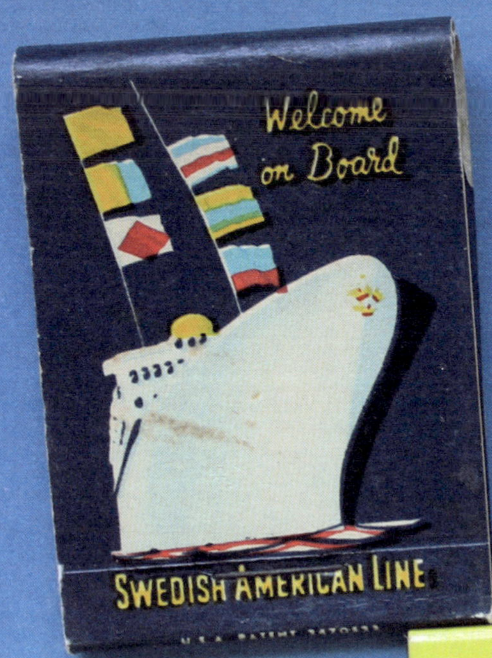
Welcome
on Board
SWEDISH AMERICAN LINE

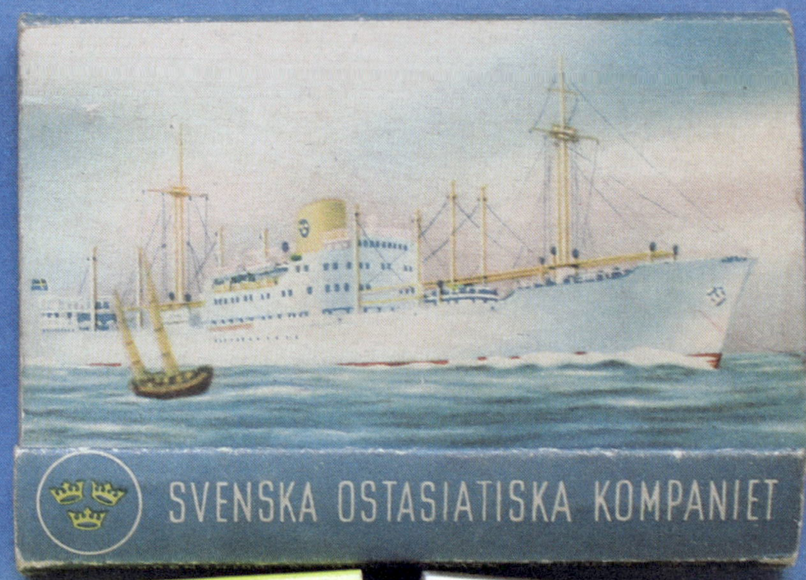
SVENSKA OSTASIATISKA KOMPANIET

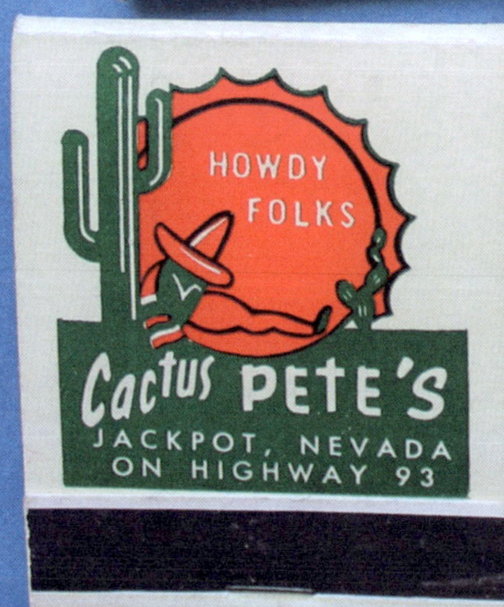
HOWDY
FOLKS
Cactus PETE'S
JACKPOT, NEVADA
ON HIGHWAY 93

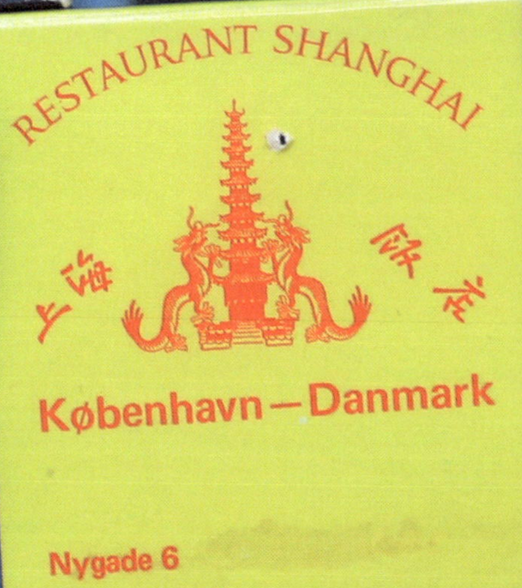
RESTAURANT SHANGHAI
København—Danmark
Nygade 6
Tlf. 121001

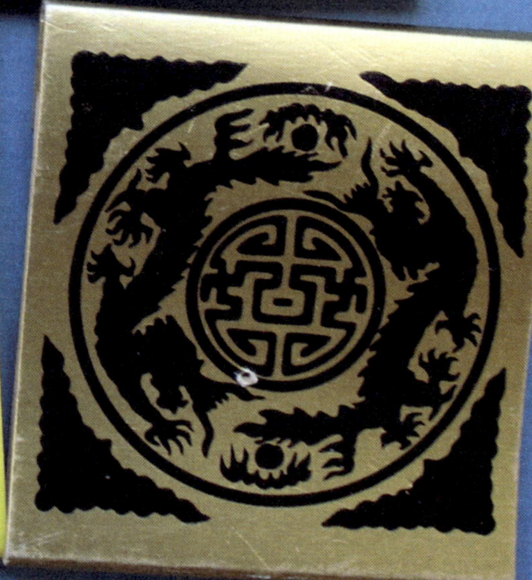

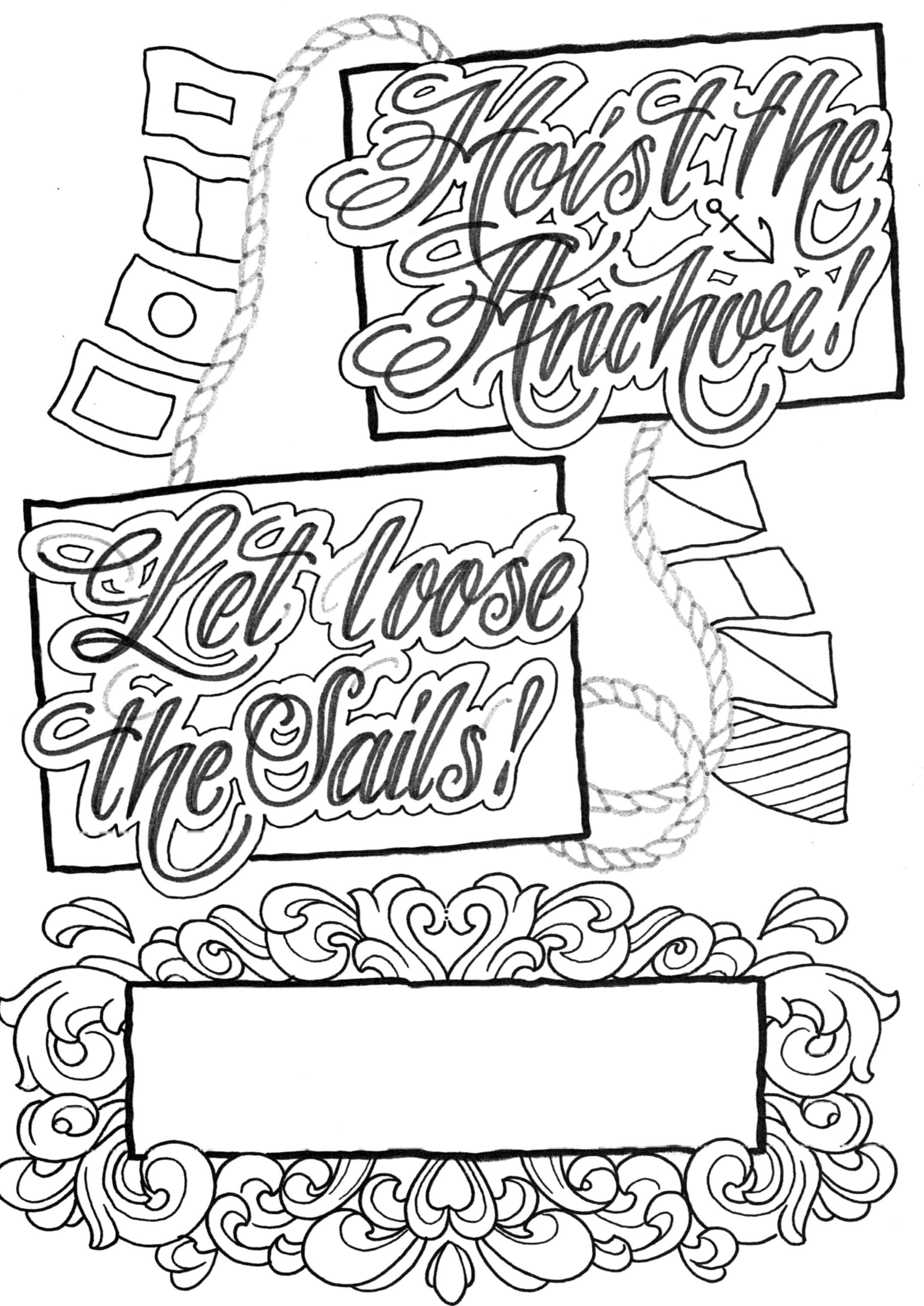
Hoist the Anchor!
Let loose the Sails!

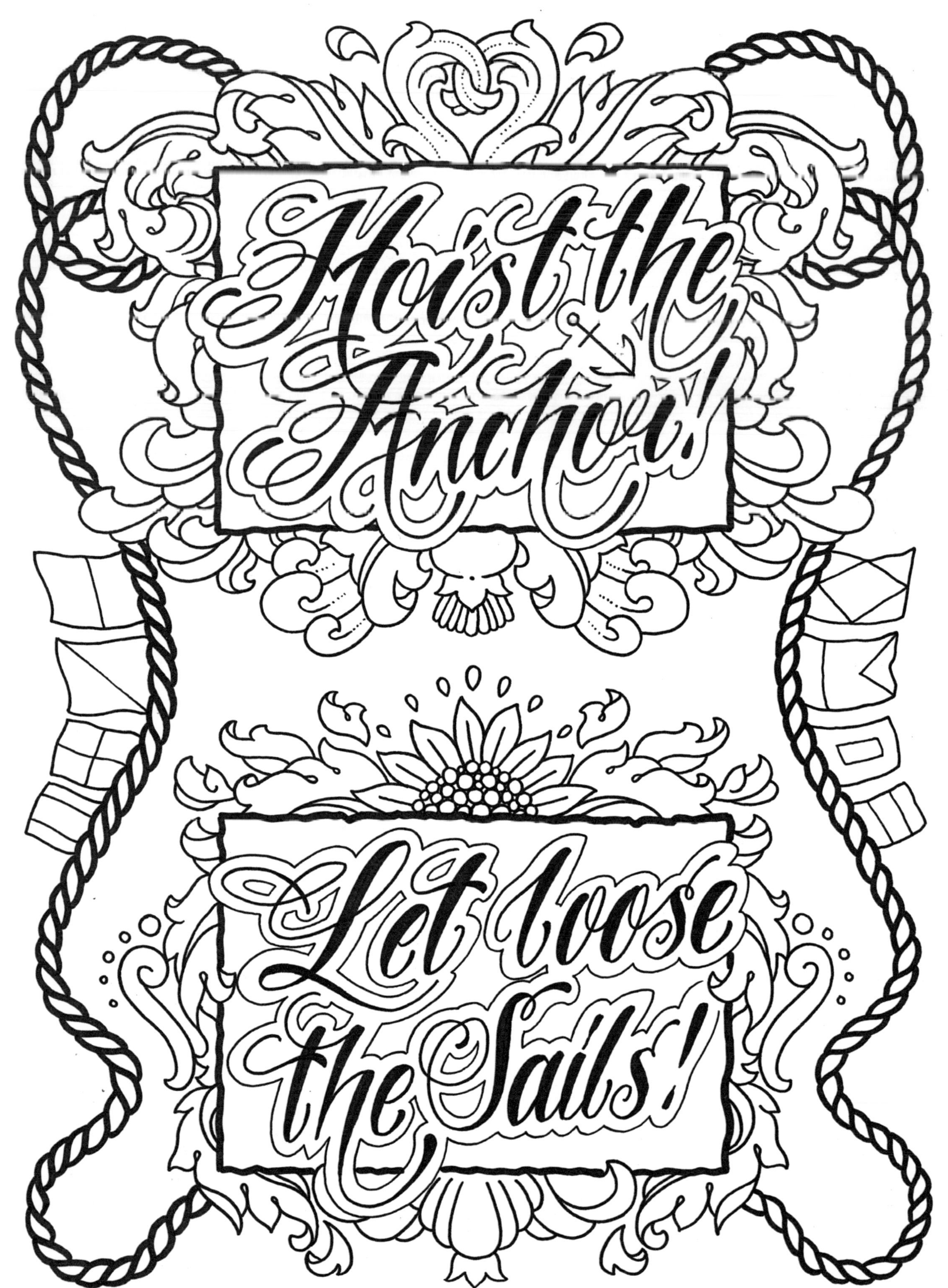
Hoist the Anchor!
Let loose the Sails!

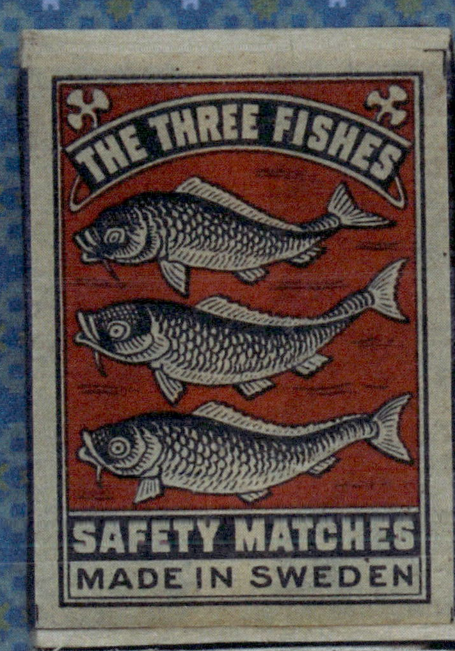
THE THREE FISHES
SAFETY MATCHES
MADE IN SWEDEN

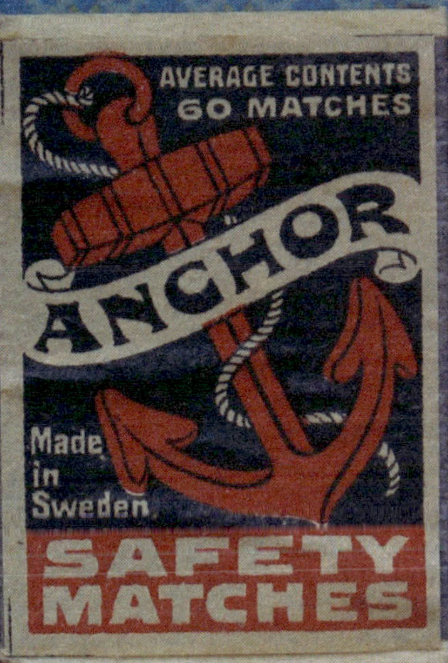
AVERAGE CONTENTS
60 MATCHES
ANCHOR
Made in Sweden
SAFETY MATCHES

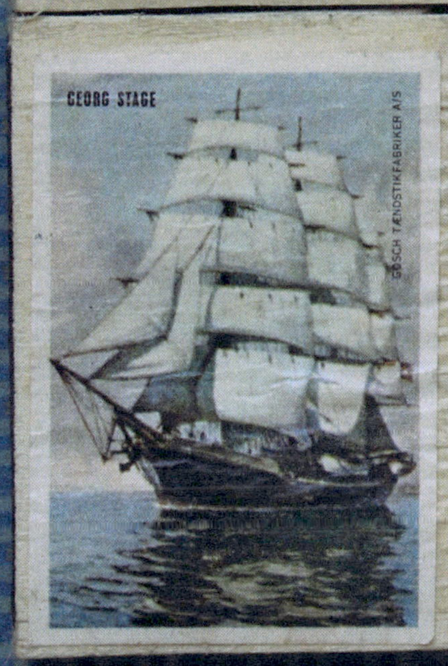
GEORG STAGE
GOSCH TÆNDSTIKFABRIKER A/S

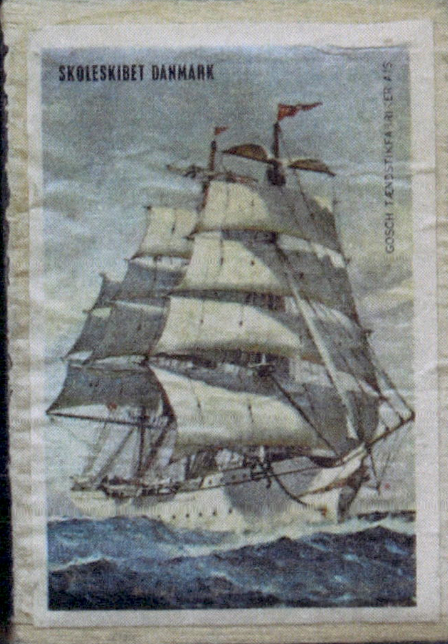
SKOLESKIBET DANMARK
GOSCH TÆNDSTIKFABRIKER A/S

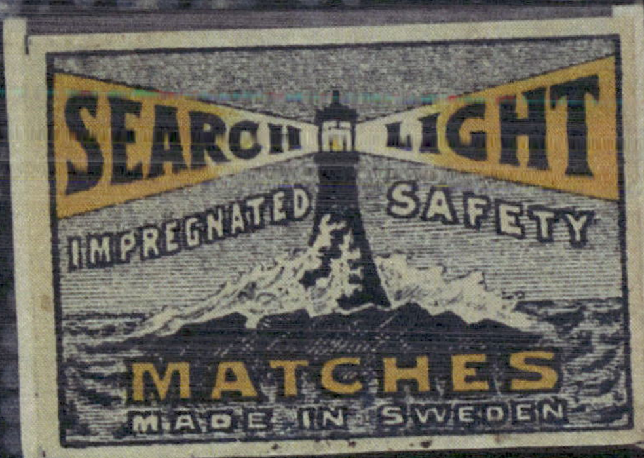
SEARCH LIGHT
IMPREGNATED SAFETY
MATCHES
MADE IN SWEDEN

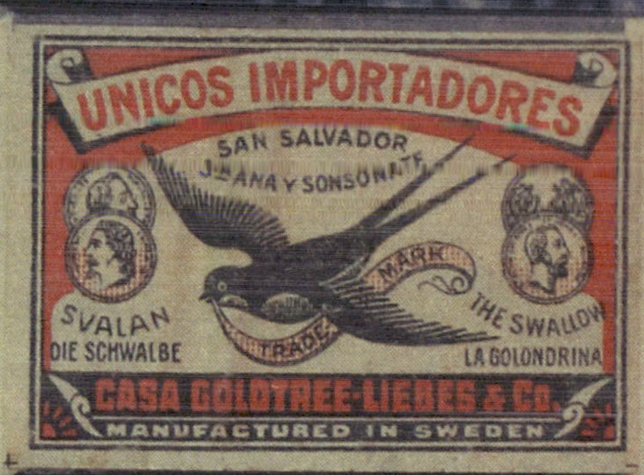
UNICOS IMPORTADORES
SAN SALVADOR
SVALAN
DIE SCHWALBE
TRADE MARK
THE SWALLOW
LA GOLONDRINA
CASA GOLDTREE-LIEBES & Co.
MANUFACTURED IN SWEDEN

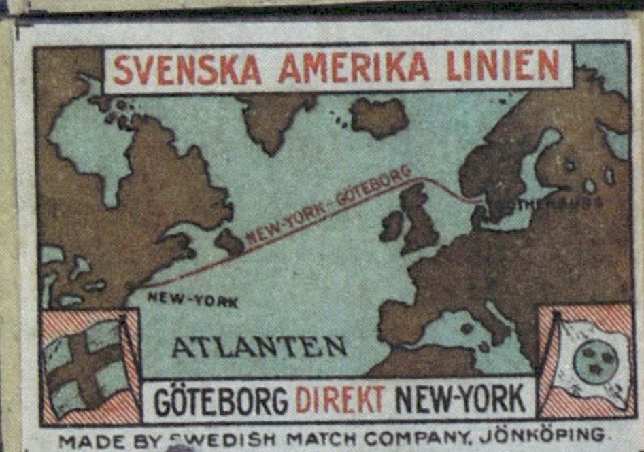
SVENSKA AMERIKA LINIEN
NEW-YORK–GÖTEBORG
NEW-YORK
ATLANTEN
GÖTEBORG DIREKT NEW-YORK
MADE BY SWEDISH MATCH COMPANY, JÖNKÖPING

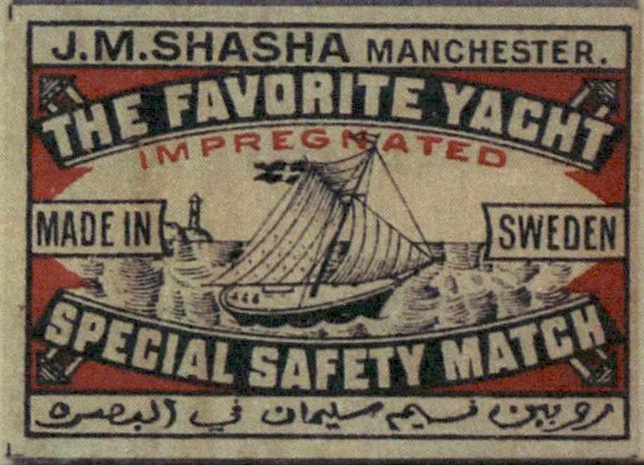
J.M.SHASHA MANCHESTER.
THE FAVORITE YACHT
IMPREGNATED
MADE IN
SWEDEN
SPECIAL SAFETY MATCH

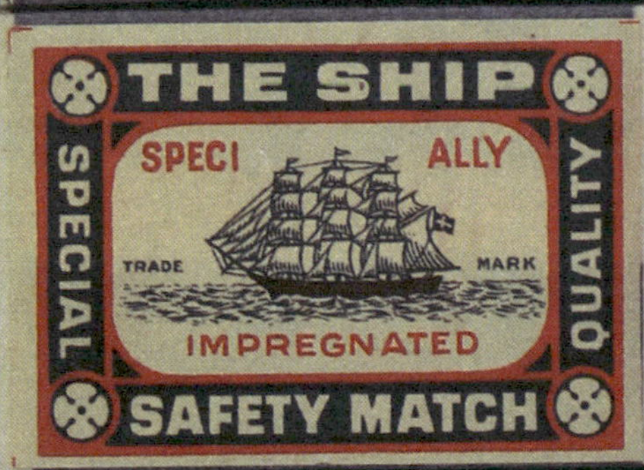
THE SHIP
SPECIAL
QUALITY
SPECI ALLY
TRADE MARK
IMPREGNATED
SAFETY MATCH

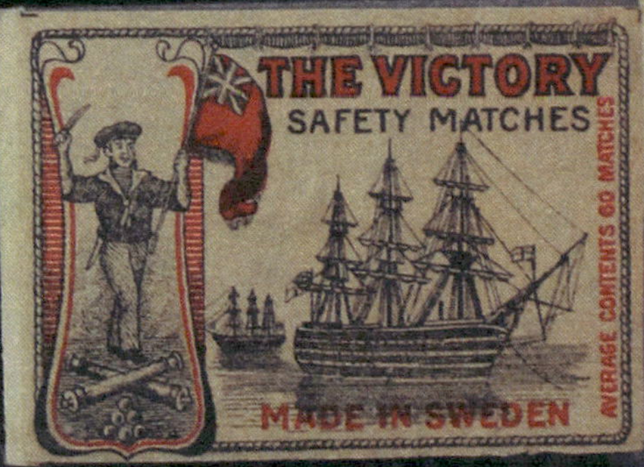
THE VICTORY
SAFETY MATCHES
AVERAGE CONTENTS 60 MATCHES
MADE IN SWEDEN

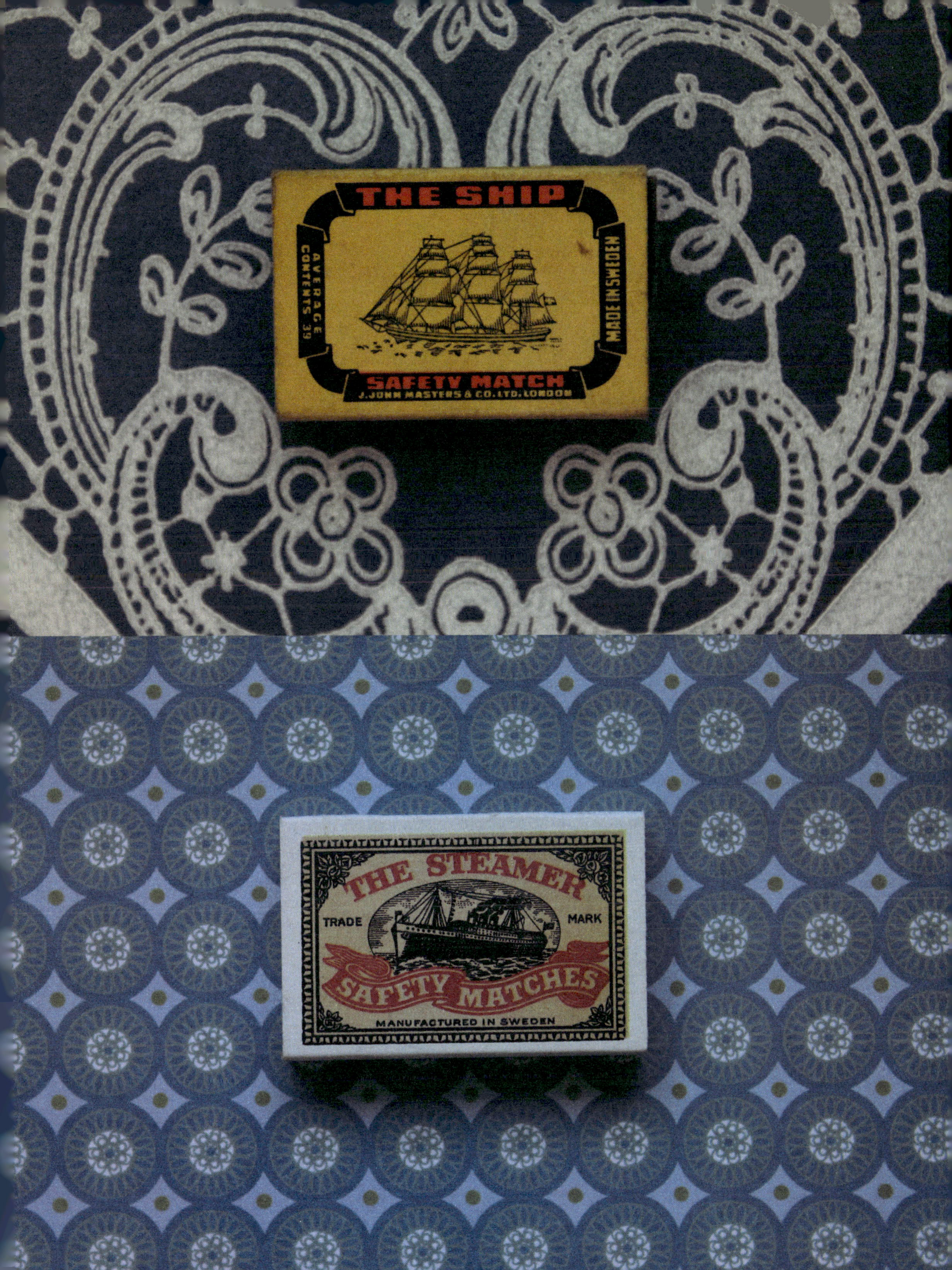
THE SHIP
AVERAGE CONTENTS 39
MADE IN SWEDEN
SAFETY MATCH
J. JOHN MASTERS & CO. LTD. LONDON
THE STEAMER
TRADE
MARK
SAFETY MATCHES
MANUFACTURED IN SWEDEN

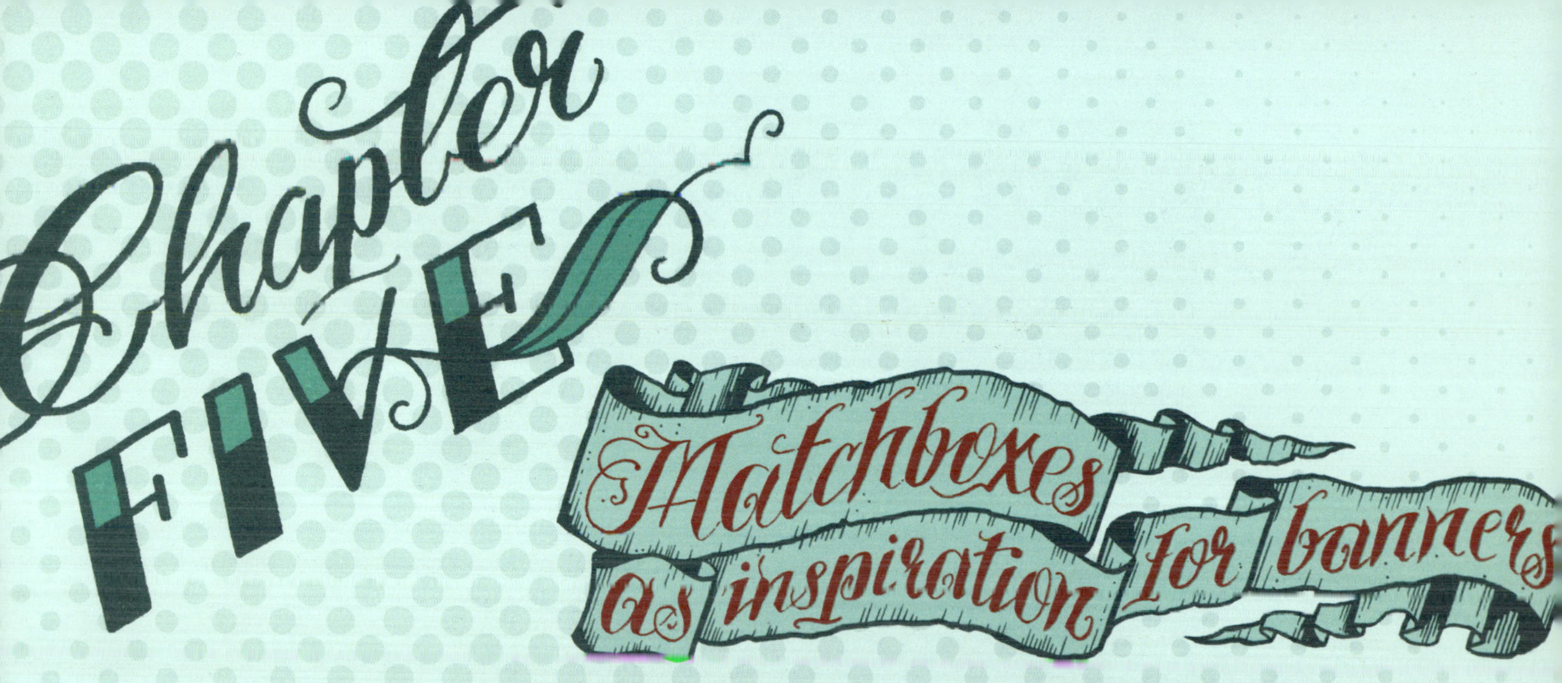

Banners are a great way to set text apart. They are an important element in lots of creative graphics. I try to save things that could be useful for inspiration later, like beautiful labels from wine bottles, tags from clothes, wrappings from candy or food. Old commercial signs, as well as labels from matchboxes and stamps, can also be used as references.

Styles of banners may vary a lot, from square boxes and scrolls to ribbons that appear almost torn by the wind. How the banner appears to move can create a feeling. Sometimes that emotion is based simply on how you let the ends of the banner fall. Ends pointing upward look more positive. A playful banner gives a lighter impression. Steady banners, with not too much emotion, show confidence.

The matchboxes shown here provide good inspiration when drawing banners and other stuff, too. Some of the boxes are Swedish and others come from all around the world. All of the boxes shown are useful design references. The wooden boxes are now mostly a thing of the past, and some of the boxes shown here are extremely rare. Once in everyone's pockets, these illustrative matchboxes are now a part of history.

A traditional tattoo I made of a swallow flying with a banner. Pink for the girls and blue for the boys.

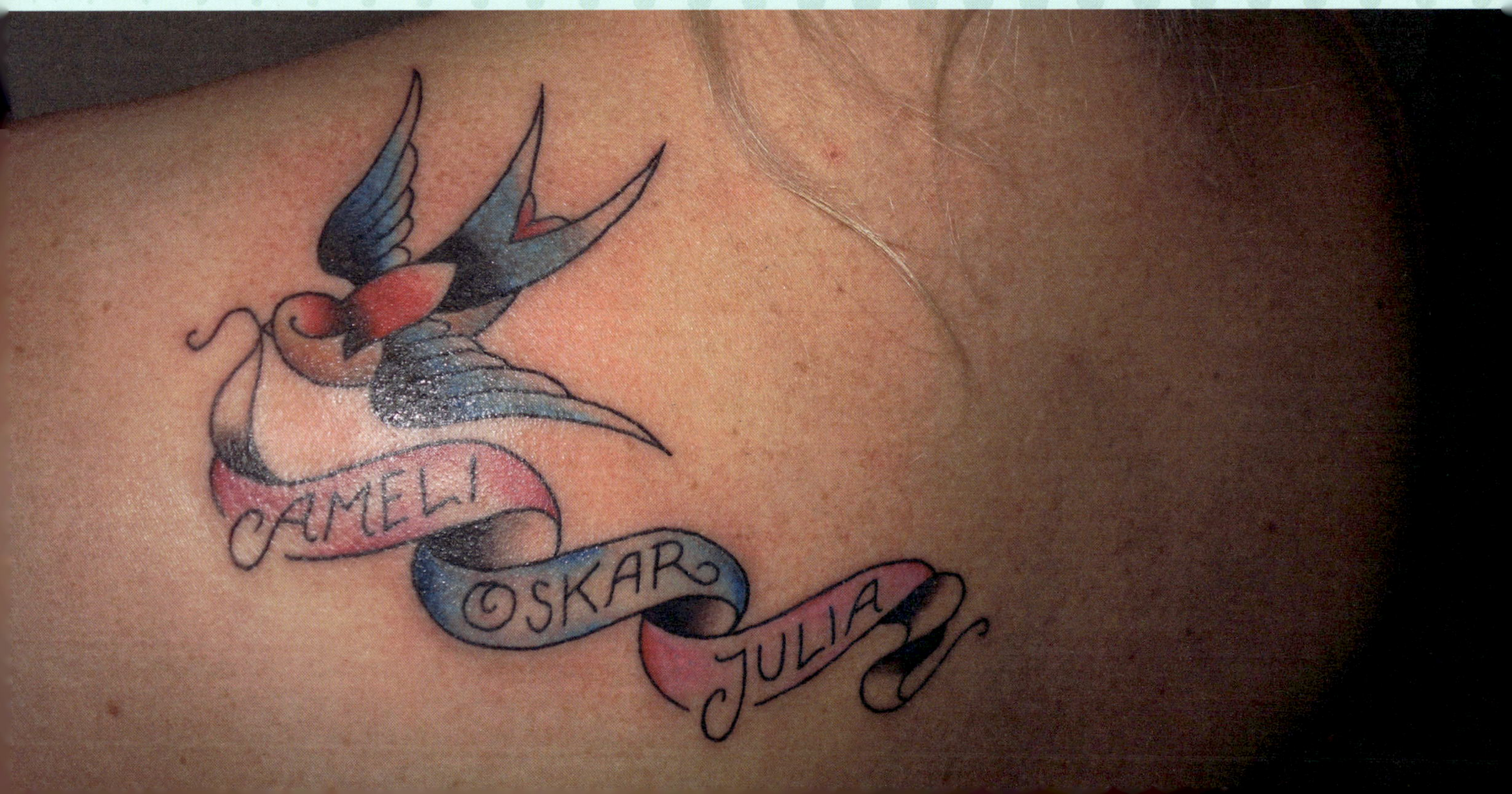

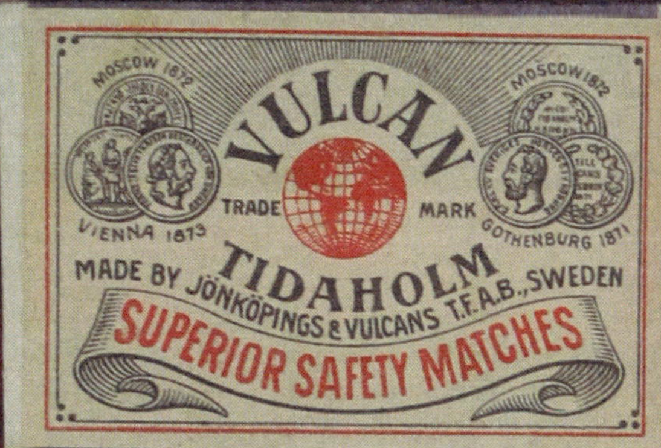
MOSCOW 1872
VIENNA 1873
VULCAN
TRADE MARK
MOSCOW 1872
GOTHENBURG 1871
TIDAHOLM
MADE BY JÖNKÖPINGS & VULCANS T.F.A.B., SWEDEN
SUPERIOR SAFETY MATCHES

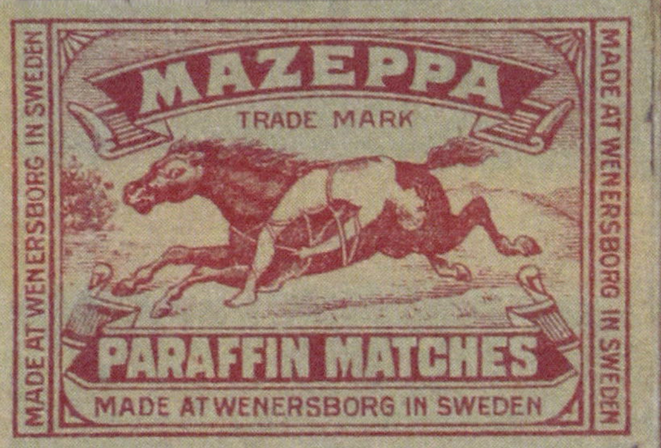
MAZEPPA
TRADE MARK
PARAFFIN MATCHES
MADE AT WENERSBORG IN SWEDEN
MADE AT WENERSBORG IN SWEDEN
MADE AT WENERSBORG IN SWEDEN

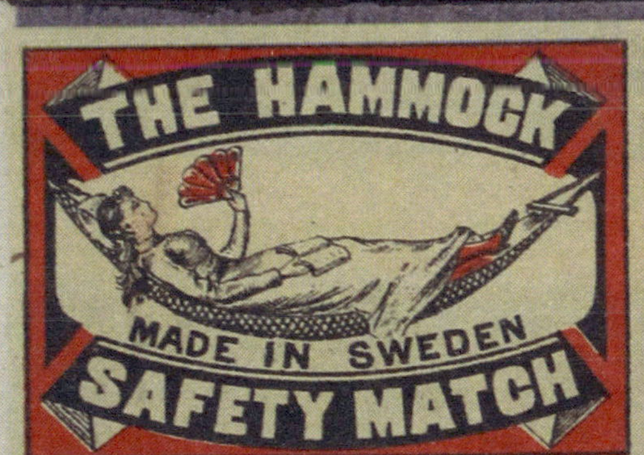
THE HAMMOCK
MADE IN SWEDEN
SAFETY MATCH

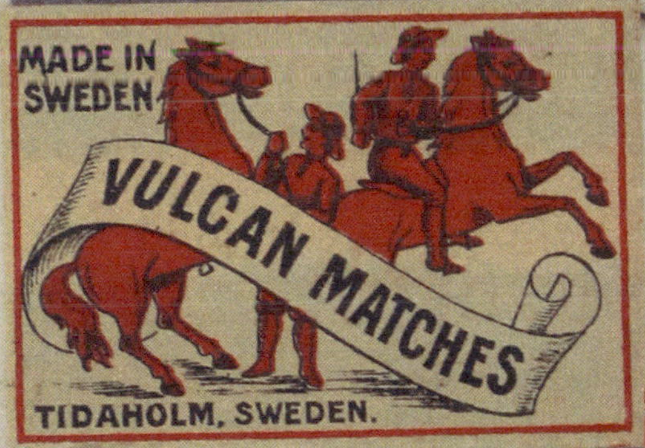
MADE IN SWEDEN
VULCAN MATCHES
TIDAHOLM, SWEDEN.

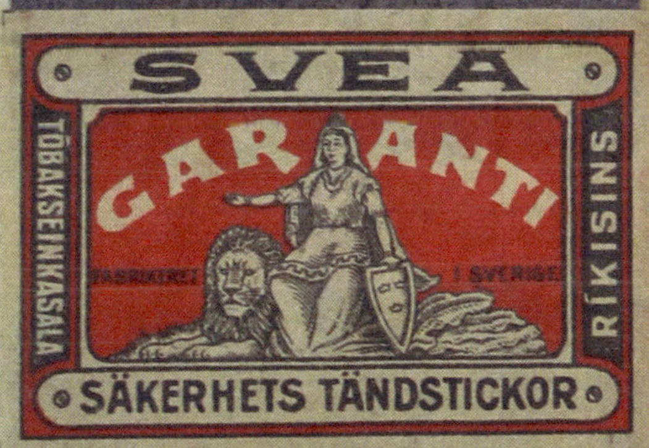
SVEA
GARANTI
TÖBAKSEINKASALA
RÍKISINS
SÄKERHETS TÄNDSTICKOR

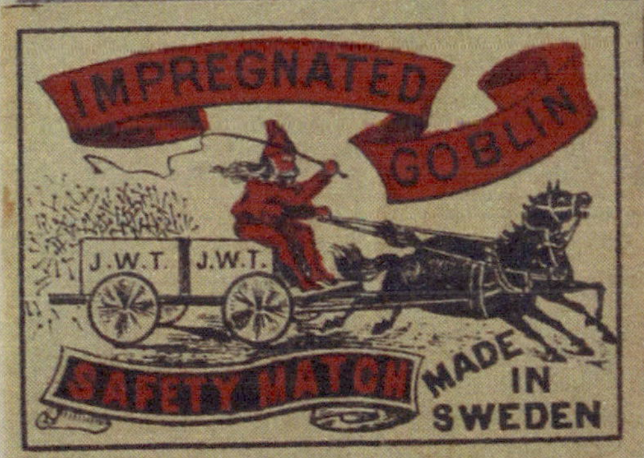
IMPREGNATED
GOBLIN
J.W.T. J.W.T.
SAFETY MATCH
MADE IN SWEDEN

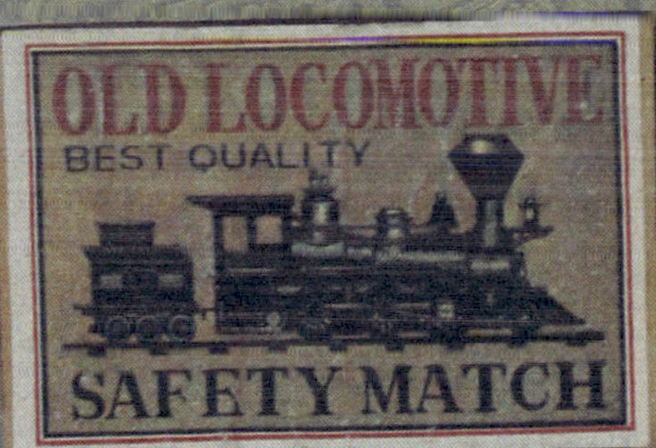
OLD LOCOMOTIVE
BEST QUALITY
SAFETY MATCH

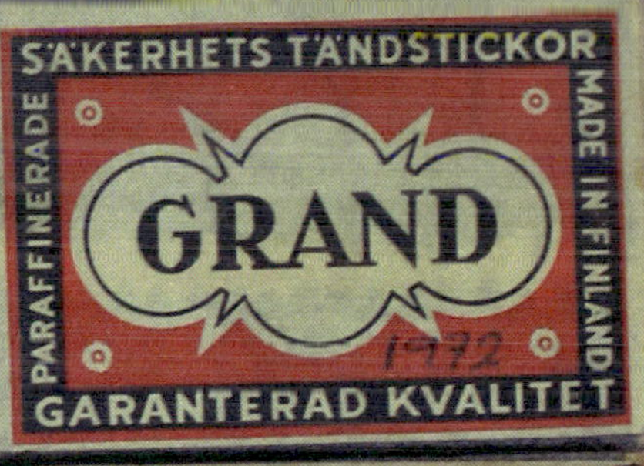
SÄKERHETS TÄNDSTICKOR
PARAFFINERADE
GRAND
MADE IN FINLAND
GARANTERAD KVALITET

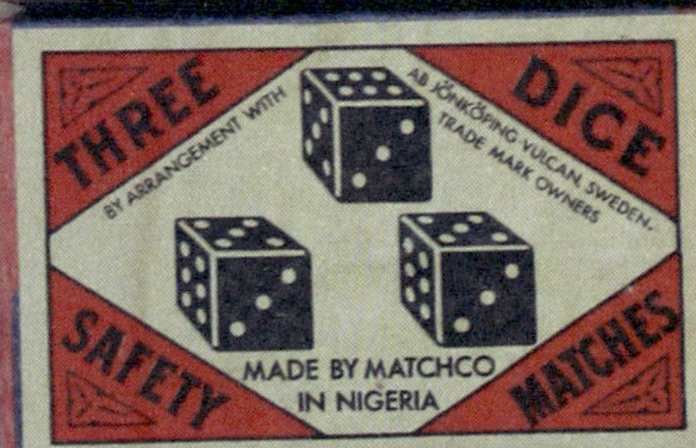
THREE
DICE
BY ARRANGEMENT WITH
AB JÖNKÖPING VULCAN SWEDEN
TRADE MARK OWNERS
MADE BY MATCHCO
IN NIGERIA
SAFETY
MATCHES

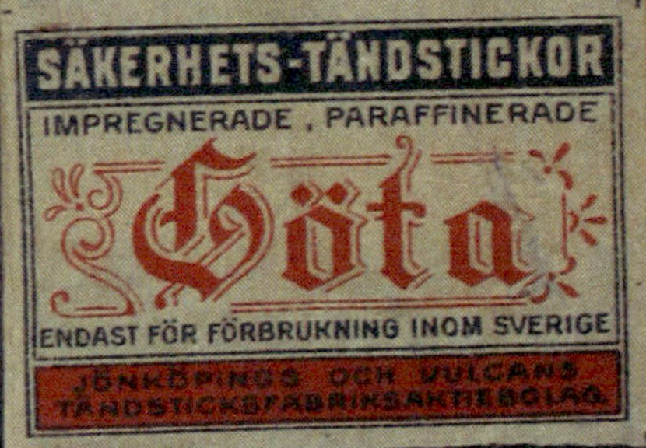
SÄKERHETS-TÄNDSTICKOR
IMPREGNERADE, PARAFFINERADE
Göta
ENDAST FÖR FÖRBRUKNING INOM SVERIGE
JÖNKÖPINGS OCH VULCANS
TÄNDSTICKSFABRIKSAKTIEBOLAG

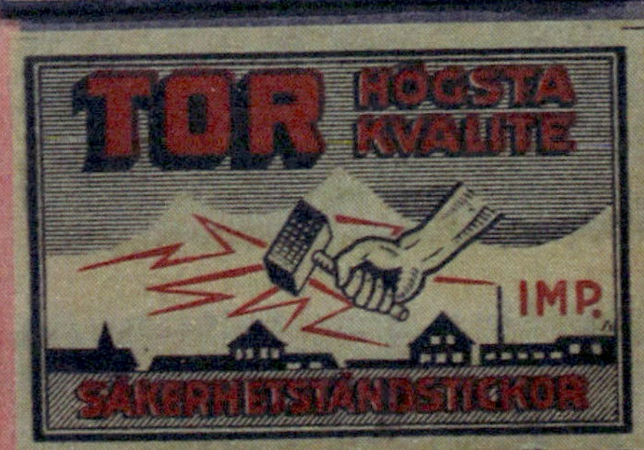
TOR
HÖGSTA
KVALITE
IMP.
SÄKERHETSTÄNDSTICKOR

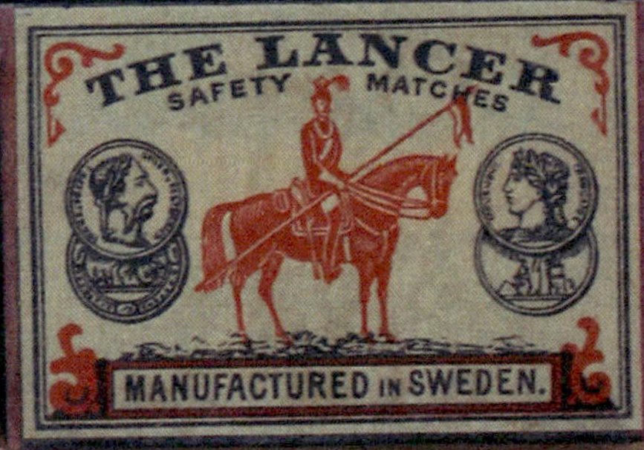
THE LANCER
SAFETY MATCHES
MANUFACTURED IN SWEDEN.

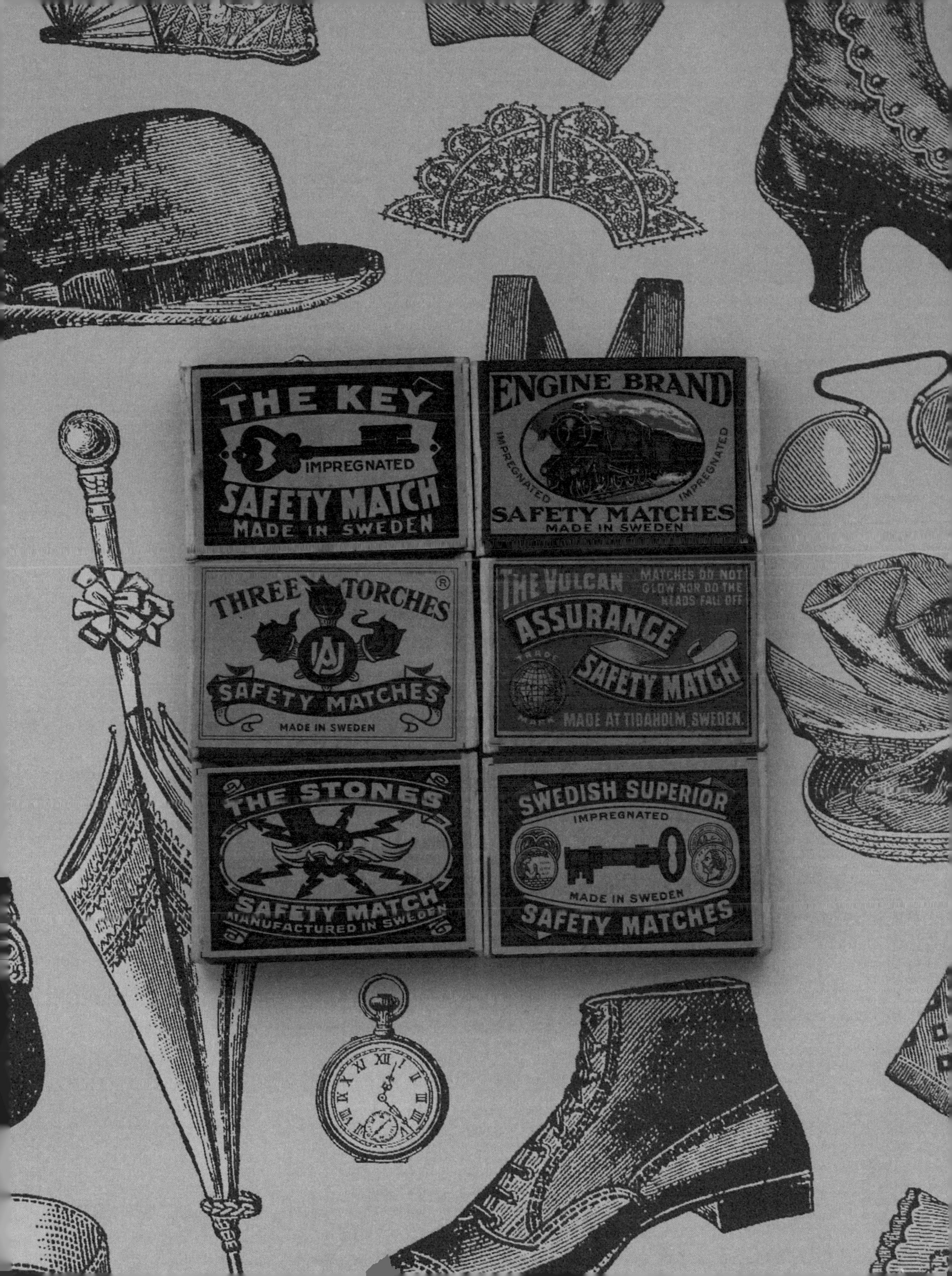
THE KEY
IMPREGNATED
SAFETY MATCH
MADE IN SWEDEN
ENGINE BRAND
IMPREGNATED
IMPREGNATED
SAFETY MATCHES
MADE IN SWEDEN
THREE TORCHES
SAFETY MATCHES
MADE IN SWEDEN
THE VULCAN
MATCHES DO NOT GLOW NOR DO THE HEADS FALL OFF
ASSURANCE
SAFETY MATCH
MADE AT TIDAHOLM SWEDEN.
THE STONES
SAFETY MATCH
MANUFACTURED IN SWEDEN
SWEDISH SUPERIOR
IMPREGNATED
MADE IN SWEDEN
SAFETY MATCHES

THREE LEGGED POT
SAFETY MATCHES
MADE IN SWEDEN.

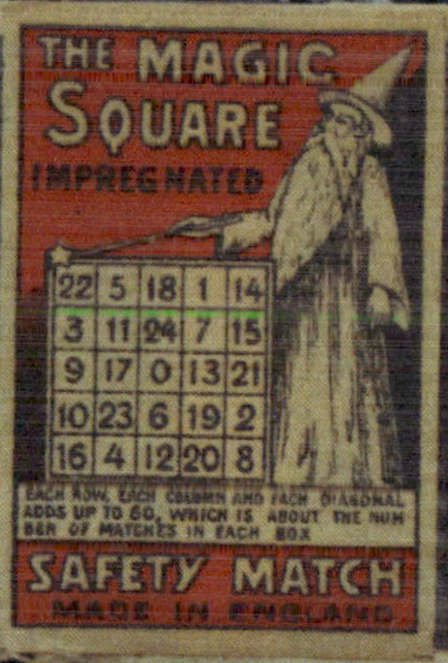
THE MAGIC SQUARE
IMPREGNATED
SAFETY MATCH
MADE IN ENGLAND

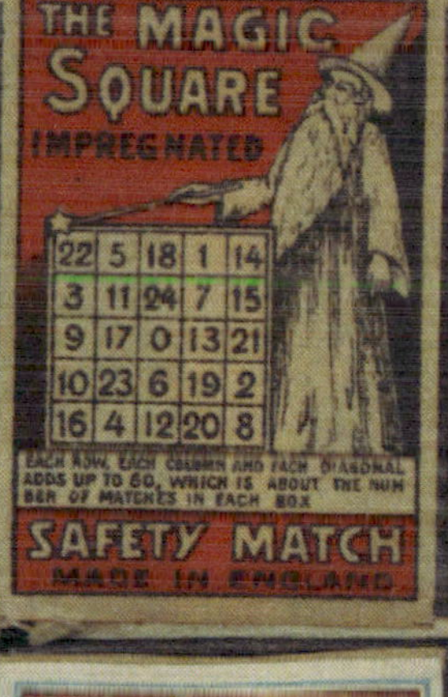

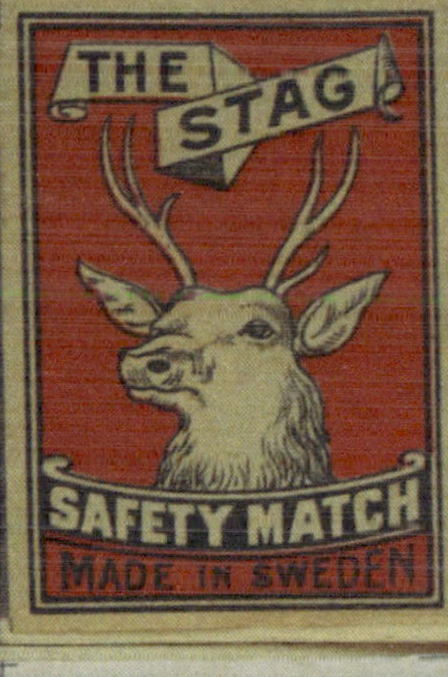
THE STAG
SAFETY MATCH
MADE IN SWEDEN

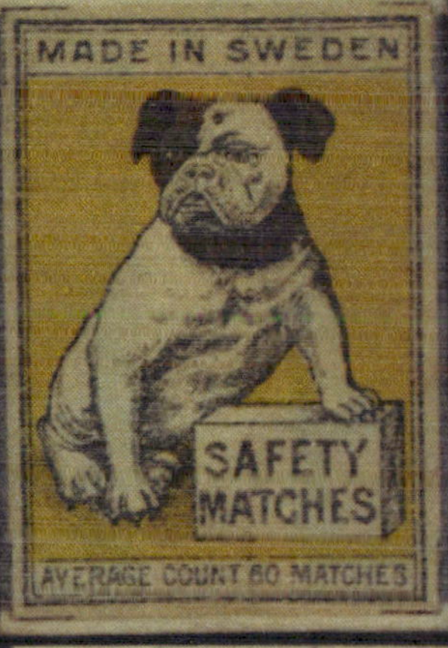
MADE IN SWEDEN
SAFETY MATCHES
AVERAGE COUNT 60 MATCHES

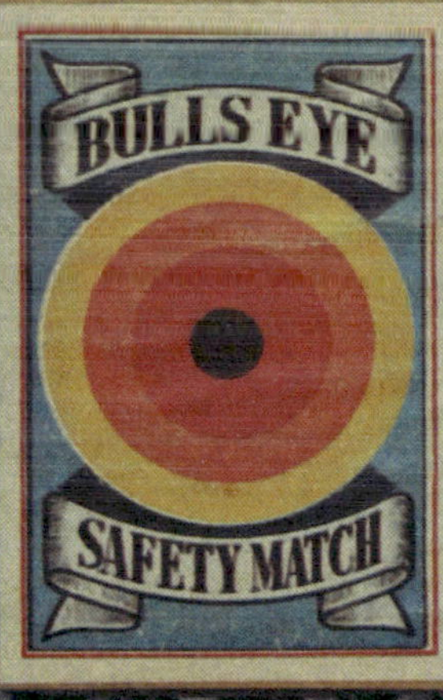
BULLS EYE
SAFETY MATCH

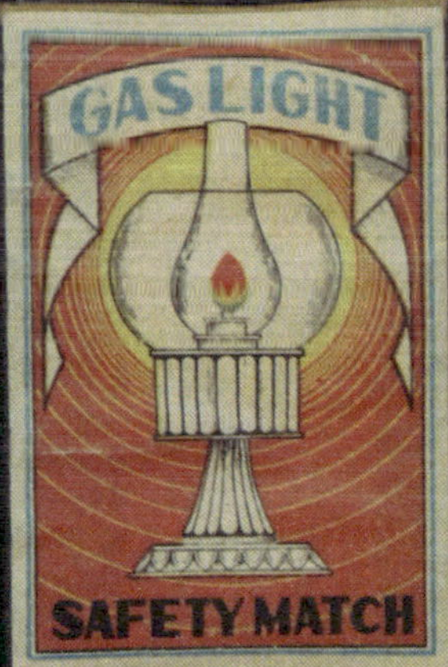
GAS LIGHT
SAFETY MATCH

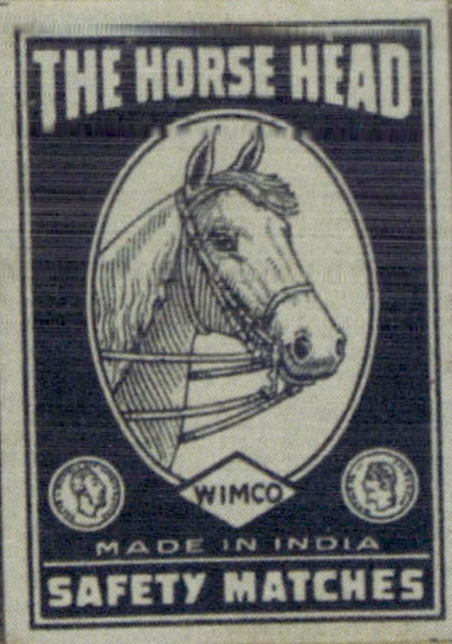
THE HORSE HEAD
WIMCO
MADE IN INDIA
SAFETY MATCHES

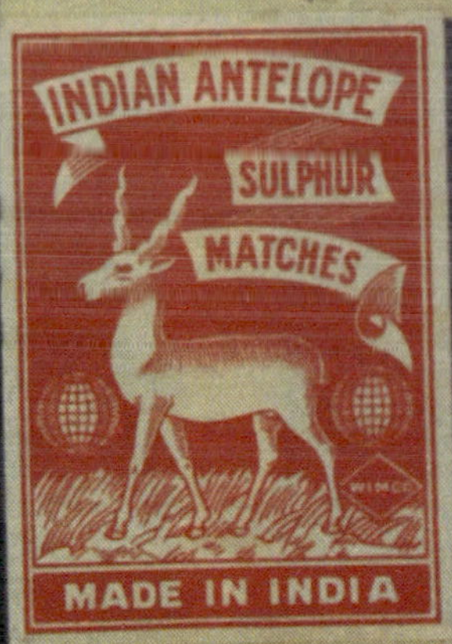
INDIAN ANTELOPE
SULPHUR
MATCHES
WIMCO
MADE IN INDIA

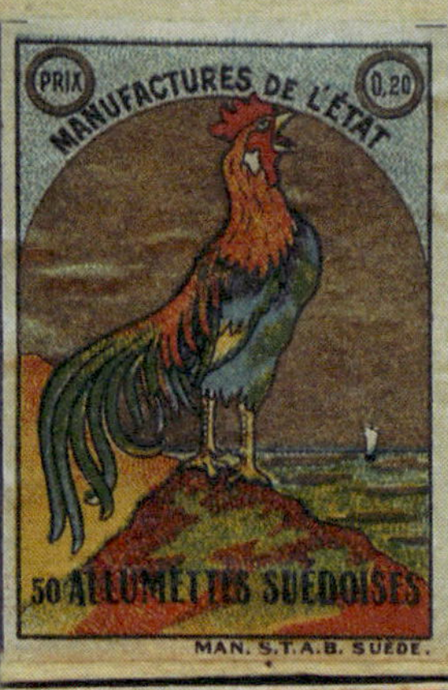
PRIX
MANUFACTURES DE L'ÉTAT
0.20
50 ALLUMETTES SUÉDOISES
MAN. S.T.A.B. SUÈDE.

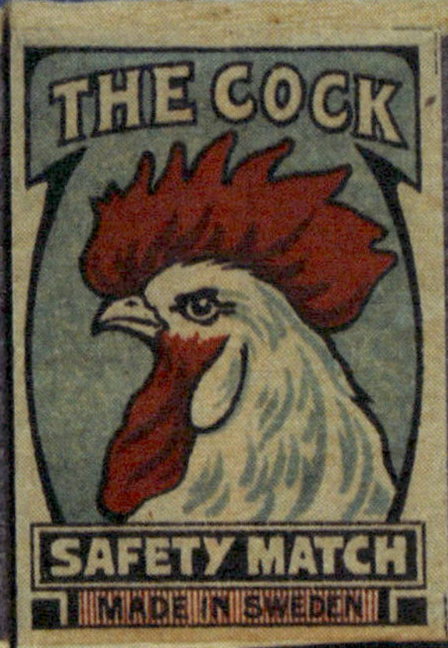
THE COCK
SAFETY MATCH
MADE IN SWEDEN

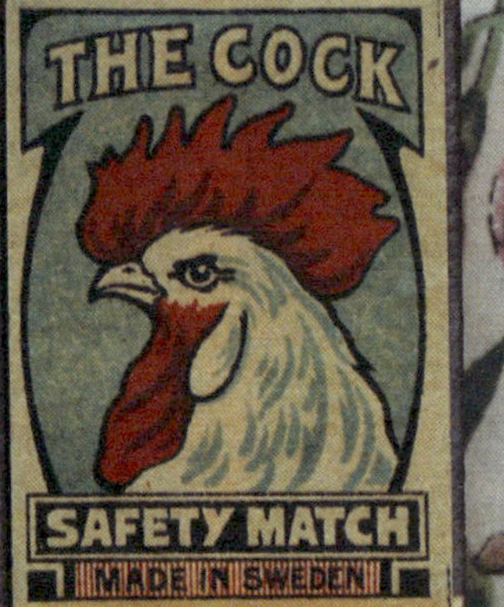

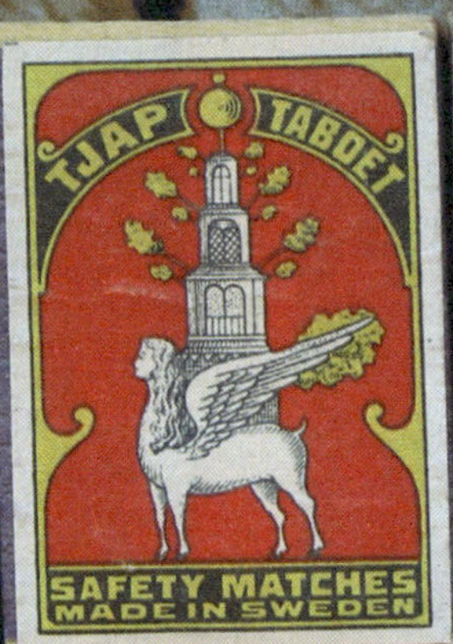
TJAP TABOET
SAFETY MATCHES
MADE IN SWEDEN

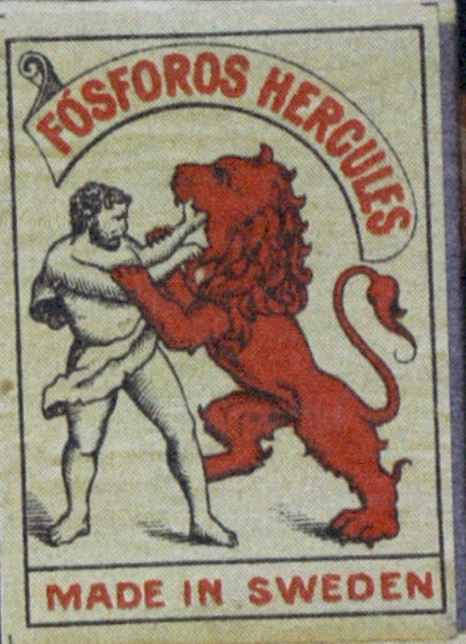
FOSFOROS HERCULES
MADE IN SWEDEN

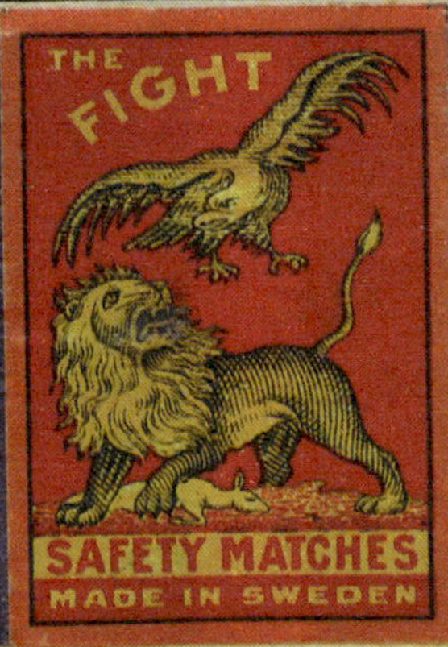
THE FIGHT
SAFETY MATCHES
MADE IN SWEDEN

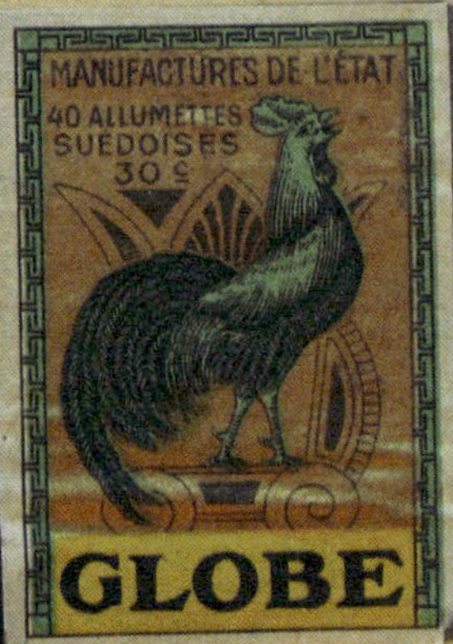
MANUFACTURES DE L'ÉTAT
40 ALLUMETTES SUÉDOISES
30 c
GLOBE

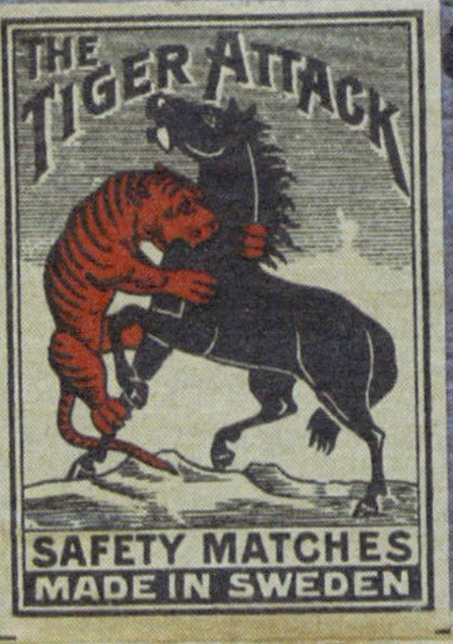
THE TIGER ATTACK
SAFETY MATCHES
MADE IN SWEDEN

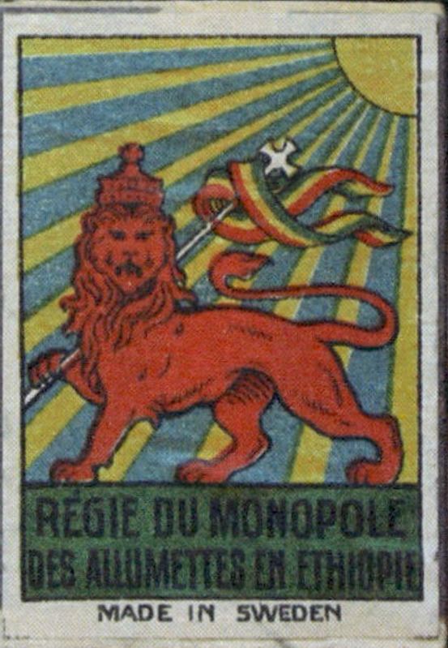
RÉGIE DU MONOPOLE
DES ALLUMETTES EN ETHIOPIE
MADE IN SWEDEN

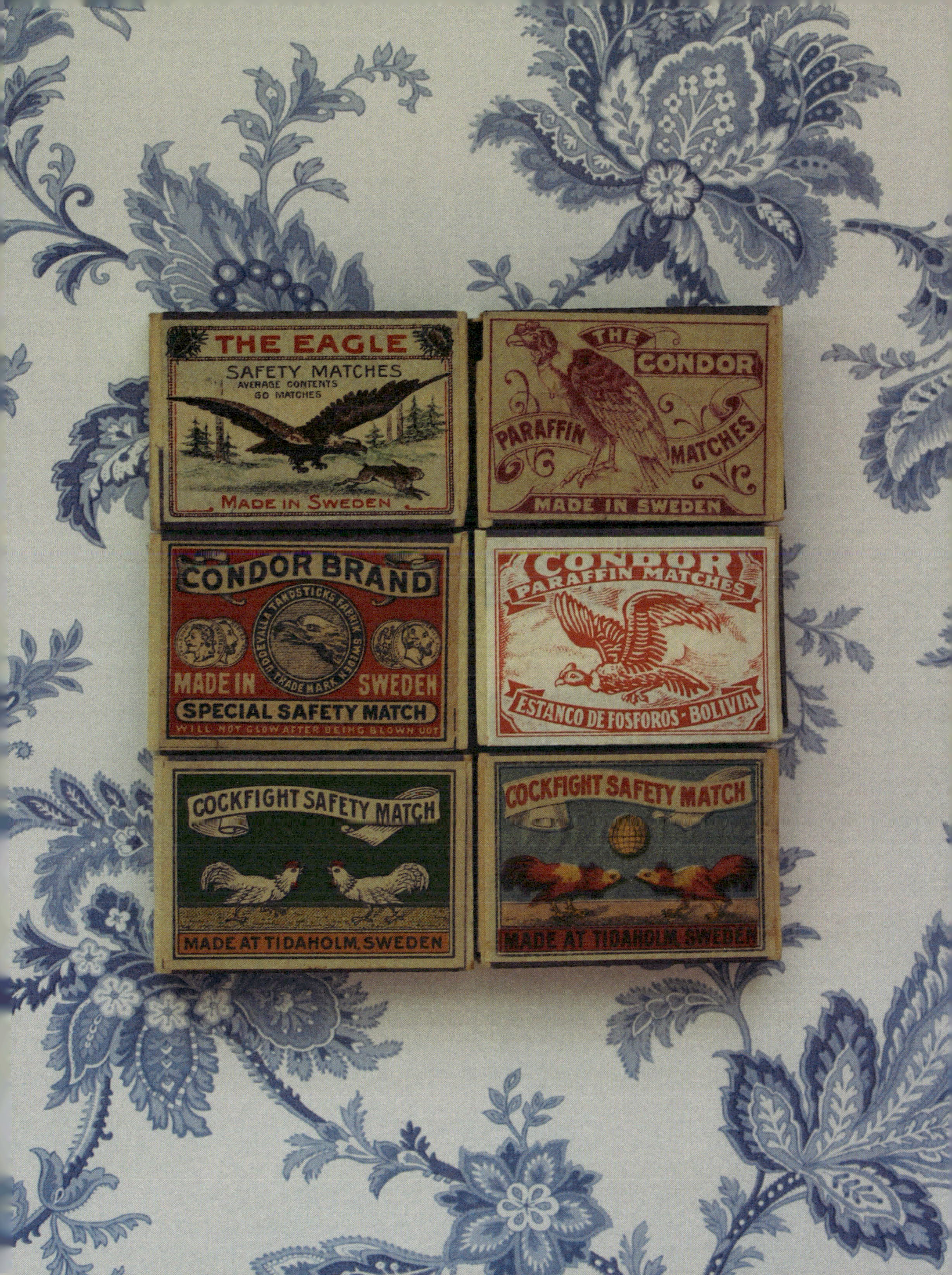
THE EAGLE
SAFETY MATCHES
AVERAGE CONTENTS
60 MATCHES
MADE IN SWEDEN
THE CONDOR
PARAFFIN MATCHES
MADE IN SWEDEN
CONDOR BRAND
MADE IN SWEDEN
SPECIAL SAFETY MATCH
WILL NOT GLOW AFTER BEING BLOWN OUT
CONDOR
PARAFFIN MATCHES
ESTANCO DE FOSFOROS - BOLIVIA
COCKFIGHT SAFETY MATCH
MADE AT TIDAHOLM, SWEDEN
COCKFIGHT SAFETY MATCH
MADE AT TIDAHOLM, SWEDEN

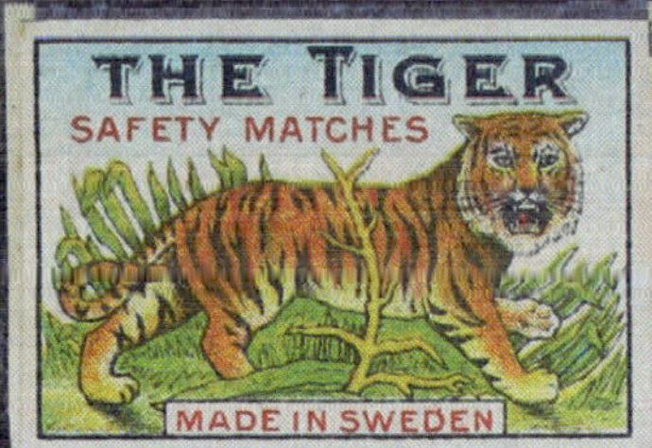
THE TIGER
SAFETY MATCHES
MADE IN SWEDEN

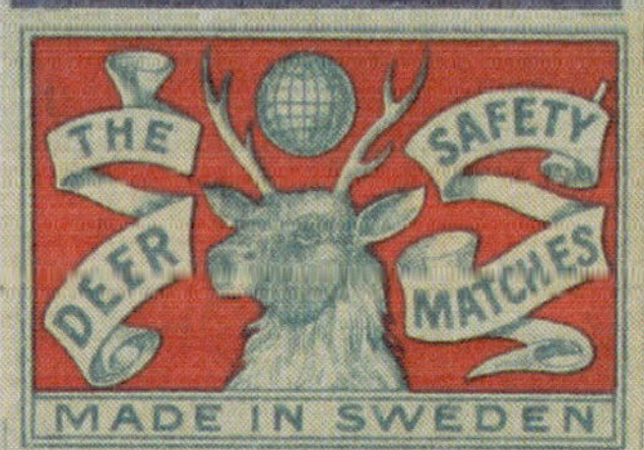
THE DEER
SAFETY MATCHES
MADE IN SWEDEN

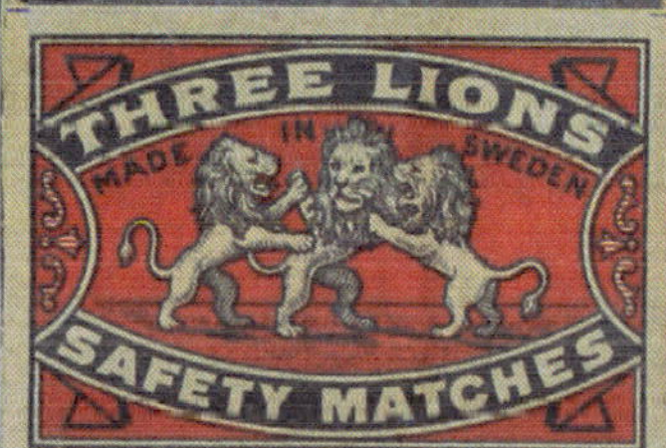
THREE LIONS
MADE IN SWEDEN
SAFETY MATCHES

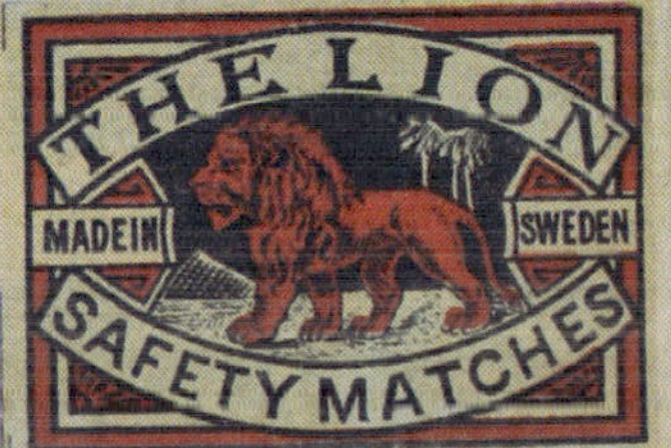
THE LION
MADE IN SWEDEN
SAFETY MATCHES

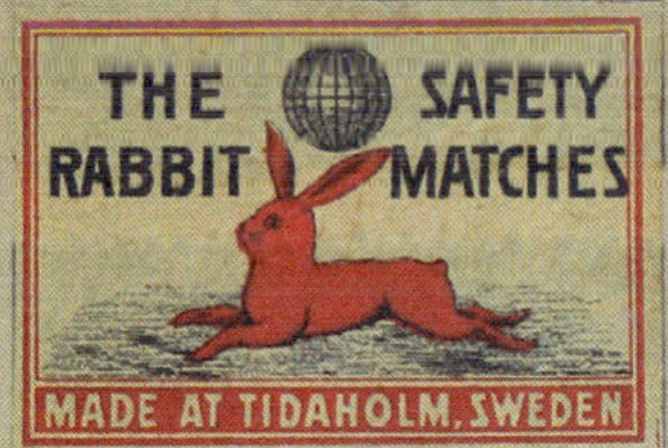
THE RABBIT
SAFETY MATCHES
MADE AT TIDAHOLM, SWEDEN

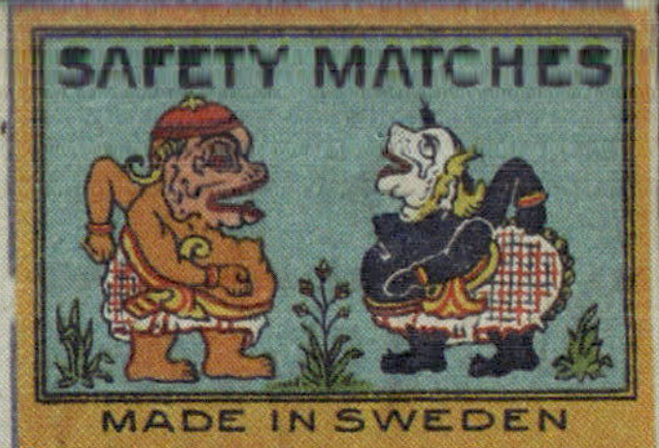
SAFETY MATCHES
MADE IN SWEDEN

THE VULTURE
SAFETY MATCH
MADE IN SWEDEN

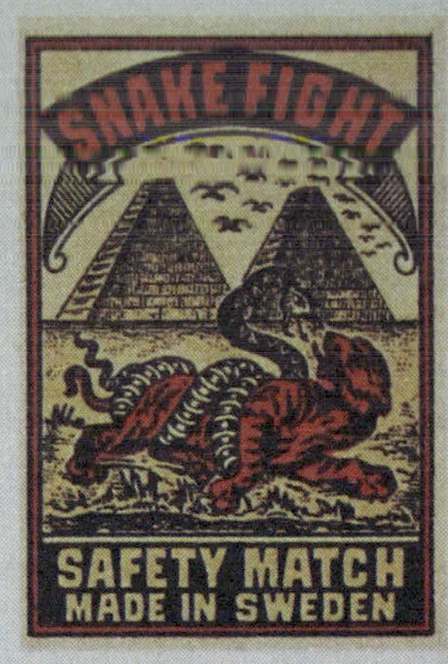
SNAKE FIGHT
SAFETY MATCH
MADE IN SWEDEN

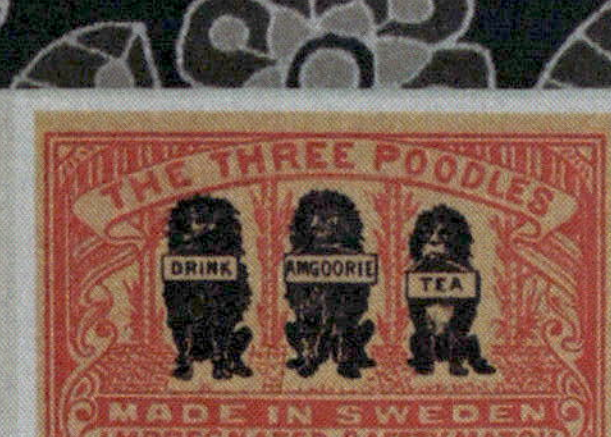
THE THREE POODLES
DRINK
TEA
MADE IN SWEDEN
IMPREGNATED SAFETY MATCH

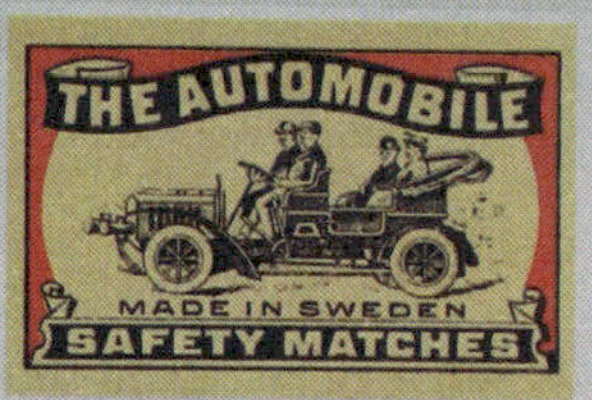
THE AUTOMOBILE
MADE IN SWEDEN
SAFETY MATCHES

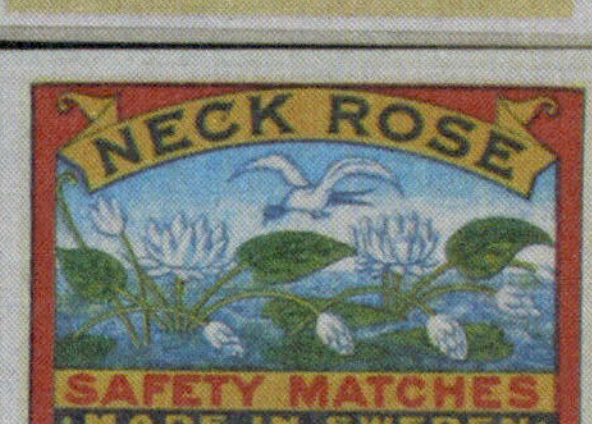
NECK ROSE
SAFETY MATCHES
MADE IN SWEDEN

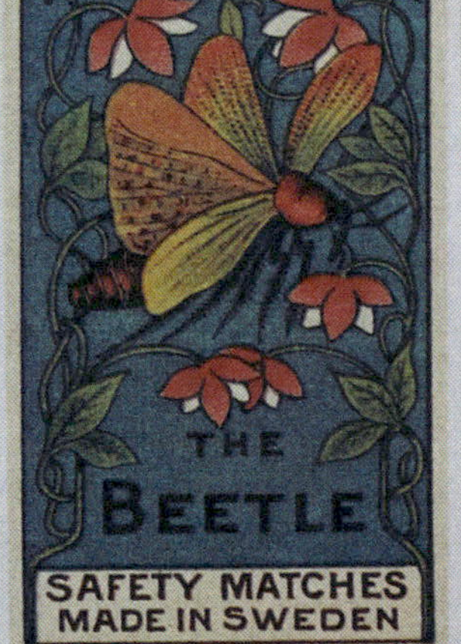
THE BEETLE
SAFETY MATCHES
MADE IN SWEDEN

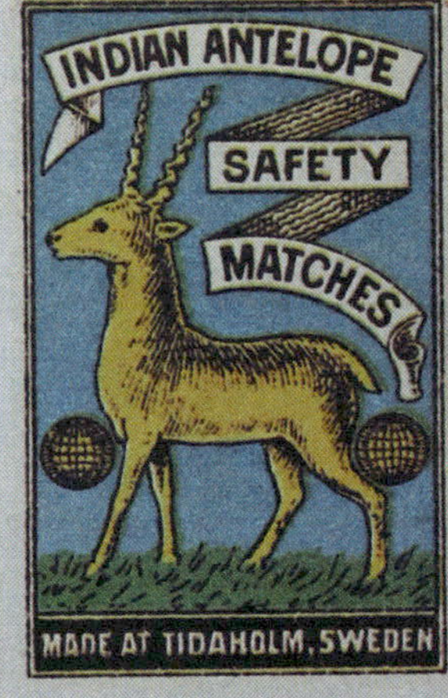
INDIAN ANTELOPE
SAFETY
MATCHES
MADE AT TIDAHOLM, SWEDEN

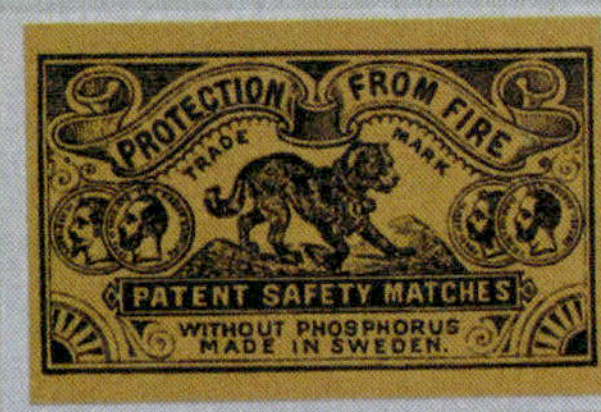
PROTECTION FROM FIRE
PATENT SAFETY MATCHES
WITHOUT PHOSPHORUS
MADE IN SWEDEN

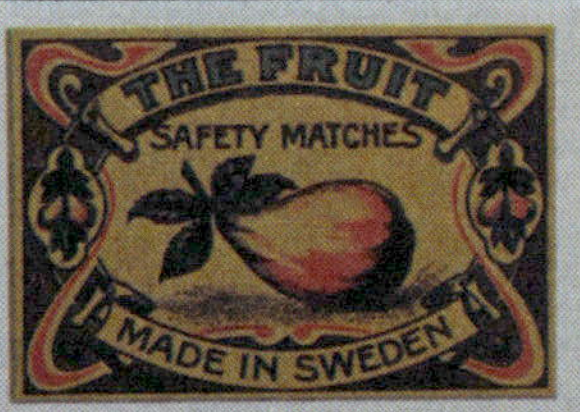
THE FRUIT
SAFETY MATCHES
MADE IN SWEDEN

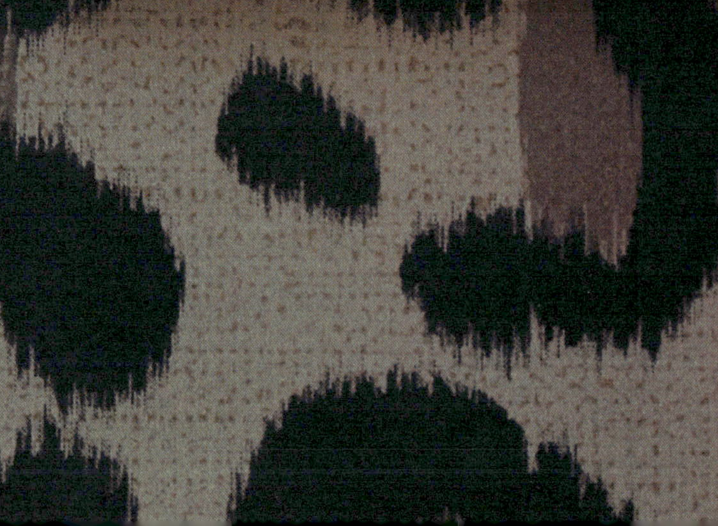

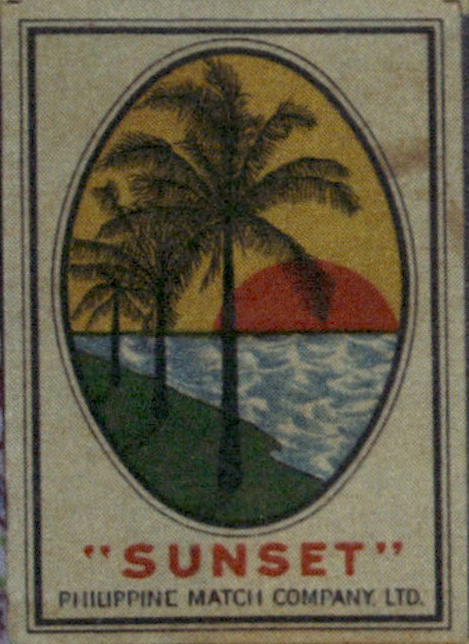
"SUNSET"
PHILIPPINE MATCH COMPANY LTD.

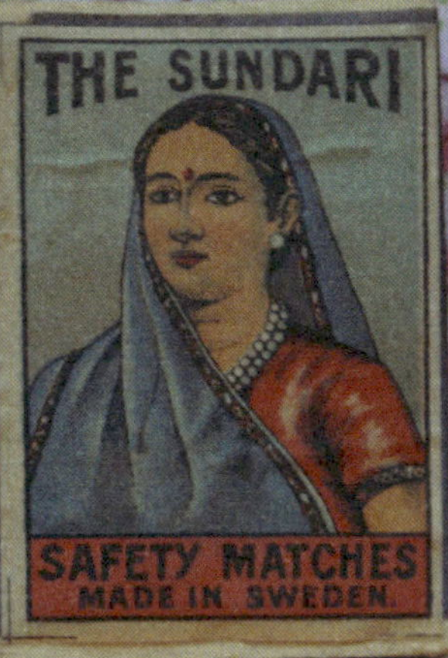
THE SUNDARI
SAFETY MATCHES
MADE IN SWEDEN

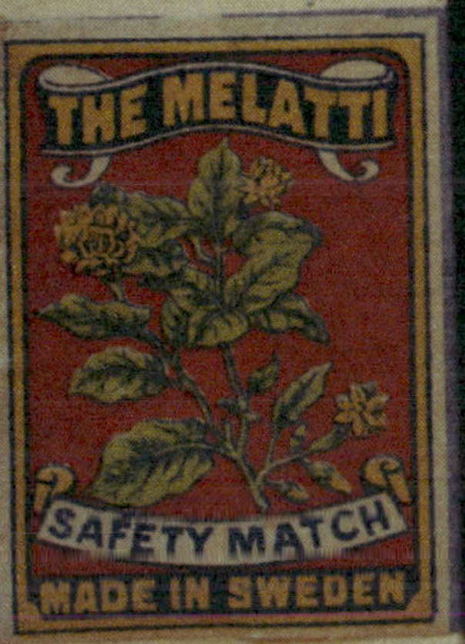
THE MELATTI
SAFETY MATCH
MADE IN SWEDEN

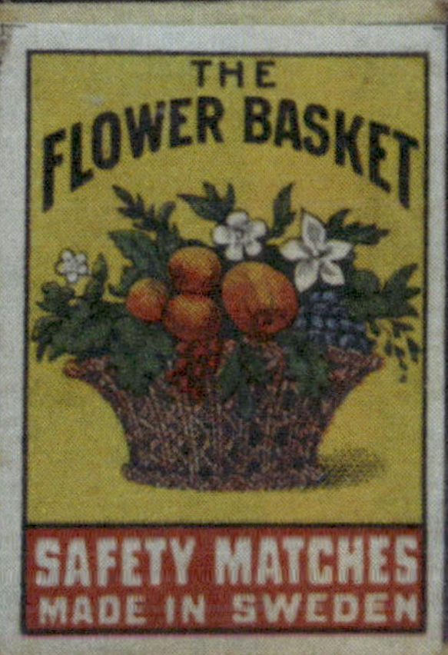
THE
FLOWER BASKET
SAFETY MATCHES
MADE IN SWEDEN

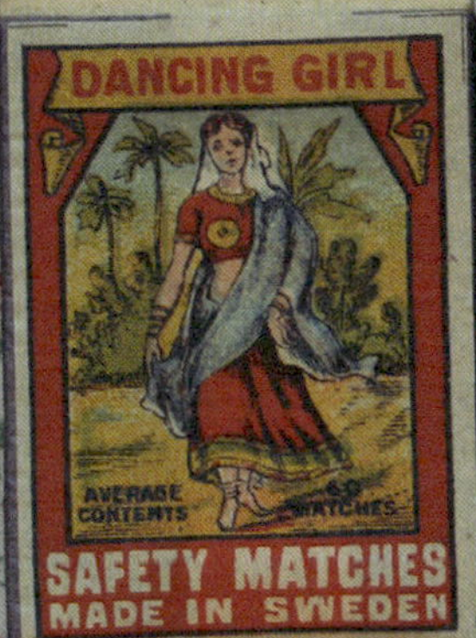
DANCING GIRL
AVERAGE CONTENTS
SAFETY MATCHES
MADE IN SWEDEN

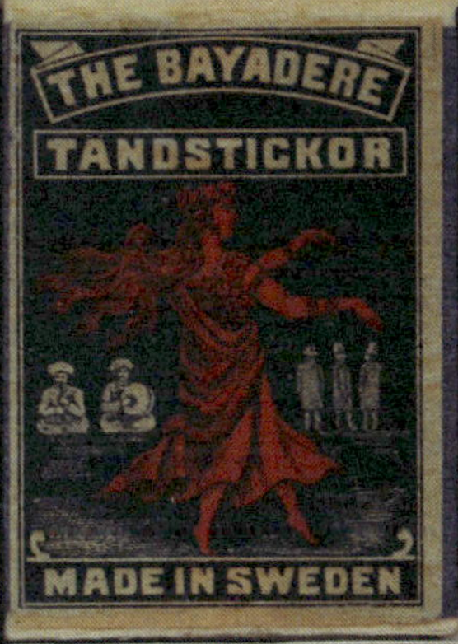
THE BAYADERE
TANDSTICKOR
MADE IN SWEDEN

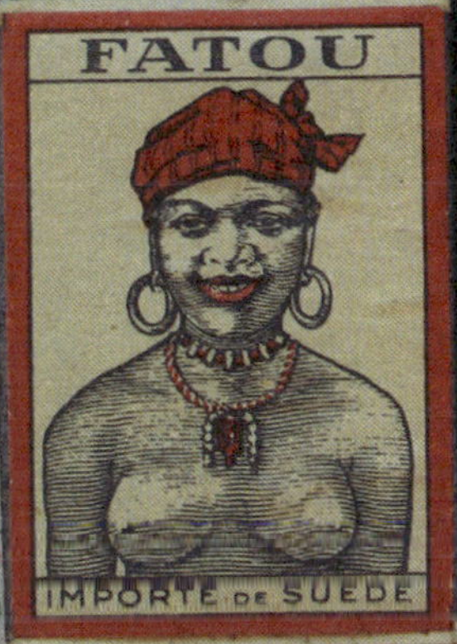
FATOU
IMPORTE DE SUEDE

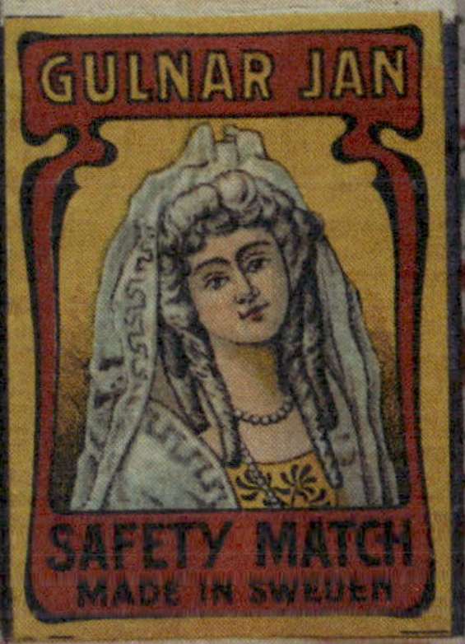
GULNAR JAN
SAFETY MATCH
MADE IN SWEDEN

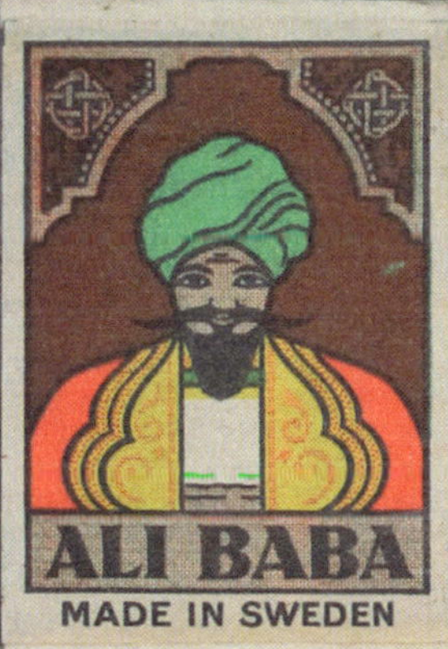
ALI BABA
MADE IN SWEDEN

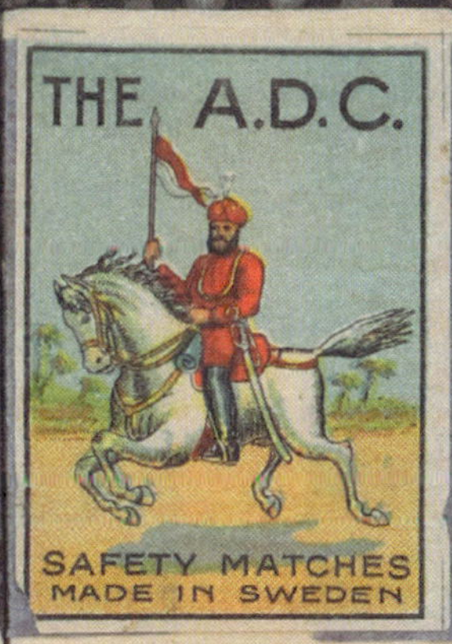
THE A.D.C.
SAFETY MATCHES
MADE IN SWEDEN

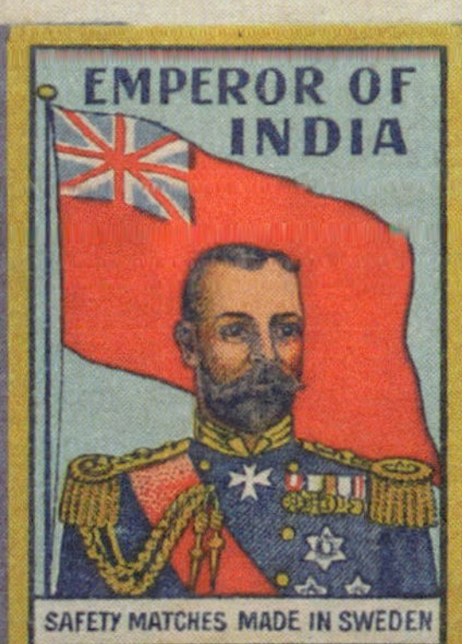
EMPEROR OF INDIA
SAFETY MATCHES MADE IN SWEDEN

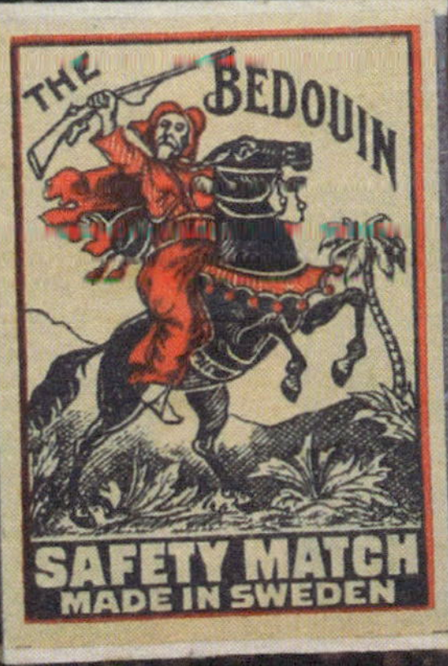
THE BEDOUIN
SAFETY MATCH
MADE IN SWEDEN

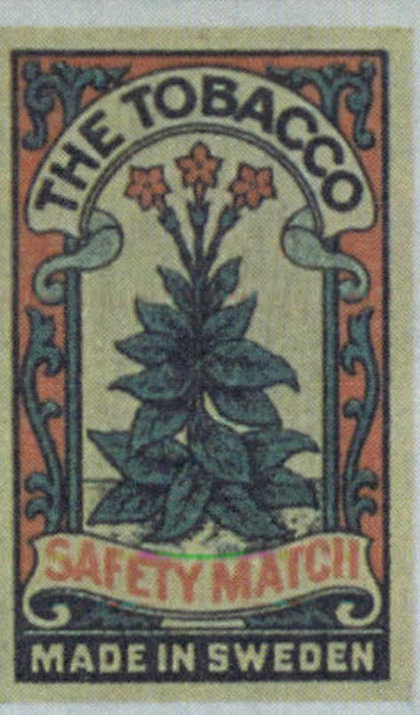
THE TOBACCO
SAFETY MATCH
MADE IN SWEDEN

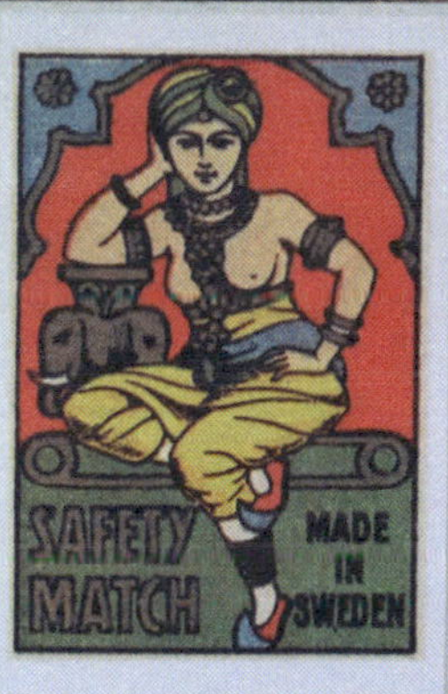
SAFETY MATCH
MADE IN SWEDEN

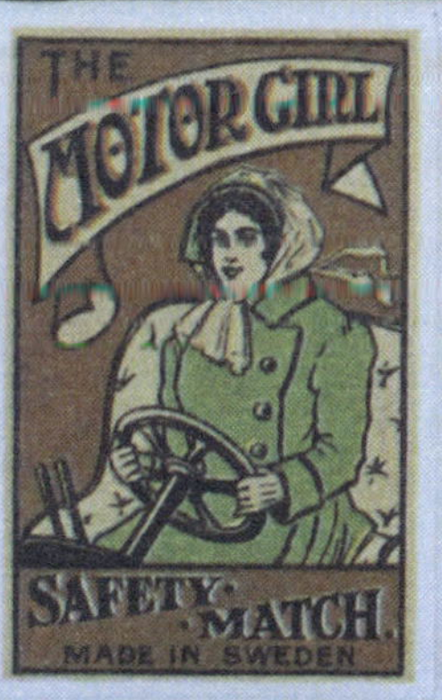
THE MOTOR GIRL
SAFETY MATCH.
MADE IN SWEDEN

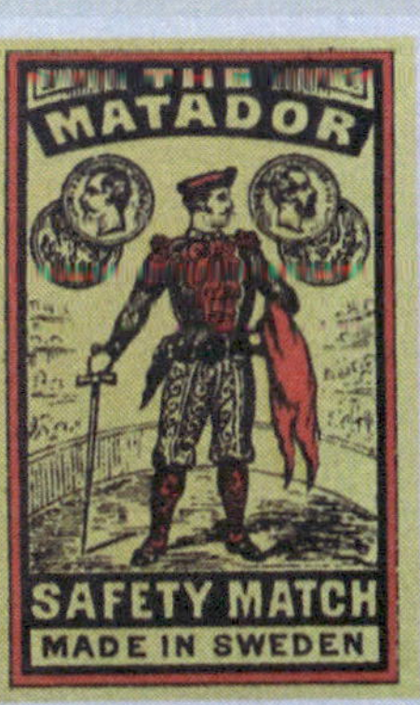
THE MATADOR
SAFETY MATCH
MADE IN SWEDEN

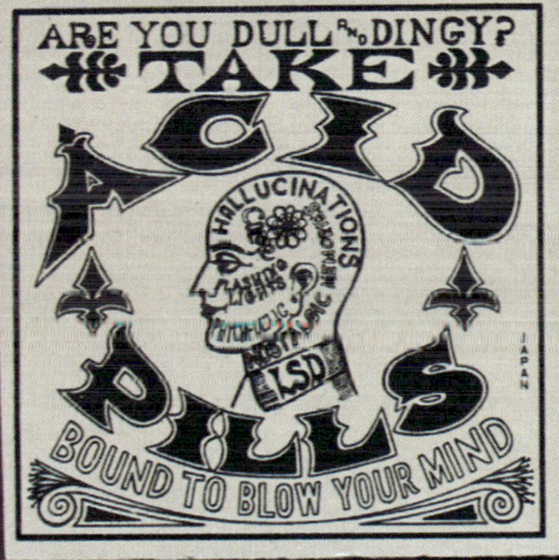
ARE YOU DULL AND DINGY?
TAKE
ACID
PILLS
HALLUCINATIONS
LSD
BOUND TO BLOW YOUR MIND
JAPAN

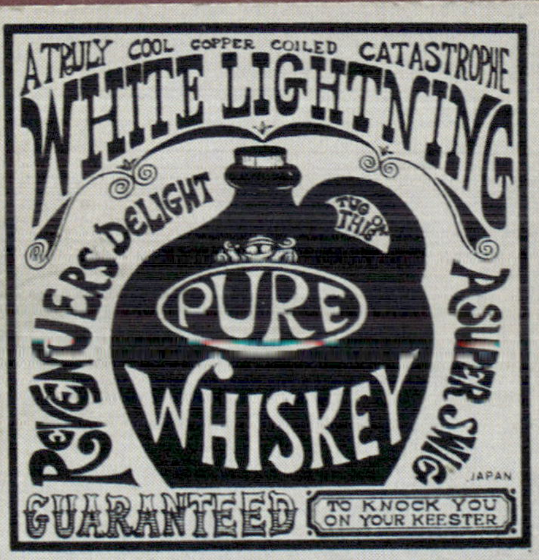
A TRULY COOL COPPER COILED CATASTROPHE
WHITE LIGHTNING
REVENUERS DELIGHT
PURE
WHISKEY
A SUPER SWIG
GUARANTEED
TO KNOCK YOU ON YOUR KEESTER
JAPAN

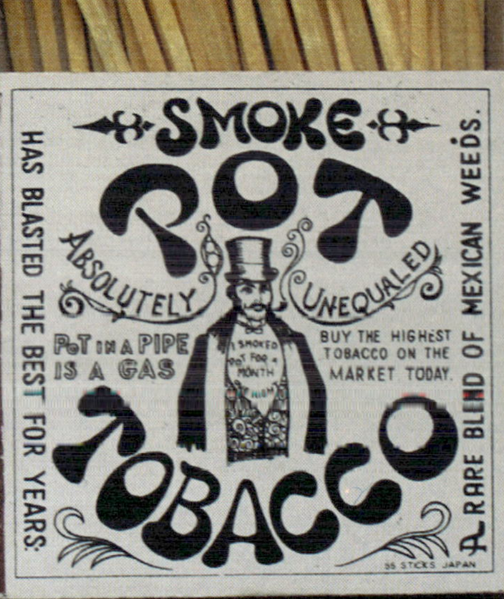
SMOKE
POT
ABSOLUTELY
UNEQUALED
POT IN A PIPE IS A GAS
BUY THE HIGHEST TOBACCO ON THE MARKET TODAY.
TOBACCO
HAS BLASTED THE BEST FOR YEARS.
A RARE BLEND OF MEXICAN WEEDS.
35 STICKS JAPAN

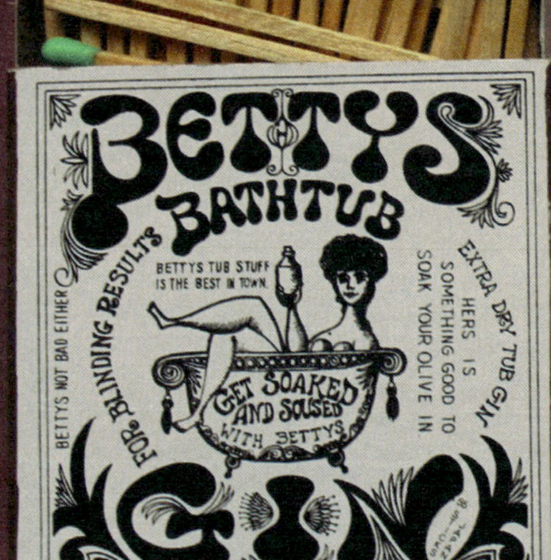
BETTYS
BATHTUB
FOR BLINDING RESULTS
BETTYS TUB STUFF IS THE BEST IN TOWN
GET SOAKED AND SOUSED WITH BETTYS
BETTYS NOT BAD EITHER
EXTRA DRY TUB GIN HERS IS SOMETHING GOOD TO SOAK YOUR OLIVE IN
GIN

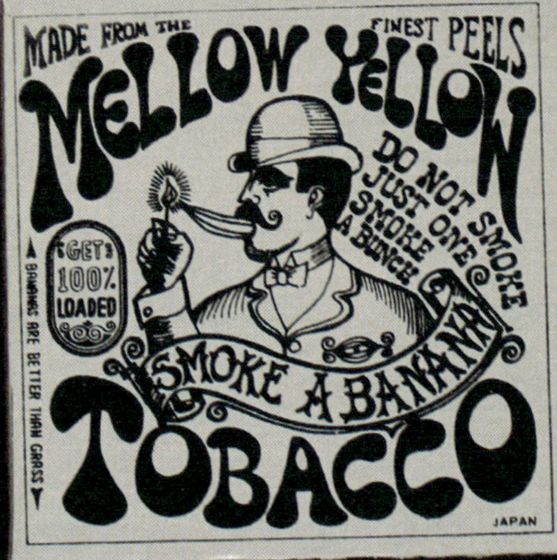
MADE FROM THE FINEST PEELS
MELLOW YELLOW
DO NOT SMOKE JUST ONE SMOKE A BUNCH
GETS 100% LOADED
BANANAS ARE BETTER THAN GRASS
SMOKE A BANANA
TOBACCO
JAPAN

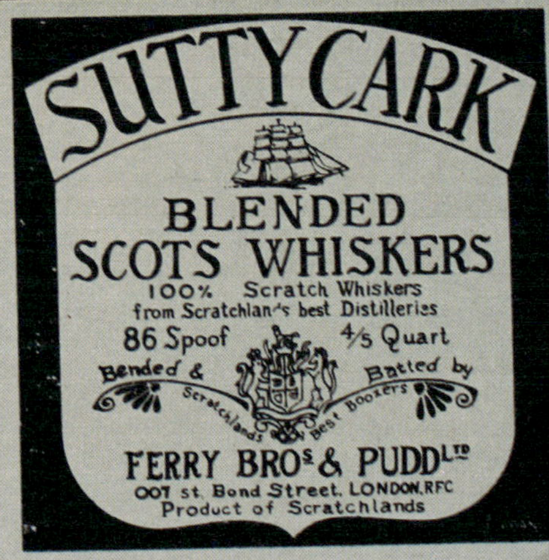
SUTTY CARK
BLENDED
SCOTS WHISKERS
100% Scratch Whiskers
from Scratchland's best Distilleries
86 Spoof
4/5 Quart
Bended & Batted by
Scratchlands Best Boozers
FERRY BROS & PUDD LTD
OOT st. Bond Street, LONDON, RFC
Product of Scratchlands

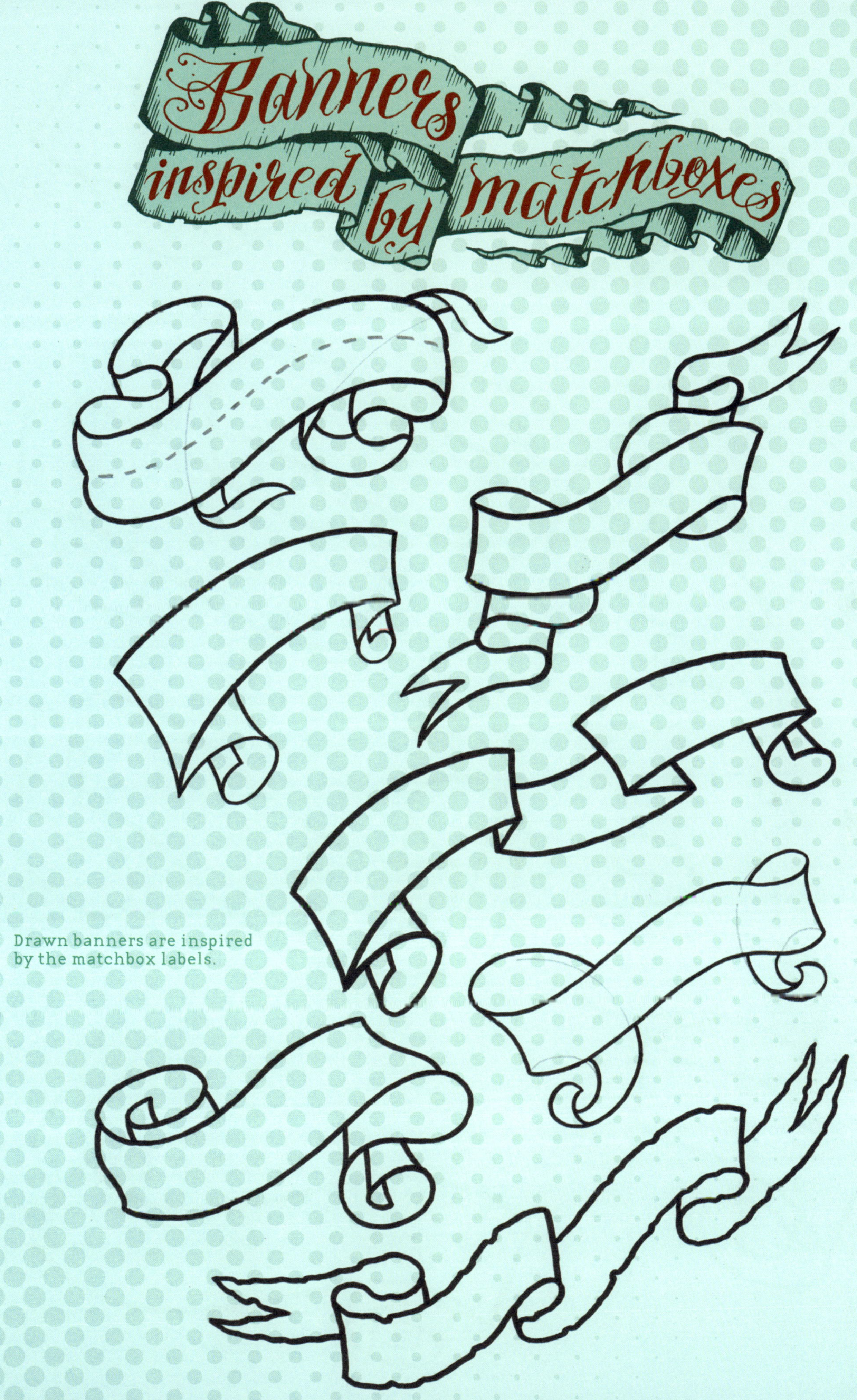

Drawn banners are inspired by the matchbox labels.

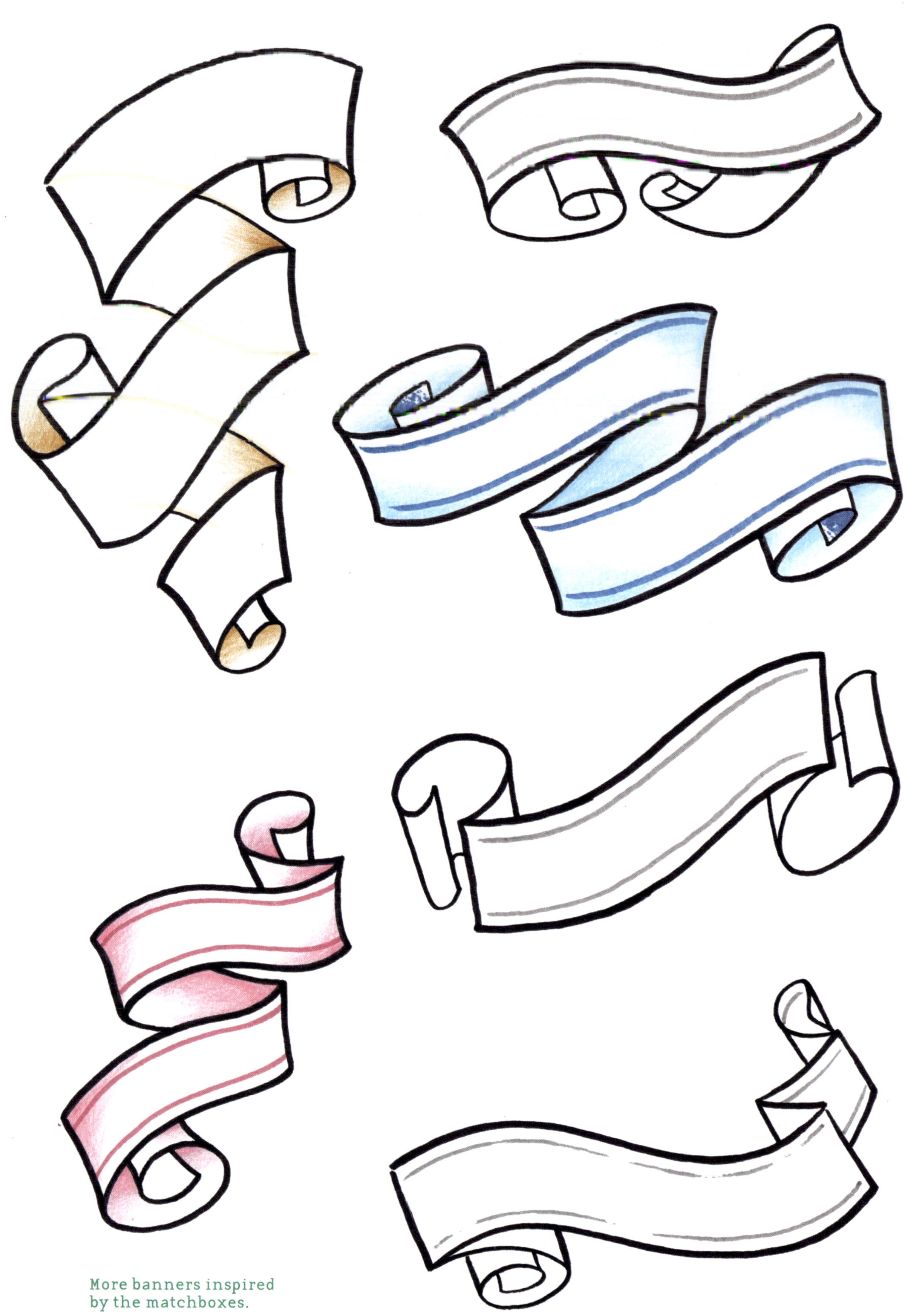

More banners inspired
by the matchboxes.

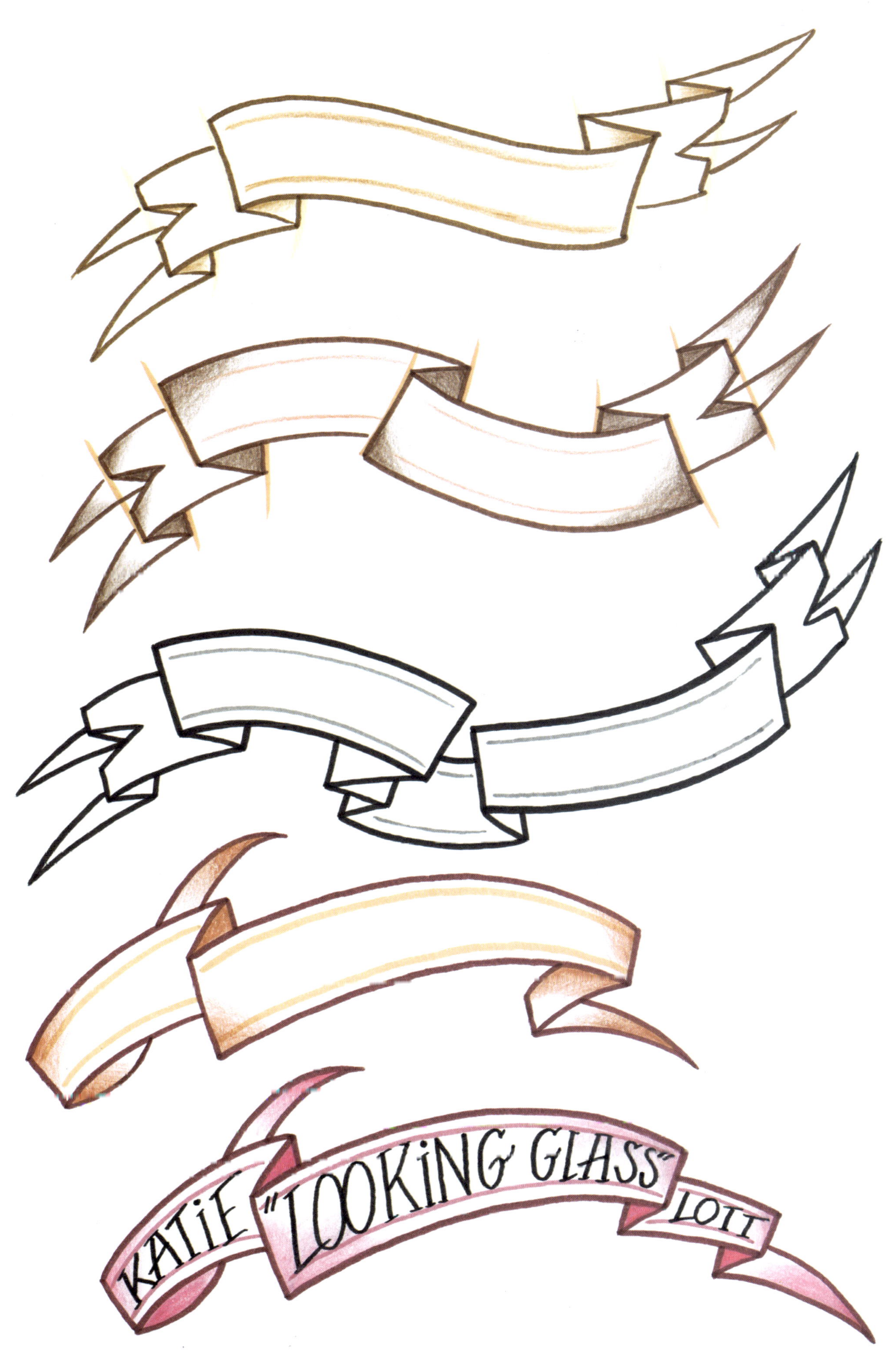
KATIE
"LOOKING GLASS"
LOTT

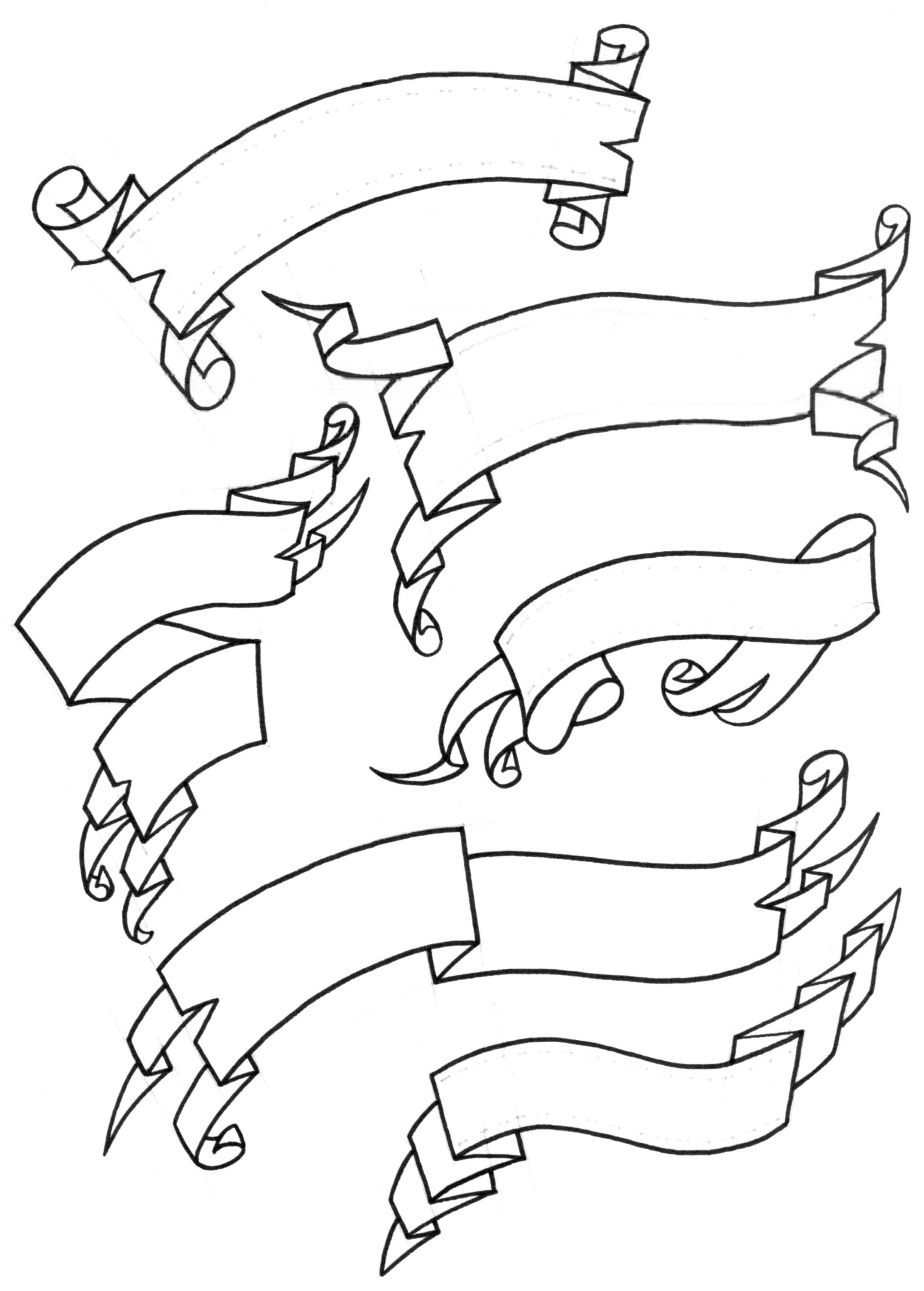

More banner examples

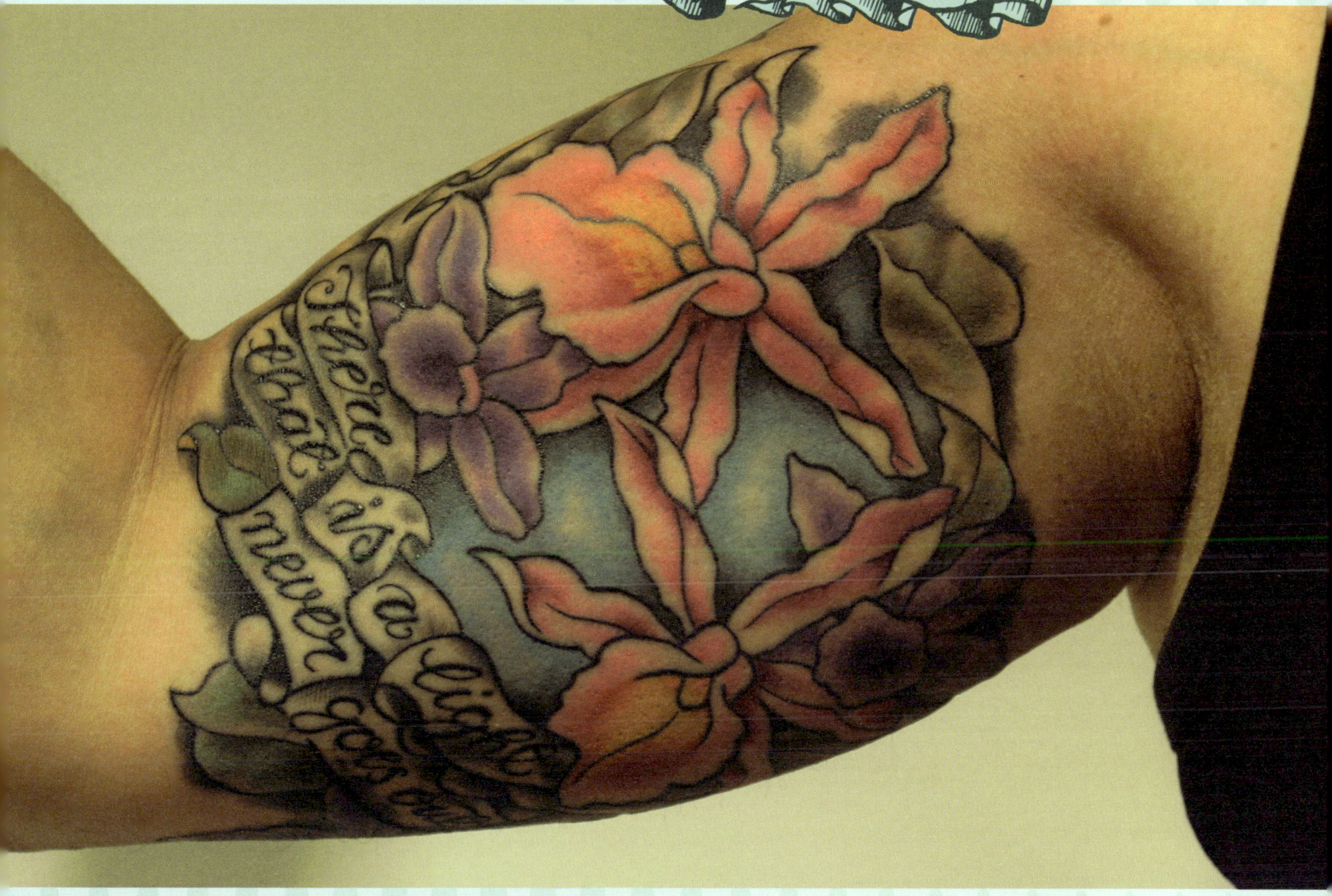

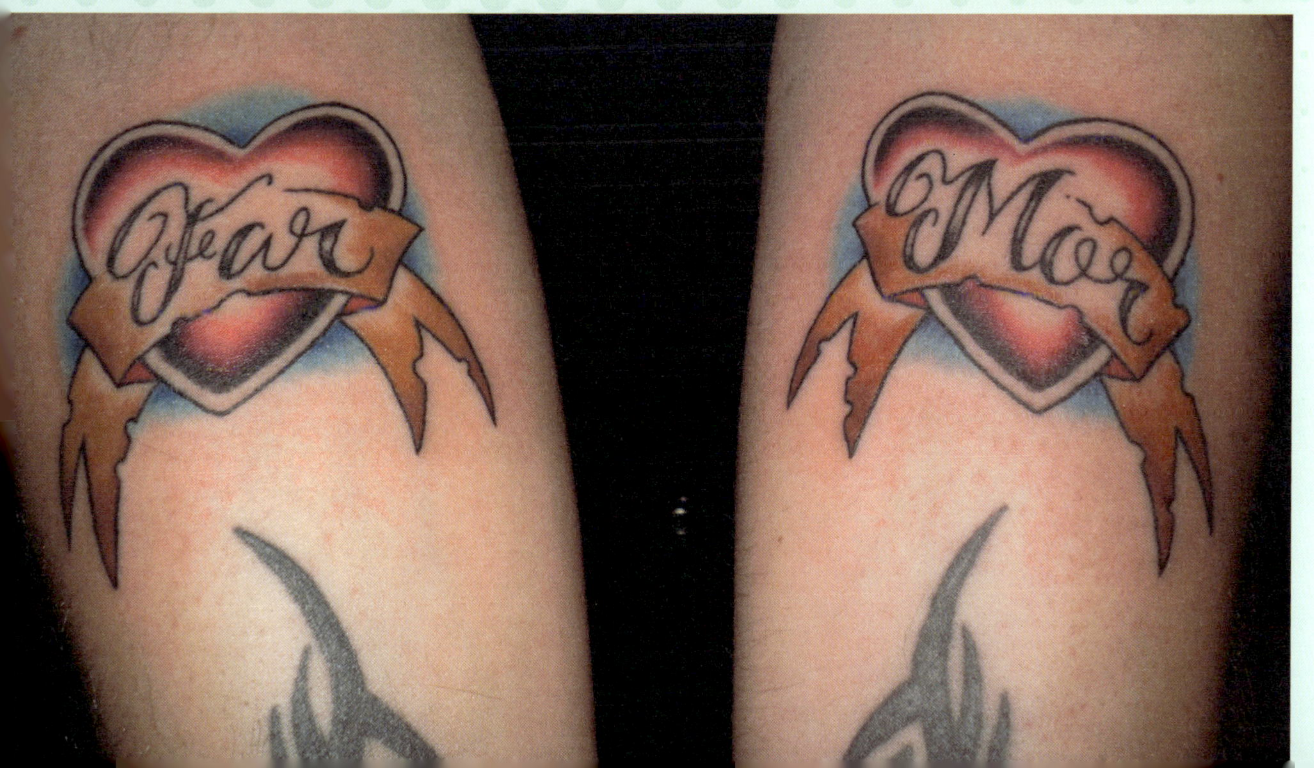

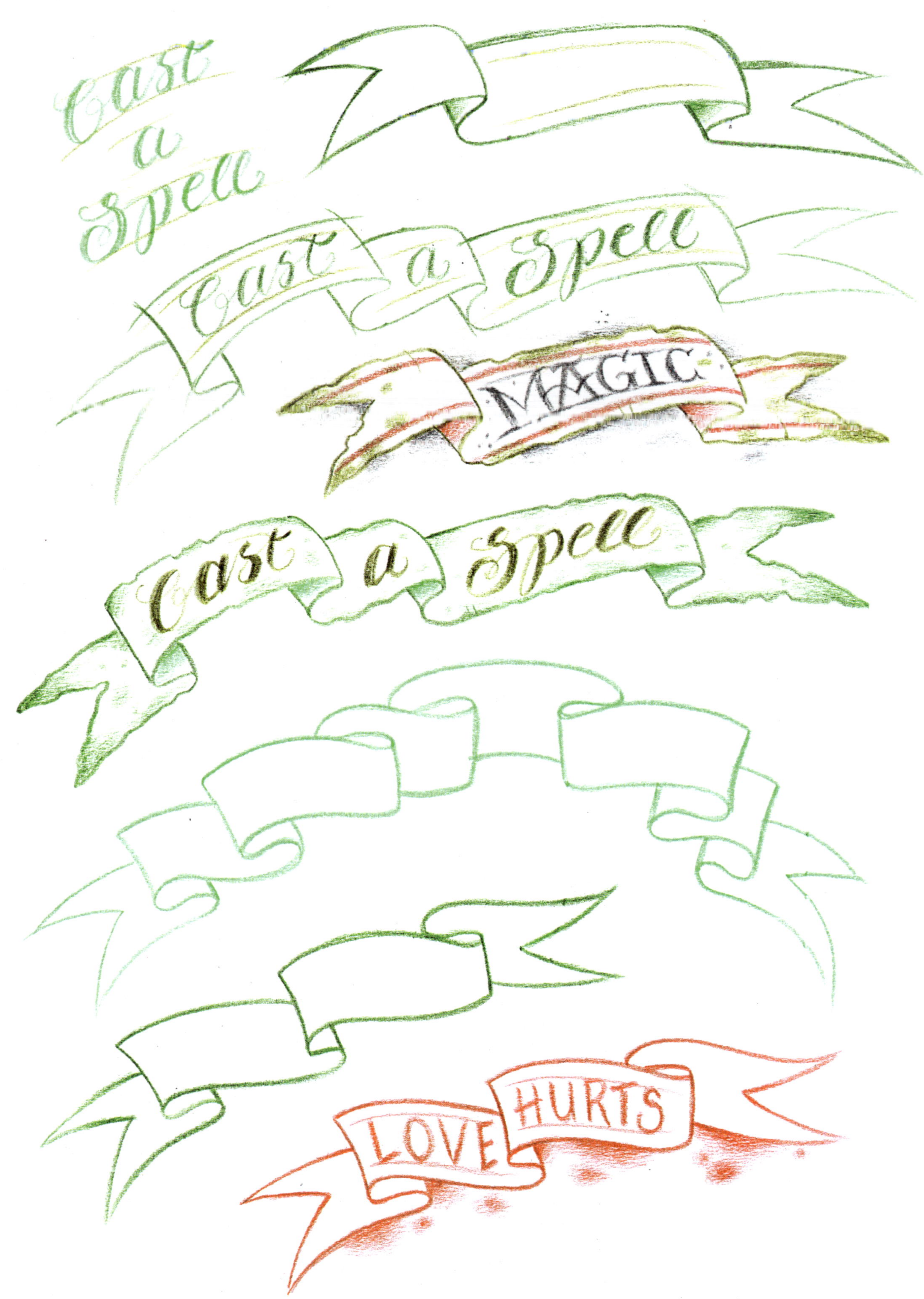
Cast
a
Spell
Cast a Spell
MAGIC
Cast a Spell
LOVE HURTS

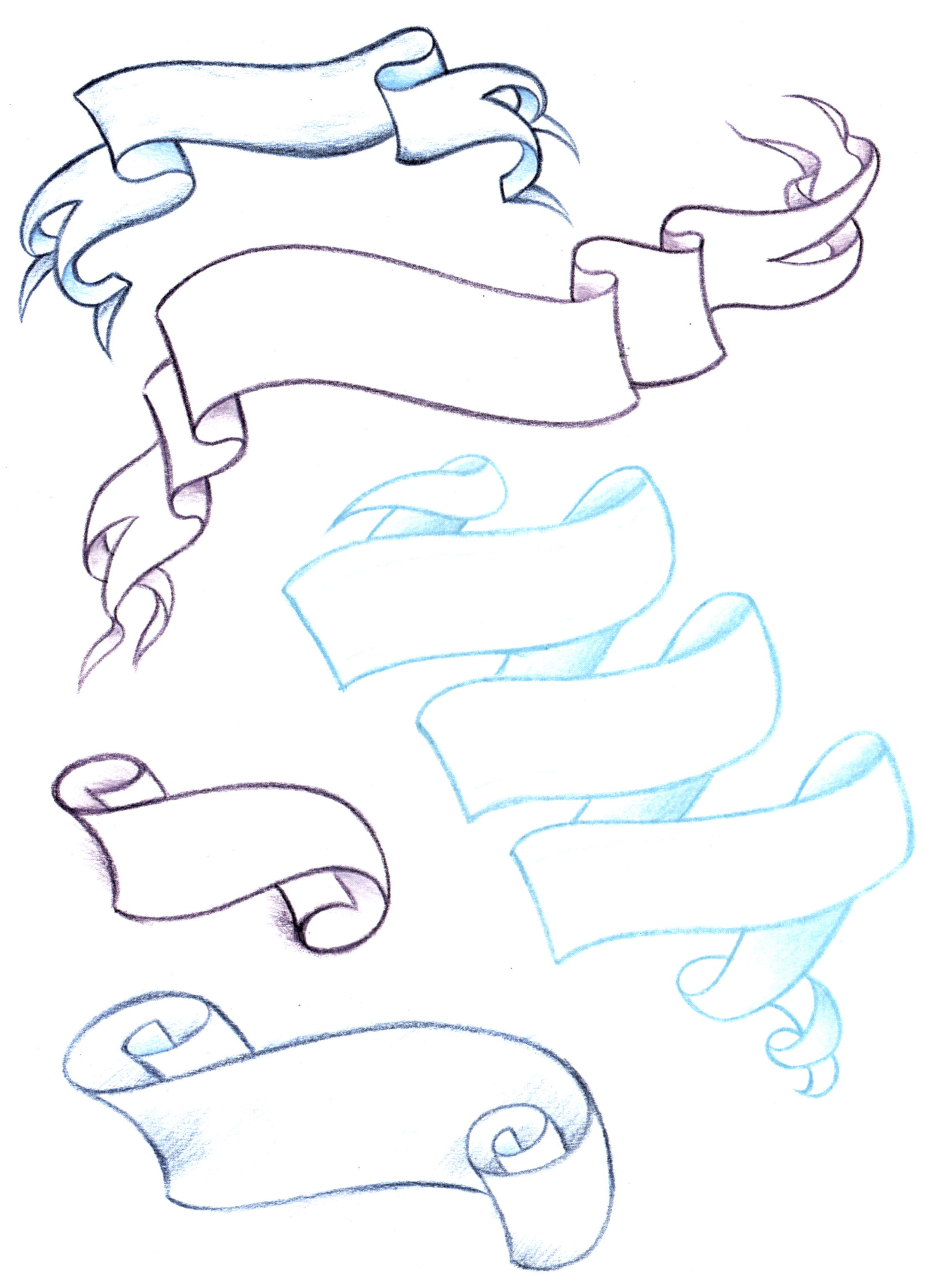

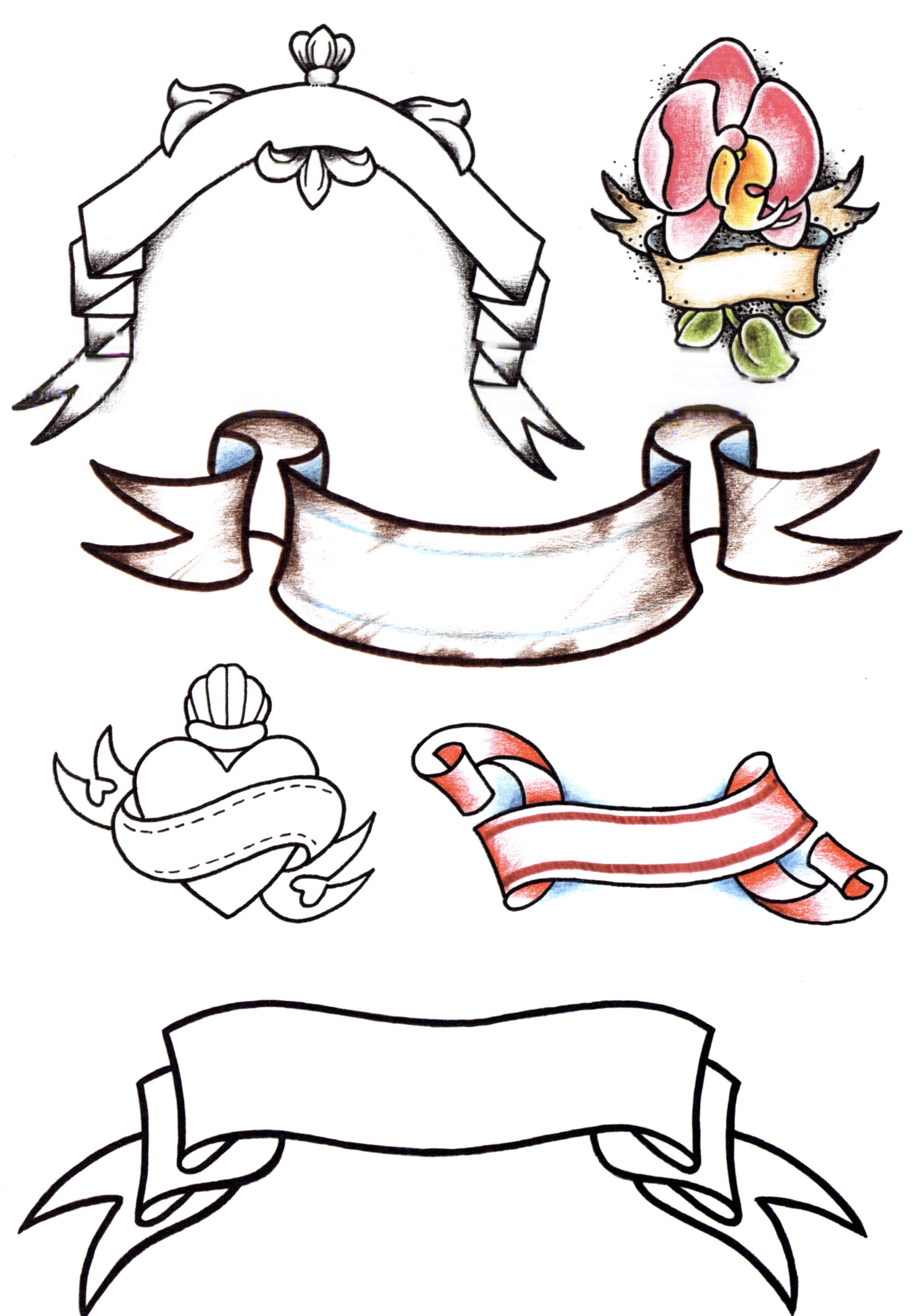

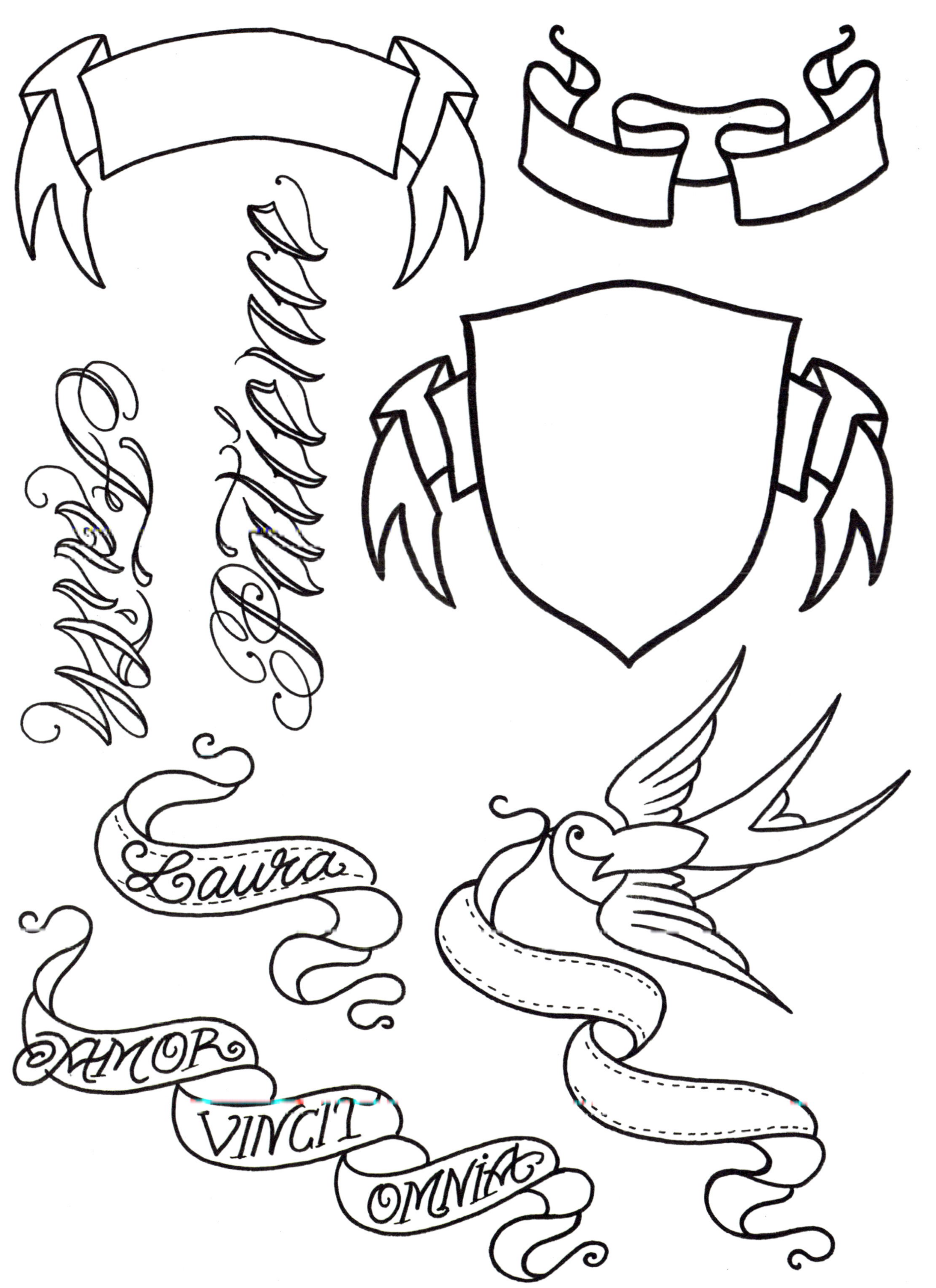

Laura
AMOR
VINCIT
OMNIA

A
WILD CHILD

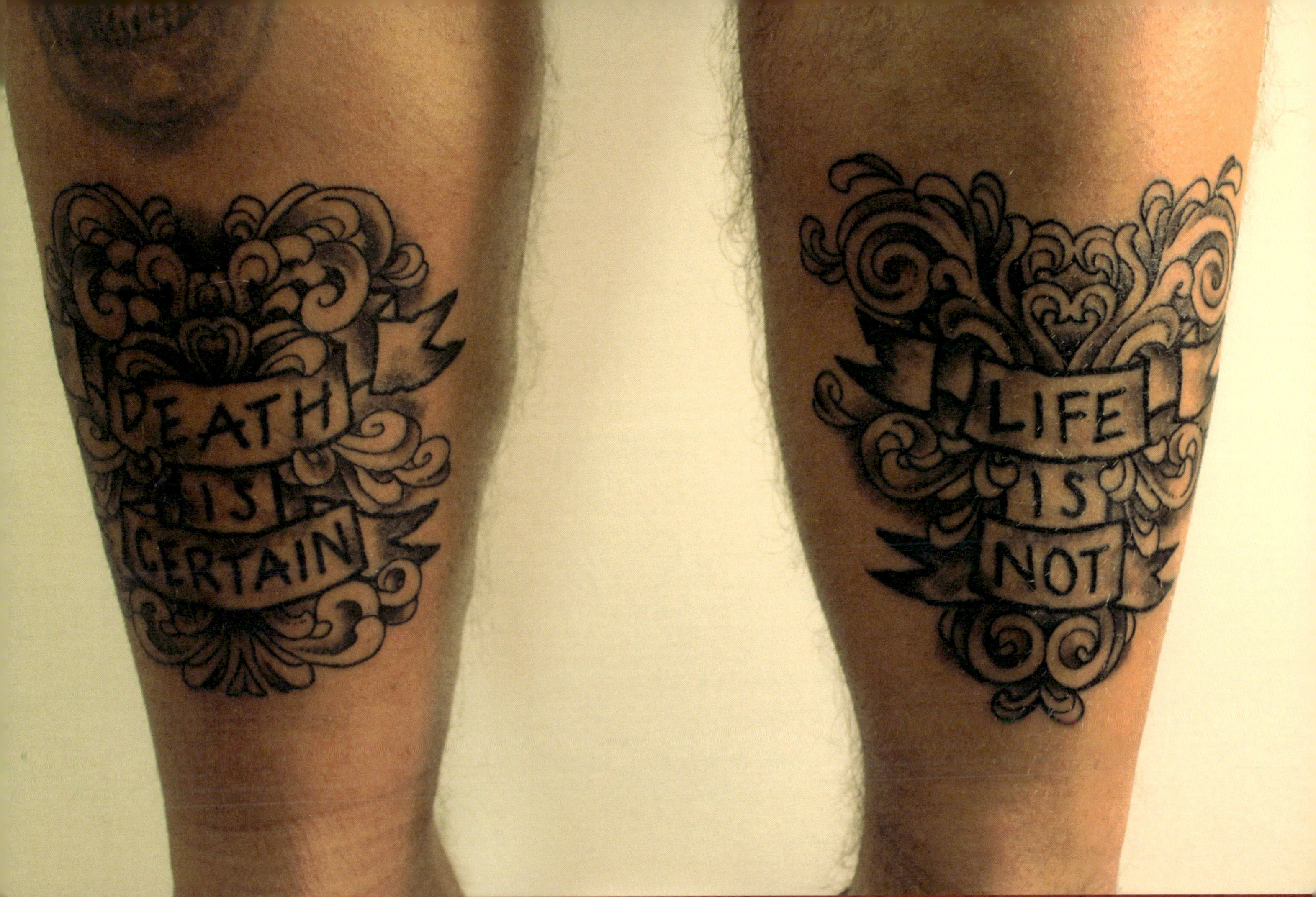

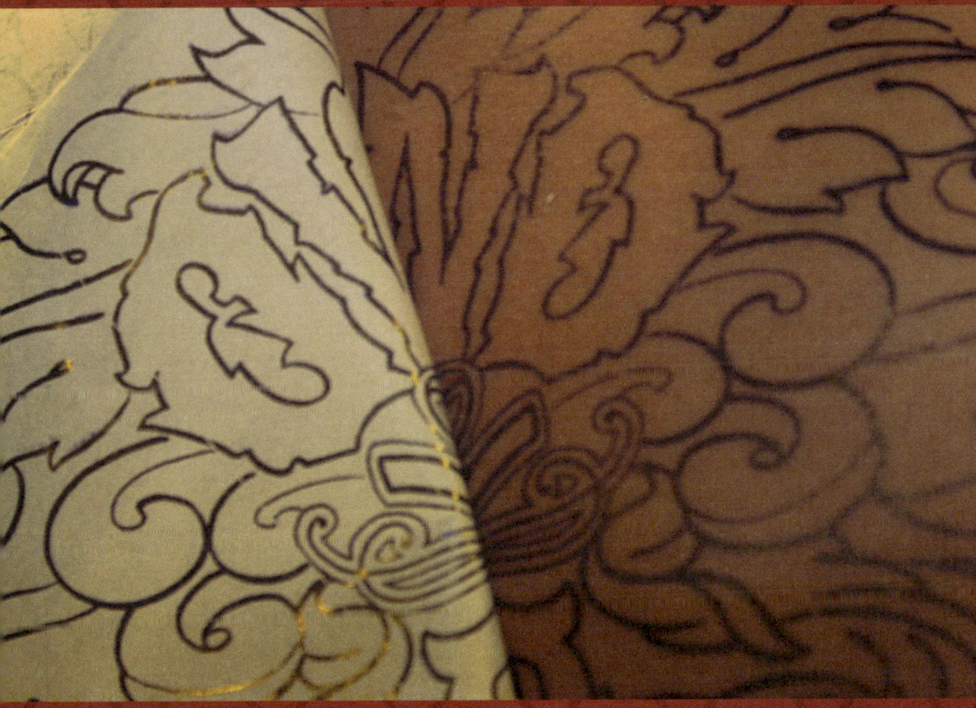

To draw these, I use a folded transparent paper. Once the banners match the text, I start drawing filigree.

Placing the stencil before starting to work.

To make these I use folded transparent paper and draw freehand, from the heart. It helps to think about fern buds or check out the late William Morris's work.

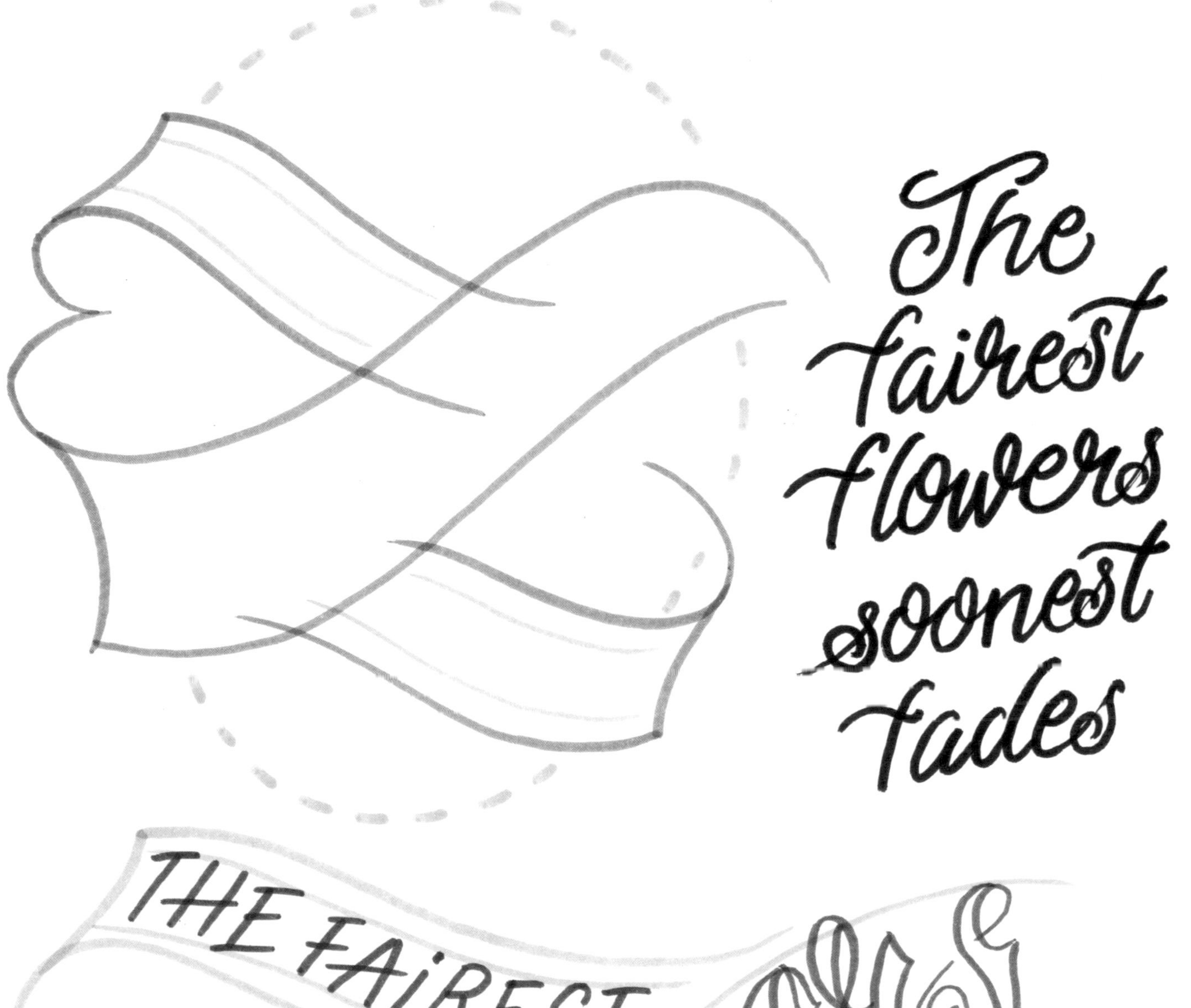

THE FAIREST

Flowers

SOONEST FADES

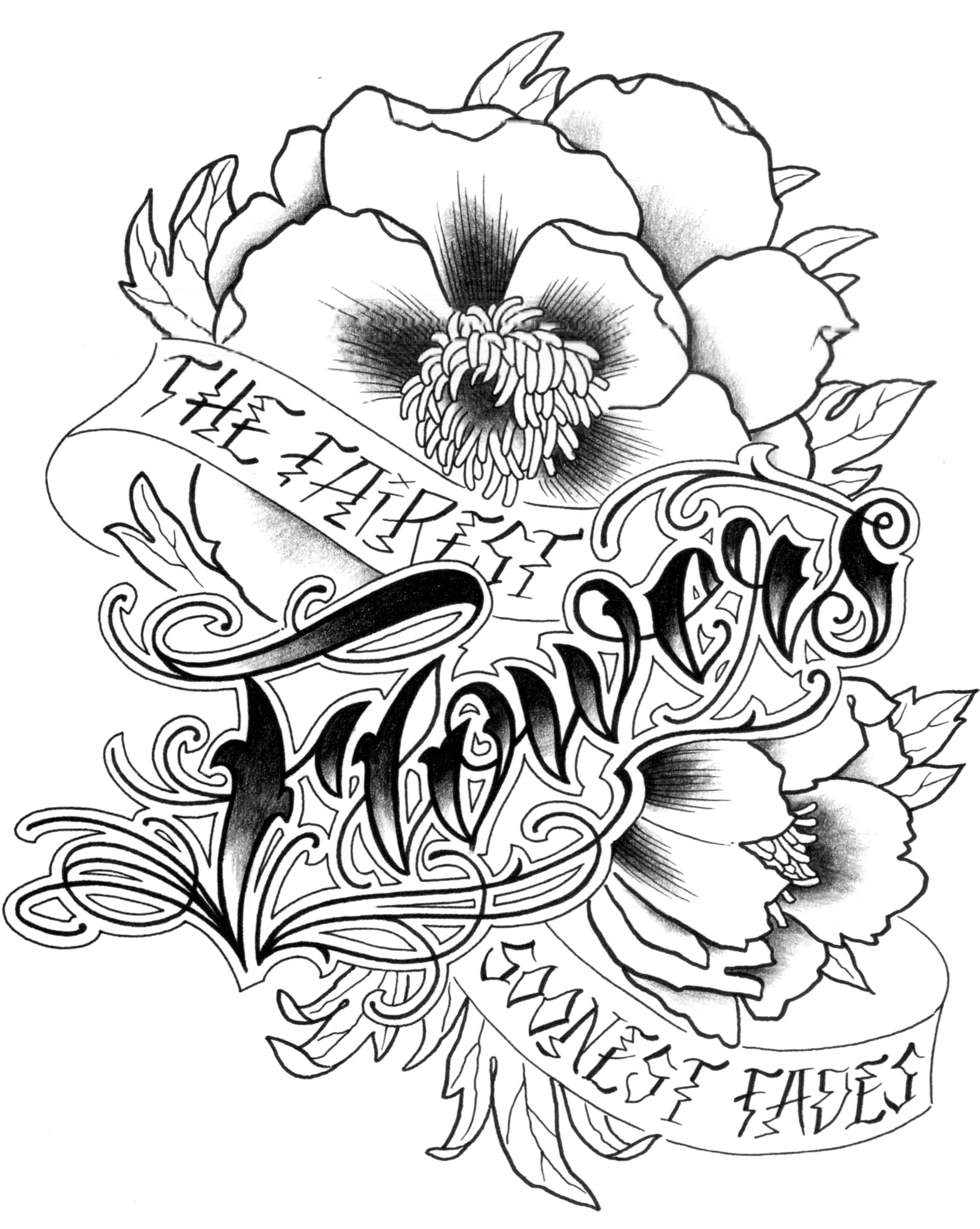
THE FAIREST
Flowers
SOONEST FADES

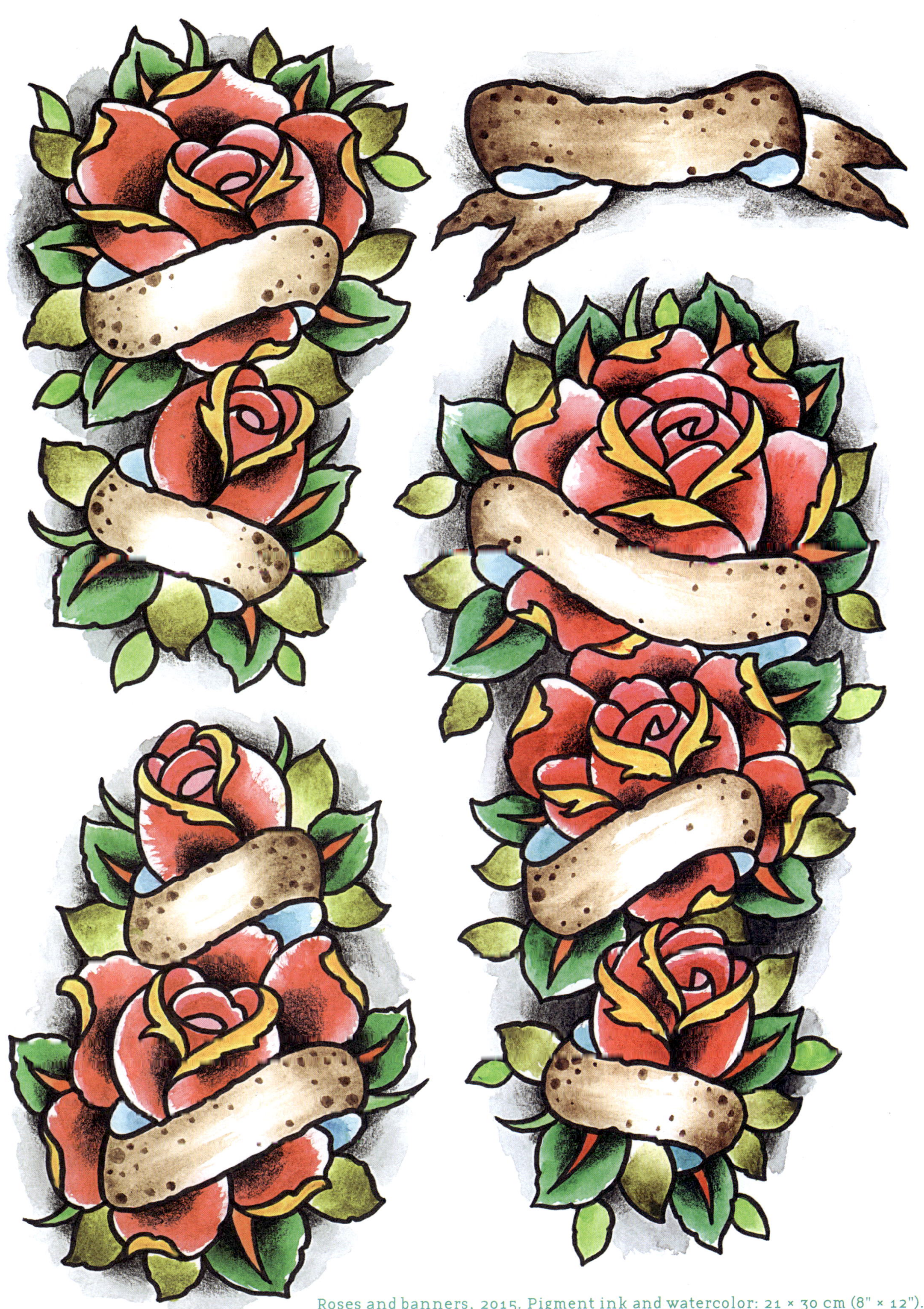

Roses and banners, 2015. Pigment ink and watercolor: 21 × 30 cm (8" × 12").

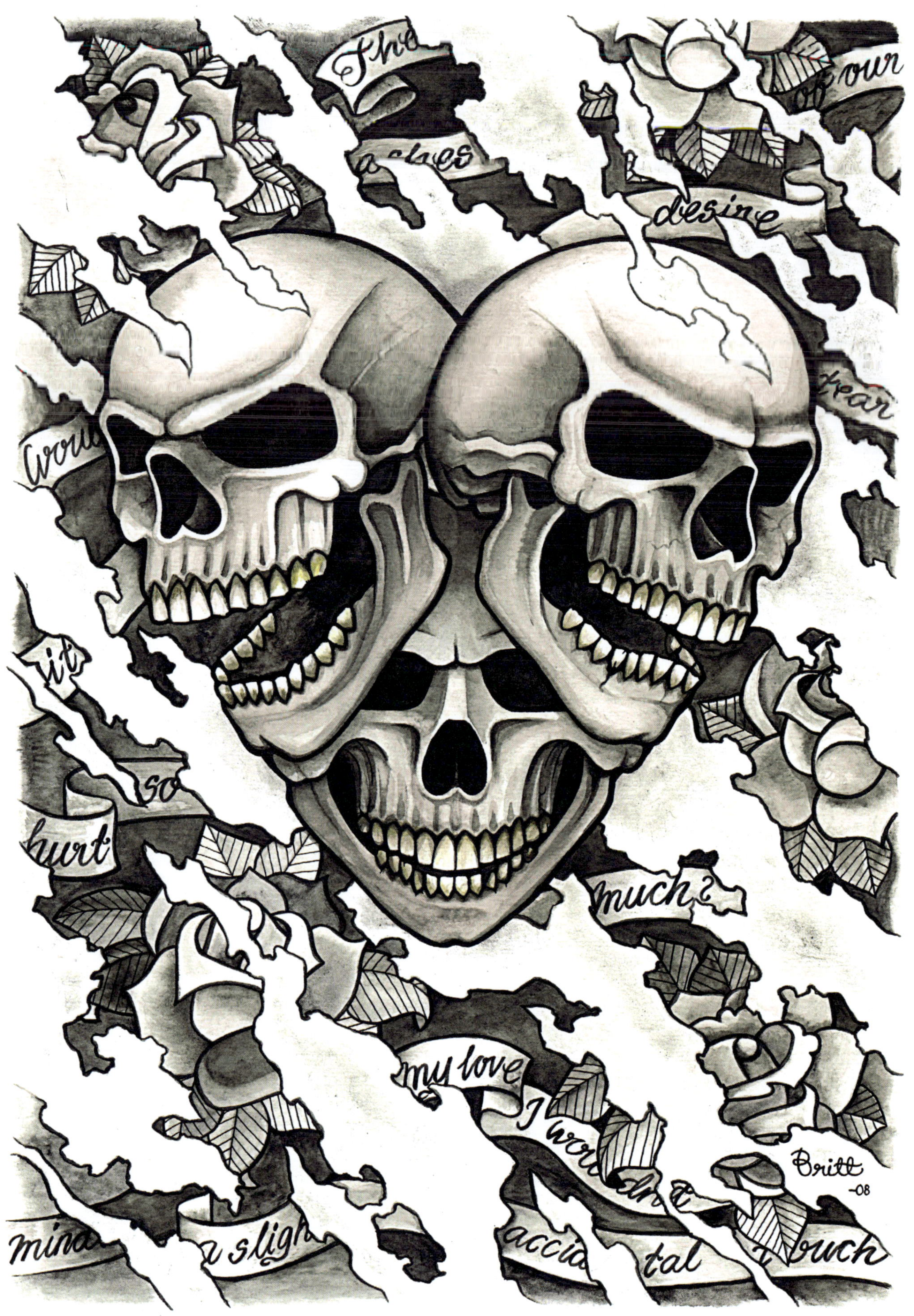

Heart of bone, 2008. Pigment ink and watercolor: 30 × 42 cm (12" × 16.5"). This painting has banners hidden in the background and torn empty spaces.

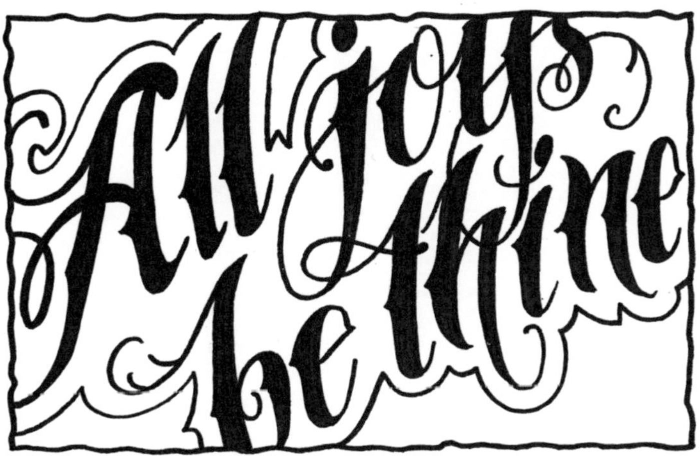

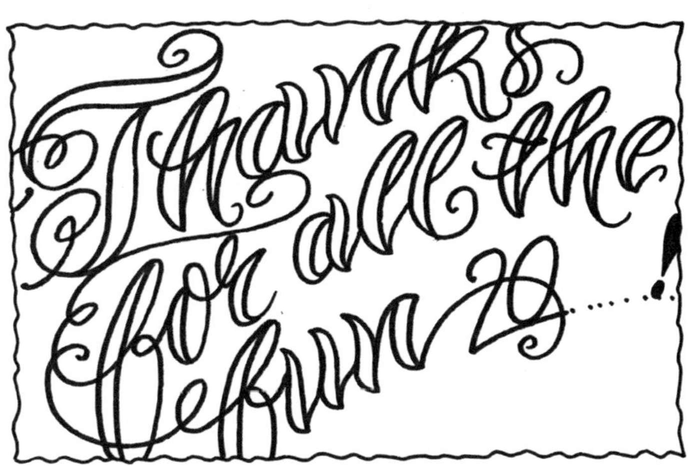

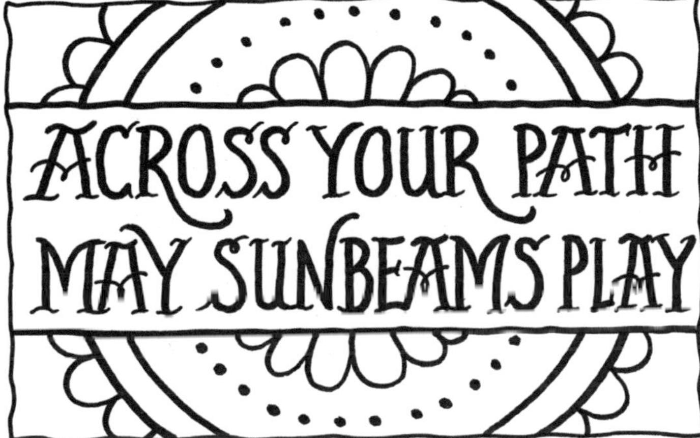

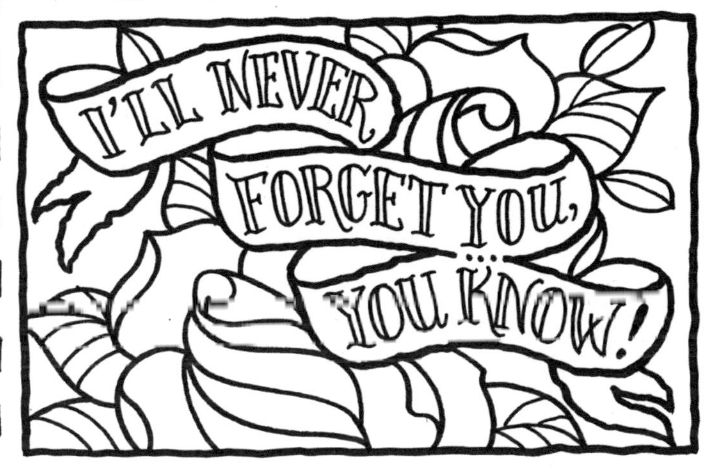

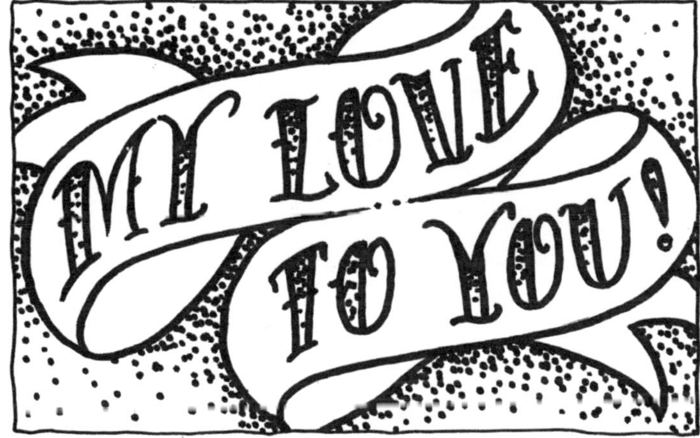

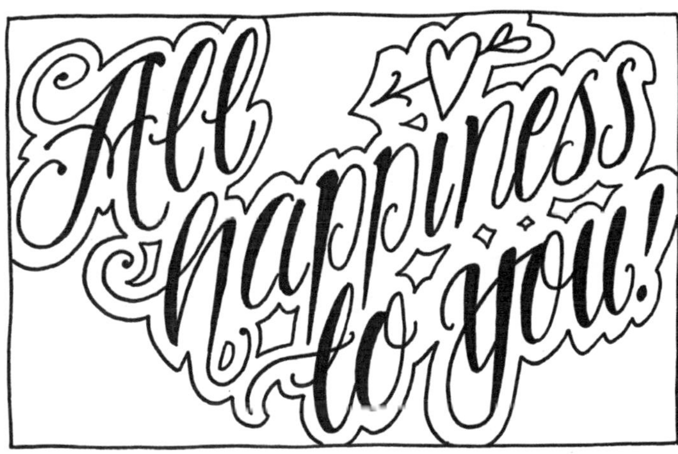

Wine, women & song!

SAFELY MAY YOU
ONWARD GLIDE
HEALTH & COMFORT
BY YOUR SIDE

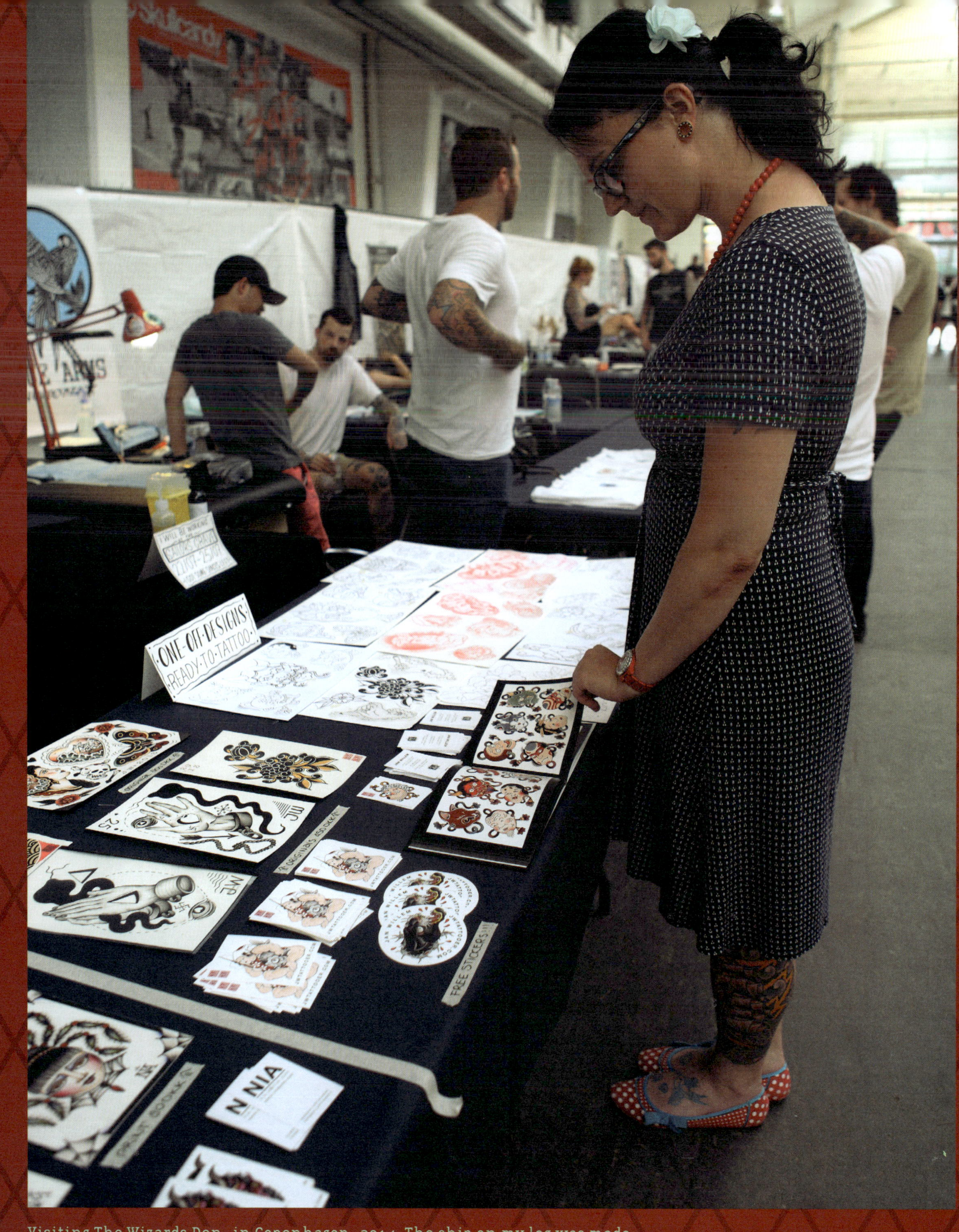

Visiting The Wizards Den, in Copenhagen, 2014. The ship on my leg was made by Judd Ripley at The Sailors Grave, Copenhagen.